COLUMBIA COLLEGE CHICAGO
C0-AVX-688

I SPEAK
OF THE CITY

COLUMBIA UNIVERSITY PRESS NEW YORK

I SPEAK OF THE CITY

POEMS OF NEW YORK

Selected by **STEPHEN WOLF**

COLUMBIA UNIVERSITY PRESS
Publishers Since 1893
New York Chichester, West Sussex

Columbia University Press wishes to express its appreciation for assistance given by the Berkeley College Faculty Development Fund toward the cost of publishing this book.

Library of Congress Cataloging-in-Publication Data

I speak of the city : poems of New York / selected by Stephen Wolf.
p. cm.
ISBN 978-0-231-14064-5 (alk. paper)—
ISBN 978-0-231-14065-2 (pbk. : alk. paper)
1. New York (N.Y.)—Poetry. 2. American poetry.
I. Wolf, Stephen, 1947– II. Title.

PS595.N45I17 2007
811 .6080974711—DC22
2006103394

Columbia University Press books are printed on permanent and durable acid-free paper. This book is printed on paper with recycled content.

Printed in the United States of America

C 10 9 8 7 6 5 4 3 2 1

DESIGN BY VIN DANG

CONTENTS

THE POEM OF THE CITY

JOHN HOLLANDER

NEW YORK CITY IS, in addition to so much else, a kind of great text, written and over-written, interpreted by itself for more than two centuries of its most recent life. For novelists, it has been everything from a self-generating, open-ended anthology of tales to a condition of life. For poets, it is a great poem itself, in an unwritten tongue that constantly needs retranslation into a poet's individual language. Cities can seem to be figures *for* poetry generally, rather than merely *in* a poem—each one configured differently, with a particular relation of hierarchies of parts to wholes within it, with histories that may or may not reveal themselves, with differing paces of life and ways of absorbing and adapting to physical topography, its dividing waters bridged or, in modern times, tunneled under. Each city becomes a smaller and more condensed version of what Walt Whitman meant when he called the United States a great poem.

"Oh could I flow like thee" wrote Sir John Denham to the river Thames in the seventeenth century, "and make thy stream / My great example, as it is my theme! / Though deep, yet clear, though gentle, yet not dull, / Strong without rage, without o'erflowing, full." Cities are not benign rivers, and the examples they can provide for poetry are of more agitated, unruly, and often violent activity as much as they are of the heavy stasis of stone and brick and steel. And perhaps better to comprehend the variety of kinds of poems, styles, genres, modes, tones, and stances taken by their speakers, it may be useful to look back over some landmarks in the history of poems "about" (always a risky word in characterizing a poem) cities.

The poetry of urban life in Western tradition starts out with two cities, one biblical and one classical, that come to a bad end. Babel (in Genesis 11, whose name is imprinted in our English word for incoherent speech,) rose to the music of ambition, aided by perfect communication among its builders because there was only one language in the world. Its overreaching tower fell, and with it Language crumbled into all the different languages. Troy is depicted by Homer under siege and, eventually, loses its war. In later portions of the Bible, Jerusalem appears as an allegorical female figure, often denounced for her loss of virtue by the prophets; Babylon, in Revelation, is the arch-whore, standing for another city, Rome, and in all these cases, the city itself is a metonymy for a whole civilization. It is, indeed, only with classical Rome and its poets that what we now feel to be the poetry of a particular city, at various stages of its existence, comes to be written: the founding of the city by Aeneas is not so much an account of the laying out of an urban actuality as it is of the founding of a civilization. This story is told by allusion and in glimpses, in Virgil and Horace, through constant comparison with its rural alternative—indeed, rurality as such is itself a concept born of the urban condition—and in the kinds of particularity we get in Juvenal's Satires, most specifically in his third one—a denunciation of the city's ways by the speaker of the poem as, his belongings loaded on a cart, he leaves the city, choosing not to live "in constant fear of fires and falling houses, the thousand perils of this savage city, as well as poets reciting in the month of August!" Ben Jonson in "Fabulous Voyage," takes a comical, mock-heroic journey through the sewers of his London, and Samuel Johnson, in "London," imitates Juvenal's poem on Rome.

It is indeed during the eighteenth century that the poetry of cities becomes more complex. Jonathan Swift, in his marvelous "Description of the Morning," moves beyond earlier satire in a poem that plays tricks on a reader's initial expectation that he or she will be presented with a rural "natural" scene; instead of sunrise, birds twittering, and so forth, his urban dawn in 1709 London begins with the first sign of urban morning, someone coming home from an all-nighter in a cab:

Now hardly here and there an Hackney-Coach
Appearing, show'd the Ruddy Morns Approach.
Now Betty from her Masters Bed had flown,
And softly stole to discompose her own.
The Slipshod Prentice from his Masters Door,
Had par'd the Dirt, and Sprinkled round the Floor.
Now Moll had whirl'd her Mop with dext'rous Airs,
Prepar'd to Scrub the Entry and the Stairs.
The Youth with Broomy Stumps began to trace
The Kennel-Edge, where Wheels had worn the Place.
The Smallcoal-Man was heard with Cadence deep,
'Till drown'd in Shriller Notes of Chimney-Sweep,
Duns at his Lordships Gate began to meet,
And Brickdust Moll had scream'd through half the Street.
The Turnkey now his Flock returning sees,
Duly let out a-Nights to Steal for Fees.
The watchful Bailiffs take their silent Stands,
And School-Boys lag with Satchels in their Hands.

The urban day is one of individual activity and enterprise, not in isolation but in a kind of concert that helps define city life itself. Swift himself admired even more his "Description of a City Shower," treating again of London in the following year. It depicts the sorts of disruption that a sudden rainfall can bring to a crowded city, including a mock-heroic glimpse of a beau impatiently sitting "boxed" in his sedan-chair and trembling as the heavy rain pounds its roof. Swift likens him to one of the Greeks inside the Trojan Horse, when "Laocoôn struck the outside with his spear, / And each imprisoned hero quaked for fear," the whole poem concluding with a memorable look at the flow of waste water from many tributary streets, all coming together in a London not yet well sewered, when

Sweepings from butchers' stalls, dung, guts and blood,
Drowned puppies, stinking sprats, all drenched in mud,
Dead cats and turnip-tops come tumbling down the flood.

And Swift's friend John Gay's marvelous *Trivia, or the Art of Walking the Streets of London* helps shape the ongoing form of describing a city through the narrative of a promenade through it, a mode that will undergo interesting variation over the next three centuries. Gay is topographically very specific about the town his long poem explores; one notes the vividness of description in such passages as this one, warning the reader about walking eastward in London in an area where the sidewalks weren't—as was usually the case—separated from the street by a row of posts:

Though expedition bids, yet never stray
Where no ranged posts defend the ragged way.
Here laden carts with thundering wagons meet,
Wheels clash with wheels, and bar the narrow street;
The lashing whip resounds, the horses strain,
And blood in anguish bursts the swelling vein.

The rhetorical modes of these poems are themselves always close to those of Roman and English urban satire, as we see in this grim urban prospect from Oliver Goldsmith's "Deserted Village," where the farmer, his livelihood compromised by the enclosure movement's privileges to nascent agribusiness, is forced off the land as so many were:

If to the city sped—What waits him there?
To see profusion that he must not share;
To see ten thousand baneful arts combined
To pamper luxury and thin mankind;
To see those joys the sons of pleasure know
Extorted from his fellow creature's woe.
Here, while the courtier glitters in brocade,
There the pale artist plies the sickly trade;
Here, while the proud their long-drawn pomps display,
There the black gibbet glooms beside the way.
The dome where Pleasure holds her midnight reign
Here, richly decked, admits the gorgeous train;
Tumultuous grandeur crowds the blazing square,
The rattling chariots clash, the torches glare.

Byron's Venice, Pushkin's St. Petersburg, Browning's Rome, and, more directly, the gritty and immediate Rome of G. G. Belli; Blake's visionary London, more the product of his relation to prophetic allegory than to observation of urban life, even as he wanders "through each chartered street / Near where the chartered Thames does flow, / And mark in every face I meet / Marks of weakness, marks of woe"; and Eliot's collage in *The Waste Land*: indeed, with hardly any exceptions, the poetry of cities was largely either satirical or topographical until the mid-nineteenth century. Only with the first modern poems—by which in this instance I mean those of the great English romantics—did a particular poet's own experience of some part of the world start to merit the same kind of speculative attention as those parts of the world themselves. In the particular case of cities, views of the whole, or visits to neighborhoods or monuments, or portraits or genre-scenes of prominent or—increasingly in the nineteenth and twentieth centuries—obscure inhabitants, all become not so much mere objects of, but very parts of, the experience, even the consciousness, of the speaker of the poem. "Things seen are things as seen," as Wallace Stevens observed, speaking for poetry from Wordsworth on. And the history of cities seems to engage in transfers of representation with the history of the poetry that at first praises, blames, scrutinizes, and analyzes but then comes to comprehend in stranger ways.

An early instance of a "New York poem"—in this case, from the 1770s—might be a typical bit of earlier eighteenth-century English verse, dutifully framed in the heroic couplets that were a default mode in the that century; a verse letter to her husband by Ann Eliza Bleecker of Albany: "To Mr. Bleecker, on His Passage to New York." It speaks only of the scenery along the Hudson valley, finally acknowledging the unnamed Manhattan as the locus of the mouth of the Hudson:

Thus having led you to the happy isle
Where waves circumfluent wash the fertile soil,
Where Hudson, meeting the Atlantic, roars,
The parting lands dismiss him from their shores.

Fifty and more years later, the city has become a far larger and more complex place, but the eighteenth century continues in the verse of Samuel Woodworth in a panegyric to the city as a home of freedom, hope, and prosperity (I would add, for some) that refuses, like most panegyrics, to give its subject a truly honest look. Instead, amid all his almost mechanical personifications,

On either hand, a mighty river glides,
Which here, at length, unite and mingle tides,
Like some fond pair, affianced in the skies,
Whose forms, as yet, ne'er met each other's eyes,
When the auspicious fated moment rolls,
They meet—they love—unite, and mingle souls.

For William Wordsworth in book 7 of *The Prelude*, London is full of things and places the poet had heard of and imagined in ways that could shape what they became for him when actually encountered, a place at once full of human wonders and of inhumanties:

Rise up, thou monstrous ant-hill on the plain
Of a too busy world! Before me flow,
Thou endless stream of men and mocing things!
Thy every-day appearance, as it strikes—
With wonder heightened, or sublimed by awe—

William Cullen Bryant, Wordsworth's artistic descendant, was a most important poet of nature, particularly in his early work, but he is not thought of as a poet of the urban imagination. Bryant, however, sees New York (once, I might add, he has become a prominent newspaper editor and public figure there), in weakly Worsdsworthian language, as a thoroughly legitimate part of Nature:

Not in the solitude
Alone may man commune with Heaven, or see,
Only in savage wood
And sunny vale, the present Deity.
Even among the multitudes,

Even here do I behold
Thy steps, Almighty!—here, amid the crowd,
. . . .
Choking the ways that wind
'Mongst the proud piles, the work of human kind.

Like rural nature, Bryant's city has become a possible site of intellectual solitude (rather than unwanted isolation), and both New York and its poetry have been fully claimed by the nineteenth century.

Two great poets—contemporaries, and an ocean apart—made another, modern kind of poetry of their own respective cities. Baudelaire's Paris, through which his poetic persona was a continual *flâneur*, and Whitman's New York, through which, as a transcendent kind of loafer (to use his own word), his poetry would walk. In Baudelaire's great poem "Le Cygne" ("The Swan") he observes, as he walks by the new Place du Carrousel, that "Old Paris is gone (a city's shape changes faster than the human heart); Only in my mind's eye can I see those huts, those piles of roughed-out capitals and columns, weeds, great blocks of stone stained green by puddles and jumbled bric-a-brac glittering in shop-windows." And then, remembering a trapped, crippled swan he had seen there the speaker's thoughts move beyond sentiment:

Paris change! mais rien de ma mélancolie
N'a bougé! Palais neufs, échafaudages, blocs,
Vieux faubourgs, tout pour moi devient allegorie,
Et mes chers souvenirs sont plus lourds que des rocs.

"Paris changes, but my melancholy is immutable. All the new buildings, scaffoldings, blocks of masonry, all the old suburbs, all become allegory, and my remembrances heavier than rocks." The new and the old per se, and the prospects wherein they overlap, become charged with significance, and in the poems of the "Paris Scenes" of his *Fleurs du mal*, moments, glimpses, presences all become allegory. Baudelaire reads the city's history into its very temper and tone and draws a boundary between verse descriptive of a city, in praise or blame, and true poetic figuration of it (whether we use the term "metaphor"—as Aristotle does—to cover the varieties of trope, or "trope" itself, or even—as Baudelaire does here—"allegory" to indicate the general non-literalness that makes a modern poem a poem rather than merely versified writing.

Baudelaire suggests that a city can be a palimpsest of its own history; Walt Whitman's New York—actually the twinned cities of Brooklyn and what he calls by its Algonquian name, Mannahatta—was allegorical, too, the experience of it continually raising questions. In cataloguing its elements of concerted human activity in "Crossing Brooklyn Ferry," Whitman is, as always, poetically incorporating the items he records as parts of himself, the walker in the city claimed by and thereby claiming what he sees and hears. This great poem ends by celebrating the energies of the river that separates and those of the "countless crowds of passengers" that cross it, but always challenging the creative consciousness, raising new questions even as it seems to offer answers to older ones:

Stand up, tall masts of Mannahatta! stand up, beautiful hills of
  Brooklyn!
Throb, baffled and curious brain! throw out questions and
  answers!
Suspend here and everywhere, eternal float of solution!
Gaze, loving and thirsting eyes, in the house or street or public
  assembly!
Sound out, voices of young men! loudly and musically call me by
  my nighest name!
Live, old life! play the part that looks back on the actor or actress!
Play the old role, the role that is great or small according as one
  makes it!

It can be noted, with some historical irony that seems to fulfill Whitman's vision rather than undermine it, that the two cities would become one after having been bridged by a magnificent span less than thirty years after this poem was written.

But again, that wonderful urban artifact itself can become allegory for the great poetry it deserves. So Hart Crane, in "To Brooklyn Bridge" (the proem to his complex visionary, *The Bridge*) addresses Roebling's masterpiece almost as a sacred image: "Unto us lowliest, sometime sweep, descend, / And of the curveship lend a myth to God." And in another part of this great long poem, "The Tunnel" represents a kind of antithetical transit, underground, a negative way. Here the imaginative bridge to poetic tradition is not the hand of Walt Whitman; nor is it the master trope of bridging and connecting—derived from Whitman's Brooklyn Ferry—that Crane conceived not only in the Brooklyn Bridge but in the general metaphor that gives his great poem its title. Rather, it is the ghost of Poe he encounters in the subway, his "eyes like agate lanterns, on and on / Below the toothpaste and the dandruff ads," and the whole of "The Tunnel" is full of echoes of Eliot's *The Waste Land*.

The same year (1883) the Brooklyn Bridge finally opened, the native New Yorker Emma Lazarus composed a sonnet for the Statue of Liberty that hails it as a "New Colossus," one to replace the famed Colossus of Rhodes, a male figure guarding a harbor, by a female one who in fact guards the new harbor's welcoming openness. Lazarus's sonnet imagines that the statue's gaze spans divisions and envisions a redemption of the past in a way beyond technology: "Her mild eyes command / The air-bridged harbor that twin cities frame"; the harbor between the cities was widening at that time, though, growing far wider than what Crane calls "the river that is East." Still the metaphor of bridging and connecting is a central one for so much modern urban poetry. The oppressive proximity of other people does little in itself to alleviate individual loneliness (as rural solitude indeed can), and connection would become more and more important in poetry about New York as the twentieth century would unroll.

Even earlier poetry—from Virgil's imagined burning of Troy onward—can dwell on cities in some degree of disruption: John Dryden wrote many stanzas on London aflame in his poem on the year 1666, *Annus Mirabilis*, telling in epic language of the famous conflagration, starting from some spark at night, which became "a prodigious fire, / Which in mean buildings first obscurely bred, / From thence did soon to open street aspire, / And straight to palaces and temples spread." And social chaos results: "Now murmuring noises rise in every street; / The more remote run stumbling with their fear, / And in the dark men jostle as they meet." Herman Melville's marvelous glimpse of Manhattan during the draft riots of July 1863 in "The House-Top" shows the city on a hot summer night (as its title, a traditional phrase for a painting of a nocturnal scene, suggests). But Melville's powerful mythopoeic imagination does not present tired neoclassical clichés but a vision of a far more Shelleyan intensity as a mythic red giant, Arson, replaces the dog-star, Sirius, and citizens becomes beasts:

No sleep. The sultriness pervades the air
And binds the brain—a dense oppression, such
As tawny tigers feel in matted shades,
Vexing their blood and making apt for ravage.
Beneath the stars the roofy desert spreads
Vacant as Libya. All is hushed near by.
Yet fitfully from far breaks a mixed surf
Of muffled sound, the Atheist roar of riot.
Yonder, where parching Sirius set in drought,
Balefully glares red Arson—there—and there.
The Town is taken by its rats—ship-rats
And rats of the wharves. All civil charms
And priestly spells which late held hearts in awe—
Fear-bound, subjected to a better sway
Than sway of self; these like a dream dissolve,
And man rebounds whole æons back in nature.

It is only with arrival of the federal troops ranged around the city that order would be restored:

Hail to the low dull rumble, dull and dead,
And ponderous drag that jars the wall.
Wise Draco comes, deep in the midnight roll
Of black artillery; he comes, though late;
In code corroborating Calvin's creed
And cynic tyrannies of honest kings;
He comes, nor parlies; and the Town, redeemed,
Gives thanks devout; nor, being thankful, heeds
The grimy slur on the Republic's faith implied,
Which holds that Man is naturally good,
And—more—is Nature's Roman, never to be scourged.

Draco, the constellation of the protector dragon, allies itself for Melville with the Athenian law giver and thus with the draconian measures needed to subdue the rioters who during the five days of violence lynched eleven black men.

But there are other privileged moments, when New York is most itself when a particular region, street, spot, prospect, or monument is given poetic significance by being the locus of what the particular poem would claim to be a shared experience with another person—a lover, a friend, a child. Thus Sara Teasdale's sense of the Woolworth Building's prominent height is from atop it, and accompanied by a beloved other person, while the building's height is comprehended from below and at some distance in other poems. Buildings in general provide points of view, in both literal and figurative senses, on other parts of the city; a monument can be felt as making present what it commemorates or canceling the referential past with its heavy presence.

The poets who have written of New York vary widely as well in their relations to the city. Some are merely pointed reporters, purportedly objective and leaving their own personal lives in the city in many ways moot; in other cases, it is just their own lives that matter deeply—whether the speaker of the poem is a native New Yorker or an adopted and adopting one (the process works both ways). Where in the city the speaker lives and whether the scene or moment that the poem addresses is local to him or her or central to everybody—the variety of these and similar questions is vast. Howard Moss, a fine poet and editor, suggested that New York poems might be by nature elegiac, at least for the writing of native New Yorkers, in that so many of the places in them were the haunts of—and then became haunted by—the poet's childhood. But there are also poets who write as visitors in their own languages, such as Lorca, Mayakovsky, Borges, Paz, and Sassoon. And yet other citizens who produce poetry in other languages about the city, including that remarkable body of earlier-twentieth-century New York poetry in the Yiddish language by poets like the great Moishe Leib Halpern, who writes of how

Like monkeys in the trees, the children
Hang in their fire-escapes, asleep;

Soot drifts down from above their heads,
Dropped by the moon, a chimney sweep.
—A little love in big Manhattan.

Alfred Corn's gaze pierces through the well-known imagery of Ellis Island immigrants in "Variousness," his moving and powerful evocation of individuation emerging from generalizations that the present makes of the past and of "the human fate given a human face." And Corn's "variousness" could be thought of as thematic of this collection—the first notable one of poetry directed toward places, people, monuments, and moments since Howard Moss's elegantly chosen *New York Poems* of twenty-five years ago. The verse in these pages maps out a kind of guidebook stroll through New York as it was, has been, and is now, from Claude Mckay's and Langston Hughes's Harlem to James Merrill's Upper East Side, and from Joseph Rodman Drake's experience of a completely rural Bronx to contemporary writers' views of Manhattan. A lot of the specific and topical poems that may give vivid glimpses of the city at various times in its history will, indeed, seem dated later on, and most of the poems of the last decades of the twentieth century reprinted here may indeed exemplify a soon-to-seem dated manner as much as the dutifully rhymed couplets of earlier nineteenth-century poems by Nathaniel Parker Willis and Emerson's friend Christopher P. Cranch, in which the name of Broadway was pronounced—as one sees from their rhyming—"Broad*way*."

Some imposing monuments and some very tall buildings, as well as many humbler and more banal ones (especially among those of the last two and a half decades) contribute diverse representations and expressions of this great city's unique way of being cosmopolitan. Poems variously of celebration, satiric disgust, or quasi-prophetic vision will frequently share the form of the catalogue so powerfully adapted by Whitman from the poetry of previous periods. Wandering through the streets of these pages, different readers will dwell variously on a historical range of sentiments and even sentimentalities, or on a variorum of tones of urban irony, whether of Ogden Nash's half-satiric delight framed in his characteristic half-doggerel, or the recent poet Joel Brouwer's amusing parody of William Carlos Williams's celebrated poem "The

Yachts"—the agenda of beauty, conflict, and cruelty is brought down to a scale appropriate to miniature boats in the shallow waters of Central Park's Conservatory Pond. Even in the ironies, the allusiveness, the formal self-reference, the simultaneous evasion and acknowledgment of literary tradition that marks the poetry of the later twentieth century, there is something of the truly urban that transcends the merely urbane. And there is something to remind us that cities—each one configured differently—can seem to be figures for poetry itself.

PREFACE

STEPHEN WOLF

ALONG THE ESPLANADE of the World Financial Center in Lower Manhattan, where the city began nearly four centuries ago, runs a low fence inscribed for twenty yards with two bronzed passages of poetry. The first is Walt Whitman's, timeless and majestic, composed when the city foresaw the epic role in the world it would soon hold: "City of the World! (for all races are here. All the lands of the earth make contributions here;) City of the Sea! city of wharves and stores! city of tall facades of marble and iron! Proud and passionate city! mettlesome, mad, extravagant city!" A century later, New York's limitless potential had far surpassed even Whitman's vision to become the financial, mercantile, entertainment, and political capital of the world. More important, to twenty-five-year-old Frank O'Hara, the capital of the art world had shifted from Paris to New York, and his poetry along the esplanade proclaims the city—its destiny fulfilled—complete unto itself: "One need never leave the confines of New York to get all the greenery one wishes—I can't even enjoy a blade of grass unless I know there's a subway handy, or a record store or some other sign that people do not totally *regret* life."

While all urban poetry shares subject matter and themes, this anthology is singularly about New York City—not merely as setting but as the collection's primary character. The earliest poem included was written two hundred years before Whitman's, when the city was still called New Amsterdam. The most recent poems in this book were written a half-century after O'Hara's. Poets who lived here, who live here still, tell New York's vast, infinitely varied, contradictory, ever-changing, yet essentially consistent and unique story: Hudson's arrival, Stuyvesant's prejudice, the city's astonishing growth and the tragic consequences that had on its people. Preserving what has vanished, poems speak from Ellis Island and of struggles even in the promised land, atop a skyscraper's thrilling observation deck and deep in teeming tenements, on sidewalks, in taxis, of decay, fear, and kindness in the subway ride. Despite the fact that Manhattan is surely the most artificially created place on earth, poets write of nature; early voices described a beautiful land of abundance quickly encroached upon by the city's growth—a crucial issue still—so that roof tops, gardens, green squares, an owl's wing, the surrounding rivers, and, supremely, Central Park become most precious and sacred in wondrous, merciless New York.

All the poems in this book speak of New York, and many poems are intrinsically American as well. The Brooklyn Bridge, Times Square, Broadway, and the Statue of Liberty (a subject of poems even before it was erected) are woven through our national identity, and because the marketing of news, business, fashion, the arts, and entertainment radiates from New York, common American experiences are New York experiences, however vicarious. The Lower East Side and Harlem, for example, are hallowed neighborhoods for many who have never walked those streets. The lure and betrayal of the American Dream originated on this island, and, though earliest legend tells of a real estate swindle of the ingenuous Lenapes—the entire island for a few coins—the city evolved not for business alone but for an ideal as fundamental to New York's conception of itself as is the Manhattan schist on which the future would rise. Those first few families seeking religious freedom colonized a remote Dutch harbor that has remained safe haven for the persecuted, the outcast, and the dreamer for nearly four centuries. Other cities have more people, taller buildings, longer bridges, or a more gleaming infrastructure, but New York remains a symbol to the world of both this nation and the modern cosmopolis as surely as the image of a skyline conjures up Manhattan, and never more so than now after what has been lost.

"The city is like poetry," wrote E. B. White in his 1948 memoir, *Here Is New York*, because "it compresses all life, all races and breeds, into a small island and adds music" that floats across bridges and boroughs from poets as dissimilar as delicate Sara Teasdale and junkie-thief Miguel Piñero, with visions as contradictory as the far bleaker New York in Allen Ginsberg's poems written only blocks from where his friend Frank O'Hara was writing love poems to the city. And both poets came to New York for the same reasons: it was New York, and other poets had arrived before them. Following the First World War there was always Greenwich Village before, after, or instead of Montmartre, and though soaring rents eventually drove poets across town to the East Side, their gatherings in such a confined space created lively dialogues, crossing neighborhoods and generations that find inspiration from the same splendor of a bridge or sanctified street. This collection includes two Nobel Prize recipients, fifteen Pulitzer Prize winners, and many others included are the most recognized in western literature. Some poets in this book were once more popular, their reputations having faded despite wonderful poems, while others have endured neglect or only now are having their voices heard, but whether writing sonnets, experiments, epics, or imagistic verse, all have been either inspired by or in conflict with New York, and sometimes even both in the same poem.

"The final measure of the greatness of all people," wrote James Weldon Johnson, "is the amount and standard of the literature and art they have produced." Although it provides only a sampling of the vast amount of literature about New York, *I Speak of the City* is a testament to the city's spirit, preserved and newly created in the most ennobling expression of the human heart.

I SPEAK OF THE CITY

JACOB STEENDAM

Known as the first poet of New Netherlands, Jacob Steendam (1616–1672) was born in Holland and came to the colony of New Amsterdam about 1653 as a clerk for the Dutch West India Company. Perhaps a farmer, he had a house on Pearl Street. This parable of the neglected child asking help from its mother was written in 1659, five years before this most valuable Dutch harbor was stolen by the English and its named changed to New York.

THE COMPLAINT OF NEW AMSTERDAM TO ITS MOTHER ☆

I'm a child of the gods
Who on th' Amstel have abodes;
Whence their orders forth are sent
Swift for aid and punishment.

I, of Amsterdam, was born,
Early of her breasts forlorn;
From her care so quickly weaned
Oft have I my fate bemoaned.

From my youth up left alone,
Naught save hardship have I known;
Dangers have beset my way
From the first I saw the day.

Think you that a cause for marvel?
This will then the thread unravel,
And the circumstances trace,
Which upon my birth took place.

Would you ask for my descent?
Long the time was it I spent
In the loins of warlike Mars.
'T seems my mother, seized with fears,

Prematurely brought me forth.
But I now am very loth
To inform how this befol;
Though 'twas thus, I know full well.

Bacchus, too,—it is a dream,
First beheld the daylight's beam
From the thigh of Jupiter.
But my reasons go too far.

My own matter must I say,
And not loiter by the way,
Yet though Bacchus oft has proven
Friend to mine in my misfortune.

Now the mid-wife who received me,
Was Bellona; in suspense, she
Long did sit in trembling fear,
For the travail was severe.

From the moment I was born,
Indian neighbors made me mourn.
They pursued me night and day,
While my mother kept away.

But my sponsors did supply
Better my necessity;
They sustained my feeble life;
They procured a bounteous wife

As my nurse, who did not spare
To my lips her paps to bare.

This was Ceres; freely she
Rendered what she nurtured me.

Her most dearly will I prize;
She has made my horns to rise;
Trained my growth through tender years,
'Midst my burdens and my cares.

True, both simple 'twas and scant,
What I had to feed my want.
Oft 't was nought except Supawn
And the flesh of buck or fawn.

When I thus began to grow,
No more care did they bestow.
Yet my breasts are full and neat,
And my hips are firmly set.

Neptune shows me his good will;
Merc'ry, quick, exerts his skill
Me t'adorn with silk and gold;
Whence I'm sought by suitors bold.

Stricken by my cheek's fresh bloom,
By my beauteous youthful form,
They attempt to seize the treasure
To enjoy their wanton pleasure.

They, my orchards too, would plunder.
Truly 'tis a special wonder,
That a maid, with such a portion,
Does not suffer more misfortune.

For, I venture to proclaim,
No one can a maiden name,
Who with richer land is blessed
Than th' estate by me possessed.

See! Two streams my garden bind,
From the East and North they wind,
Rivers pouring in the sea,
Rich in fish, beyond degree.

Milk and butter; fruits to eat
No one can enumerate;
Ev'ry vegetable known;
Grain the best that e'er was grown.

All the blessings man e'er knew,
Here does our Great Giver strew,
(And a climate ne'er more pure)
But for me,—yet immature,

Fraught with danger; for the swine
Trample down these crops of mine;
Up-root, too, my choicest land;
Still and dumb, the while, I stand,

In the hope, my mother's arm
Will protect me from the harm.
She can succor my distress.
Now my wish, my sole request,

Is for men to till my land;
So I'll not in silence stand.
I have lab'rors almost none;
Let my household large become;

I'll my mother's kitchen furnish
With my knicknacks, with my surplus;
With tobacco, furs and grain;
So that Prussia she'll disdain.

TRANS. HENRY C. MURPHY

PHILIP FRENEAU

Referred to in his day as the "father of American poetry," and certainly one of New York's earliest important writers, Philip Freneau (1752–1832) was born on Frankfort Street in New York City, a descendant of French Huguenots and orthodox Calvinists, when the city was still an English colony. A political writer for independence, a militiaman, and a British prisoner (subject of his poem "The British Prison-Ship"), the poet writes here of an issue still a concern to New Yorkers over two centuries later.

ON THE CITY ENCROACHMENT ON THE HUDSON RIVER, 1800

Where Hudson, once, in all his pride
In surges burst upon the shore
They plant amidst his flowing tide
Moles to defy his loudest roar;
And lofty mansions grow where late
Half Europe might discharge her freight.

From northern lakes and wastes of snow
The river takes a distant rise,
Now marches swift, now marches slow,
And now adown some rapid flies
Till join'd the *Mohawk*, in their course
They travel with united force.

But cease, nor with too daring aim
Encroach upon this giant flood;
No rights reserved by nature, claim,
Nor on his ancient bed intrude:—
The river may in rage awake
And time restore him all you take.

SAMUEL WOODWORTH

Born in Massachusetts, son of an impoverished farmer and Revolutionary War fighter, Samuel Woodworth (1785–1842) spent the first ten years of his life as an indentured servant to a Boston printer. He brought the skills he learned to New York in 1809, where he and George Pope Morris founded *New-York Mirror* in 1823, one of the thriving newspapers published along Publishers' Row (where Park Row and Centre are now). This poem tells of the grandeur and promise, impossibly idealized and with a blind eye, of early New York.

NEW YORK

Hail! happy city! where the arts convene
And busy commerce animates the scene;
Where taste, and elegance, with wealth combine,
To perfect art, in every bright design;
Where splendid mansions that attract the eye,
Can boast, what opulence could never buy,
The generous wish that springs to Virtue's goal,
The liberal mind, the high, aspiring soul;
The freeborn wish that warms the patriot's breast,
The chaste refinements that make beauty blest:
These are the charms that give Industry, here,
A pleasing relish, and a hope sincere;
And while they bid the sighs of anguish cease,
Strew Labor's pillow with the flowers of peace.

When the sad exile, freed from ocean's storm,
First treads our shore, what hopes his bosom warm!
For welcome meets him with an honest smile,
And kind attentions every care beguile.
No dread of tyrants here his peace annoys,
No fears of fetters mar his bosom's joys;
No dark suspicions on his steps attend,
He only needs one, here, to find a friend;

He finds, at once, a refuge and a home,
Nor longer mourns the cause that bade him roam.

Where'er he turns, on every side are traced
The marks of genius, and enlightened taste;
He sees in every portico and dome,
The architectural grace of Greece and Rome;
And finds, in our unrivaled promenades,
Charms that may vie with Athen's classic shades.
That rural scene that skirts the loveliest bay
That ever sparkled in the solar ray;
Where the rude engines of relentless Mars,
Once frowned, in ranks, beneath Columbia's stars,
But which have since for ever yielded place
To fashion, beauty, elegance, and grace—
That lovely scene first greets the wanderer's eye,
And cheats his bosom of a passing sigh,
So like some spots upon his native shore,
By him, perhaps, to be enjoyed no more!

On either hand, a mighty river glides,
Which here, at length, unite and mingle tides,
Like some fond pair, affianced in the skies,
Whose forms, as yet, ne'er met each other's eyes,
When the auspicious fated moment rolls,
They meet—they love—unite, and mingle souls.

Magnific piles, the monuments of art,
And lofty spires, adorn this splendid mart,
Where Piety erects her sacred shrine,
And pays her homage to the power divine;
Where heaven-born "genius wings his eagle flight,
Rich dew-drops shaking from his wings of light;"
Where Science opens wide his boundless store
Of classic sweets and antiquated lore;
Where freedom, virtue, knowledge, all unite
To make the scene an Eden of delight;

Where pulpit, press, and bar, are all combined
To mend the heart, and elevate the mind.

Nor do these mighty engines toil alone,
By other hands the seeds of taste are sown.
The Drama opes its bright, instructive scenes;
Its object *use*—amusement but the *means*:
For though the muse resort to fiction's aid,
Fiction is here, but truth is masquerade,
And thousands, who her grave entreaties shun,
Are, by her borrowed smiles, allured and won.

FITZ-GREENE HALLECK

Born in Connecticut and moving with his family to New York in 1811, Fitz-Greene Halleck (1790–1867) wrote, along with Joseph Rodman Drake, "The Croakers," a series of local satires for the *New York Evening Post*, and his 1819 poem "Fanny" was a satire of New York society. He edited both *The Works of Byron in Prose and Verse* (1833) and *Selection of British Poets* (1840), served as vice president of Authors Club of New York (Washington Irving, president). Known as the Knickerbocker Poet and, according to William Cullen Bryant, "the favorite poet of the city of New York," he had a Bronx street named after him, and there is a statue of him along Literary Mall in Central Park.

SONG

There's a barrel of porter at Tammany Hall ☆
And the bucktails are swigging it all the night long;
In the time of my boyhood 'twas pleasant to call
For a seat and segar, mid the jovial throng.

That beer and those bucktails I never forget;
But oft, when alone, and unnoticed by all,

I think, is the porter cask foaming there yet?
  Are the bucktails still swigging at Tammany Hall?

No! the porter was out long before it was stale,
  But some blossoms on many a nose brightly shone,
And the speeches inspired by the fumes of the ale,
  Had the fragrance of porter when porter was gone.

How much Cozzens will draw of such beer ere he dies,
  Is a question of moment to me and to all;
For still dear to my soul, as 'twas then to my eyes,
  Is that barrel of porter at Tammany Hall.

WILLIAM CULLEN BRYANT

Born in a log cabin in Massachusetts, William Cullen Bryant (1794–1878) wrote "Thanatopsis," which many consider the first important truly American poem, when he was seventeen. He moved to New York at thirty and became an editor at the *New York Evening Post*. Soon he was chief editor, a position he held the rest of his life and which he used as a platform for city reform, civic leadership, and the city's desperate need for a large public space, his vision later realized in Central Park. A statue of Bryant behind the Public Library is in the park that bears his name.

HYMN OF THE CITY

  Not in the solitude
Alone may man commune with heaven, or see,
  Only in savage wood
And sunny vale, the present Deity;
  Or only hear His voice
Where the winds whisper and the waves rejoice.

  Even here do I behold
Thy steps, Almighty!—here, amidst the crowd,

Through the great city rolled,
With everlasting murmur deep and loud—
Choking the ways that wind
'Mongst the proud piles, the work of human kind.
Thy golden sunshine comes
From the round heaven, and on their dwellings lies,
And lights their inner homes;
For them thou fill'st with air the unbounded skies,
And givest them the stores
Of ocean, and the harvests of its shores.

Thy spirit is around,
Quickening the restless mass that sweeps along;
And this eternal sound—
Voices and footfalls of the numberless throng—
Like the resounding sea,
Or like the rainy tempest, speaks of thee.
And when the hours of rest
Come, like a calm upon the mid-sea brine,
Hushing its billowy breast—
The quiet of that moment too is thine;
It breathes of Him who keeps
The vast and helpless city while it sleeps.

JOSEPH RODMAN DRAKE

Born in New York City, Joseph Rodman Drake (1795–1820) wrote "The American Flag," a poem which became a standard patriotic declamation. Although a prominent physician, he, along with the Knickerbocker Poet Fitz-Greene Halleck, wrote satirical, daily, and anonymous verses for the *New York Evening Post*. This poem about recollections of his childhood is perhaps the first to mention the Bronx as not merely a river but a place to live. His death at only twenty-five from tuberculosis led to Halleck's elegy "Green be the turf above thee," and he is buried in Joseph Rodman Drake Park in the Bronx.

BRONX, 1818 ☆

I sat me down upon a green bank-side,
  Skirting the smooth edge of a gentle river,
Whose waters seemed unwillingly to glide,
  Like parting friends, who linger while they sever;
Enforced to go, yet seemingly still unready,
  Backward they wind their way in many a wistful eddy.

Grey o'er my head the yellow-vested willow
  Ruffled its hoary top in the fresh breezes,
Glancing in light, like spray on a green billow,
  Or the fine frost-work which young winter freezes;
When first his power in infant pastime trying,
  Congeals sad autumn's tears on the dead branches lying.

From rocks around hung the loose ivy dangling,
  And in the clefts sumach of liveliest green,
Bright ising-stars the little beach was spangling,
  The gold-cup sorrel from his gauzy screen
Shone like a fairy crown, enchased and beaded,
  Left on some morn, when light flashed in their eyes unheeded.

The hum-bird shook is sun-touched wings around,
  The bluefinch caroll'd in the still retreat;
The antic squirrel capered on the ground
  Where lichens made a carpet for his feet:
Through the transparent waves, the ruddy minkle
  Shot up in glimmering sparks his red fin's tiny twinkle.

There were dark cedars with loose mossy tresses,
  White powdered dog-trees, and stiff hollies flaunting
Gaudy as rustics in their May-day dresses,
  Blue pelloret from purple leaves upslanting
A modest gaze, like eyes of a young maiden
  Shining beneath dropt lids the evening of her wedding.

The breeze fresh springing from the lips of morn,
  Kissing the leaves, and sighing so to lose 'em,
The winding of the merry locust's horn,
  The glad spring gushing from the rock's bare bosom:
Sweet sights, sweet sounds, all sights, all sounds excelling,
  Oh! 'twas a ravishing spot formed for a poet's dwelling.

And did I leave thy loveliness, to stand
  Again in the dull world of earthly blindness?
Pained with the pressure of unfriendly hands,
  Sick of smooth looks, agued with icy kindness?
Left I for this thy shades, where none intrude,
  To prison wandering thought and mar sweet solitude?

Yet I will look upon thy face again,
  My own romantic Bronx, and it will be
A face more pleasant than the face of men.
  Thy waves are old companions, I shall see
A well-remembered form in each old tree,
  And hear a voice long loved in thy wild minstrelsy.

RALPH WALDO EMERSON

Born in Boston, Harvard-educated, and, like his father, an ordained minister, Ralph Waldo Emerson (1803–1882) gradually developed a faith in the individual's moral sentiment rather than in conventional religion, and his reading of Samuel Taylor Coleridge's *Aides to Reflection* provided a basis for "intuitive reason" over "understanding" and influenced his idealistic philosophy of transcendentalism. In his essay "The Poet," Emerson states that the poet "appraises us not of his wealth but of the common wealth," and he believed early in Walt Whitman to whom he wrote, after reading the first edition of *Leaves of Grass*, that "I greet you at the beginning of a great career." His *Journals and Miscellaneous Notebooks*, where the following poem remained only a penciled version and was never published, reveal a spiritual life in nineteenth-century America.

"HE WALKED THE STREETS OF GREAT NEW YORK"

He walked the streets of great New York
Full of men, the men were full of blood
Signs of powers, signs of worth,
Yet all seemed trivial
As the ceaseless cry
Of the newsboys in the street
Now men do not listen after
The voice in the breast
Which makes the thunder mean
But the Great God hath departed
And they listen after Scott & Byron
I met no gods—I harboured none,
As I walked by noon & night alone
The crowded ways
And yet I found in the heart of the town
A few children of God nestling in his bosom
Not detached as all the crowd appeared
each one a sutlers boat
Cruising for private gain
But these seemed undetached united
Lovers of Love, of Truth,
And as among Indians they say
The One the One is known
So under the eaves of Wall Street
Brokers had met the Eternal
In the city of surfaces
Where I a swain becomes a surface
I found & worshipped Him.
Always thus neighbored well
The two contemporaries dwell
The World which by the world is known
And Wisdom seeking still its own
I walked with men
Who seemed as if they were chairs or stools
Tables or shopwindows or champagne baskets

For these they loved & were if truly seen
I walked with others of their wisdom gave me proof
Who brought the starry heaven
As near as the house roof

NATHANIEL PARKER WILLIS

Born in Portland, Maine, but raised in Boston, Nathaniel Parker Willis (1806–1867) published his first poem at age seventeen in his father's newspaper. A journalist after graduating Yale, he moved to New York in 1831, where he became a contributing editor to the *New-York Mirror*. Although known as a chronicler of fashionable New York life, he befriended Edgar Allan Poe, whose reputation he defended from Rufus Griswold's attacks. A playwright and writer of light fiction as well as a poet, he also edited, along with George Pope Morris, *The Prose and Poetry of Europe and America* (1857).

CITY LYRICS ☆

Argument.— The poet starts from the Bowling Green to take his sweet-heart up to Thompson's for an ice, or (if she is inclined for more) ices. He confines his muse to matters which any every-day man and young woman may see in taking the same promenade for the same innocent refreshment.

Come out, love—the night is enchanting!
  The moon hangs just over Broadway;
The stars are all lighted and panting—
  (Hot weather up there, I dare say!)
'Tis seldom that "coolness" entices,
  And love is no better for chilling—
But come up to Thompson's for ices,
  And cool your warm heart for a shilling!

What perfume comes balmily o'er us?
  Mint juleps from City Hotel!
A loafer is smoking before us—

(A nasty cigar, by the smell!)
Oh Woman! thou secret past knowing!
Like lilachs that grow by the wall,
You breathe every air that is going,
Yet gather but sweetness from all!

On, on! by St. Paul's, and the Astor!
Religion seems very ill-plann'd!
For one day we list to the pastor,
For six days we list to the band!
The sermon may dwell on the future,
The organ your pulses may calm—
When—pest!—that remember'd cachucha
Upsets both the sermon and psalm!

Oh, pity the love that must utter
While goes a swift omnibus by!
(Though sweet is *I scream*[*] when the flutter
Of fans shows thermometers high)—
But if what I bawl, or I mutter,
Falls into your ear but to die,
Oh, the dew that falls into the gutter
Is not more unhappy than I!

[*] *Query.* Should this be *Ice cream*, or I scream?—*Printer's Devil.*

LAUGHTON OSBORN

Born in New York, an 1827 graduate of Columbia University, Laughton Osborn (1809–1878) wrote poems in French and Italian and was a skilled painter and an eccentric literary recluse. Here he writes of the notorious slum—known also as "Den of Thieves" and "Murderer's Alley"—where "you will see," wrote the reformer Lydia Maria Child in 1844, "nearly every form of human misery, every sign of human degradation," and tenements were called such ominous names as the Gates of Hell or Brickbat Mansion.

FIVE POINTS, 1838

☆

Fast by the dike, where frown the granite eaves
Of the huge dome Manhattan rears for thieves,
A range of filthy dwelling houses stood,
Fac'd with dull brick, and bridg'd with steps of wood.
Here, in chalk'd spaces, seven feet by four,
Crowd various families a common floor;
The night's straw sack their musty couch by day,
While on the loathsome plank their broken victuals lay.
Dogs, cats, and children in one litter cry,
And mud-cak'd pigs encroach upon the sky.
Without, all wreck and nastiness; within,
Starvation, sickness, vermin, stench, and sin.
Such hives as still are found, with ev'n less room,
In Laurens Street, the southern side of Broom.

CHRISTOPHER PEARSE CRANCH

An ordained Unitarian minister who left the clergy for poetry, Christopher Pearse Cranch (1813–1892) was connected to the New England transcendentalist poets and appeared frequently in their journal, *The Dial*. Although written nearly a century and a half ago, this poem tells of the timeless disparity in wealth visible in New York.

THE OLD APPLE-WOMAN: A BROADWAY LYRIC

She sits by the side of a turbulent stream
That rushes and rolls forever
Up and down like a weary dream
In the trance of a burning fever.
Up and down through the long Broadway
If flows with its tiresome paces—
Down and up through the noisy day,

A river of feet and of faces.
Seldom a drop of that river's spray
Touches her withered features;
Yet still she sits there day by day
In the throng of her fellow-creatures.
Apples and cakes and candy to sell,
Daily before her lying.
The ragged newsboys know her well—
The rich never think of buying.
Year in, year out, in her dingy shawl
The wind and the rain she weathers,
Patient and mute at her little stall;
But few are the coppers she gathers.
Still eddies the crowd intent on gain.
Each for himself is striving
With selfish heart and seething brain—
An endless hurry and driving.
The loud carts rattle in thunder and dust;
Gay Fashion sweeps by in its coaches.
With a vacant stare she mumbles her crust,
She is past complaints and reproaches.
Still new faces and still new feet—
The same yet changing forever;
They jostle along through the weary street,
The waves of the human river.
Withered and dry like a leafless bush
That clings to the bank of the torrent,
Year in, year out, in the whirl and the rush,
She sits, of the city's current.
The shrubs of the garden will blossom again
Though far from the flowing river;
But the spring returns to her in vain—
Its bloom has nothing to give her.
Yet in her heart there buds the hope
Of a Father's love and pity;
For her the clouded skies shall ope,
And the gates of a heavenly city.

HERMAN MELVILLE

Bookkeeper, clerk, teacher, lecturer, shipmate on whaling vessels, and later deputy inspector of customs for the port of New York, Herman Melville (1819–1891) was born in New York City, the grandson of the American Revolutionary general Peter Gansevoort. After publishing financially successful fictional adventures of his sailing experiences, Melville wrote *Moby-Dick* (1851), the great novel of the American romantic age, though it met with indifference and doomed his long remaining literary career. His short novel "Bartleby, the Scrivener: A Story of Wall Street" (1853) is a powerful indictment of the cold-hearted, business-oriented city, and this poem is a roof-top view of the bloodiest urban riots in American history: the three days' disturbances that followed Lincoln's Conscription Act of 1863. Melville is buried in the Bronx.

THE HOUSE-TOP ☆

A Night Piece
(JULY, 1863)

No sleep. The sultriness pervades the air
And binds the brain—a dense oppression, such
As tawny tigers feel in matted shades,
Vexing their blood and making apt for ravage.
Beneath the stars the roofy desert spreads
Vacant as Libya. All is hushed near by.
Yet fitfully from far breaks a mixed surf
Of muffled sound, the Atheist roar of riot.
Yonder, where parching Sirius set in drought,
Balefully glares red Arson—there—and there.
The Town is taken by its rats—ship-rats
And rats of the wharves. All civil charms
And priestly spells which late held hearts in awe—
Fear-bound, subjected to a better sway
Than sway of self; these like a dream dissolve,
And man rebounds whole æons back in nature.

Hail to the low dull rumble, dull and dead,
And ponderous drag that shakes the wall.
Wise Draco comes, deep in the midnight roll
Of black artillery; he comes, though late;
In code corroborating Calvin's creed
And cynic tyrannies of honest kings;
He comes, nor parlies; and the Town, redeemed,
Gives thanks devout; nor, being thankful, heeds
The grimy slur on the Republic's faith implied,
Which holds that Man is naturally good,
And—more—is Nature's Roman, never to be scourged.

WALT WHITMAN

Born in West Hills, Long Island, in 1819 and moving with his family to Brooklyn when he was three, Walt Whitman watched New York evolve from a harbor of 50,000 to become, when he died in 1892, the largest city in the world, a symbol of the Industrial Age, and—to Whitman's limitless delight and wonder—the home of more than 2.5 million people, with another million before the decade was out. Printer, newsman, editor, medical assistant during the Civil War, father of modern poetry, he expressed in his essay "Human and Heroic New York"—as he did in his poetry— a fascination with "the crowds, the streets . . . Broadway, the ferries, the west side of the city, democratic Bowery—human appearances and manners as seen in all these, and along the wharves . . . or in Wall and Nassau streets by day—in the places of amusement at night—bubbling and whirling and moving like its own environment of waters—endless humanity in all phases." Still the greatest influence on other poets writing of New York and a model for poets today, Whitman wrote in the final line of his preface to the first edition of *Leaves of Grass* (1855)—poems written "out of my life in Brooklyn and New York"—that "the proof of a poet is that his country absorbs him as affectionately as he has absorbed it."

MANNAHATTA ☆

I was asking for something specific and perfect for my city,
Whereupon, lo! upsprang the aboriginal name!
Now I see what there is in a name, a word, liquid, sane,
 unruly, musical, self-sufficient;
I see that the word of my city is that word from of old,
Because I see that word nested in nests of water-bays, superb,
Rich, hemm'd thick all around with sailships and steamships,
 an island sixteen miles long, solid-founded.
Numberless crowded streets, high growth of iron, slender,
 strong, light, splendidly uprising toward clear skies,
Tides swift and ample, well-loved by me, toward sundown,
The flowing sea-currents, the little islands, larger adjoining
 islands, the heights, the villas,
The countless masts, the white shore-steamers, the lighters,
The down-town streets, the jobbers' houses of business, the
 houses of business of the ship-merchants and money-
 brokers, the river-streets,
Immigrants arriving, fifteen or twenty thousand in a week,
The carts hauling goods, the manly race of drivers of horses, the
 brown-faced sailors,
The summer air, the bright sun shining, and the sailing clouds
 aloft,
The winter snows, the sleigh-bells, the broken ice in the river,
 passing along up or down with the flood-tide or ebb-tide,
The mechanics of the city, the masters, well-form'd, beautiful-
 faced, looking you straight in the eyes,
Trottoirs throng'd, vehicles, Broadway, the women, the shops
 and shows,
A million people—manners free and superb—open voices—
 hospitality—the most courageous and friendly young men,
City of hurried and sparkling waters! city of spires and masts!
City nested in bays! my city!
The city of such women, I am mad to be with them! I will return
 after death to be with them!
The city of such young men, I swear I cannot live happy, without
 I often go talk, walk, eat, drink, sleep, with them!

from GIVE ME THE SPLENDID SILENT SUN ☆

2

Keep your splendid silent sun,
Keep your woods O Nature, and the quiet places by the woods,
Keep your fields of clover and timothy, and your corn-fields and
orchards,
Keep the blossoming buckwheat fields where the Ninth-month
bees hum;
Give me faces and streets—give me these phantoms incessant and
endless along the trottoirs!
Give me the interminable eyes—give me women—give me
comrades and lovers by the thousands!
Let me see new ones every day—let me hold new ones by the
hand every day!
Give me such shows—give me the streets of Manhattan!
Give me Broadway, with the soldiers marching—give me the
sound of the trumpets and drums!
(The soldiers in companies or regiments—some starting away,
flush'd and reckless,
Some, their time up, returning with thinn'd ranks, young yet very
old, worn, marching, noticing nothing;)
Give me the shores and wharves heavy-fringed with black ships!
O such for me! O an intense life, full to repletion and varied!
The life of the theatre, bar-room, huge hotel, for me!
The saloon of the steamer! the crowded excursion for me! the
torchlight procession!
The dense brigade bound for the war, with high piled military
wagons following;
People, endless, streaming, with strong voices, passions,
pageants,
Manhattan streets with their powerful throbs, with beating drums
as now,
The endless and noisy chorus, the rustle and clank of muskets,
(even the sight of the wounded),
Manhattan crowds, with their turbulent musical chorus!
Manhattan faces and eyes forever for me.

from CROSSING BROOKLYN FERRY ☆

8

Ah, what can ever be more stately and admirable to me than
mast-hemm'd Manhattan?
River and sunset and scallop-edg'd waves of flood-tide?
The sea-gulls oscillating their bodies, the hay-boat in the twilight,
and the belated lighter?
What gods can exceed these that clasp me by the hand, and with
voices I love call me promptly and loudly by my nighest
name as I approach?
What is more subtle than this which ties me to the woman
or man that looks in my face?
Which fuses me into you now, and pours my meaning into
you?

We understand then do we not?
What I promis'd without mentioning it, have you not accepted?
What the study could not teach—what the preaching could not
accomplish is accomplish'd, is it not?

9

Flow on, river! flow with the flood-tide, and ebb with the ebb-tide!
Frolic on, crested and scallop-edg'd waves!
Gorgeous clouds of the sunset! drench with your splendor me, or
the men and women generations after me!
Cross from shore to shore, countless crowds of passengers!
Stand up, tall masts of Mannahatta! stand up, beautiful hills of
Brooklyn!
Throb, baffled and curious brain! throw out questions and
answers!
Suspend here and everywhere, eternal float of solution!
Gaze, loving and thirsty eyes, in the house or street or public
assembly!
Sound out, voices of young men! loudly and musically call me by
my nighest name!
Live, old life! play the part that looks back on the actor or actress!

Play the old role, the role that is great or small according as one makes it!
Consider, you who peruse me, whether I may not in unknown ways be looking upon you;
Be firm, rail over the river, to support those who lean idly, yet haste with the hasting current;
Fly on, sea-birds! fly sideways, or wheel in large circles high in the air;
Receive the summer sky, you water, and faithfully hold it till all downcast eyes have time to take it from you!
Diverge, fine spokes of light, from the shape of my head, or any one's head, in the sunlit water!
Come on, ships from the lower bay! pass up or down, white-sail'd schooners, sloops, lighters!
Flaunt away, flags of all nations! be duly lower'd at sunset!
Burn high you fires, foundry chimneys! cast black shadows at nightfall! cast red and yellow light over the tops of the houses!
Appearances, now or henceforth, indicate what you are,
You necessary film, continue to envelop the soul,
About my body for me, and your body for you, be hung out divinest aromas,
Thrive, cities—bring your freight, bring your shows, ample and sufficient rivers,
Expand, being than which none else is perhaps more spiritual,
Keep your places, objects than which none else is more lasting.
You have waited, you always wait, you dumb, beautiful ministers,
We receive you with free sense at last, and are insatiate henceforward;
Not you any more shall be able to foil us, or withhold yourselves from us,
We use you, and do not cast you aside—we plant you permanently within us,
We fathom you not—we love you—there is perfection in you also,
You finish your parts toward eternity;
Great or small, you furnish your parts toward the soul.

EMMA LAZARUS

Publishing her first book of poetry (praised by Emerson) when she was only seventeen, Emma Lazarus (1849–1887) came from one of the oldest and most wealthy of the city's Jewish families but was deeply moved by immigrant Jews fleeing pogroms in Czarist Russia. Her articles in *Critic* and *Century* were passionate articulations on the need for decent housing on the Lower East Side. "The New Colossus," written in 1883, was her response to the committee formed to raise awareness and needed funds for the pedestal of the world's largest statue—Frederic-Auguste Bartholdi's "Liberty Enlightening the World." Dying of Hodgkin's disease, the poet would never see the statue nor ever know that in 1903 her sonnet was carved into the pedestal she had so lovingly helped twenty years before.

THE NEW COLOSSUS ☆

Not like the brazen giant of Greek fame,
With conquering limbs astride from land to land;
Here at our sea-washed, sunset gates shall stand
A mighty woman with a torch, whose flame
Is the imprisoned lightning, and her name
Mother of Exiles. From her beacon-hand
Glows world-wide welcome; her mild eyes command
The air-bridged harbor that twin cities frame.
"Keep, ancient lands, your storied pomp!" cries she
With silent lips. "Give me your tired, your poor,
Your huddled masses yearning to breathe free,
The wretched refuse of your teeming shore.
Send these, the homeless, tempest-tost to me,
I lift my lamp beside the golden door!"

HENRY VAN DYKE

Henry Van Dyke (1852–1933) served as pastor of the Brick Presbyterian Church in New York City before he was a professor of

English literature at Princeton. In this leap back and forth in time, the poet sails with the Dutch East India Company in 1609, searching for a northern passage to the Pacific with Englishman Henry Hudson, the first European to step foot on Manhattan. "Never have I beheld," Hudson wrote in his first official report, "such a rich and pleasant land."

HUDSON'S LAST VOYAGE

Son, have you forgot
Those mellow autumn days, two years ago,
When first we sent our little ship *Half-Moon*,—
The flag of Holland floating at her peak,—
Across a sandy bar, and sounded in
Among the channels, to a goodly bay
Where all the navies of the world could ride?
A fertile island that the redmen called
Manhattan, lay above the bay: the land
Around was bountiful and friendly fair.
But never land was fair enough to hold
The seaman from the calling of the sea.
And so we bore to westward of the isle,
Along a mighty inlet, where the tide
Was troubled by a downward-flowing flood
That seemed to come from far away,—perhaps
From some mysterious gulf of Tartary?

Inland we held our course; by palisades
Of naked rock where giants might have built
Their fortress; and by rolling hills adorned
With forests rich in timber for great ships;
Through narrows where the mountains shut us in
With frowning cliffs that seemed to bar the stream;
And then through open reaches where the banks
Sloped to the water gently, with their fields
Of corn and lentils smiling in the sun.
Ten days we voyaged through that placid land,
Until we came to shoals, and sent a boat

Upstream to find,—what I already knew,—
We traveled on a river, not a strait.

But what a river! God has never poured
A stream more royal through a land more rich.
Even now I see it flowing in my dream,
While coming ages people it with men
Of manhood equal to the river's pride.
I see the wigwams of the redmen changed
To ample houses, and the tiny plots
Of maize and green tobacco broadened out
To prosperous farms, that spread o'er hill and dale
The many-coloured mantle of their crops;
I see the terraced vineyard on the slope
Where now the fox-grape loops its tangled vine;
And cattle feeding where the red deer roam;
And wild-bees gathered into busy hives,
To store the silver comb with golden sweet;
And all the promised land begins to flow
With milk and honey. Stately manors rise
Along the banks, and castles top the hills,
And little villages grow populous with trade,
Until the river runs as proudly as the Rhine,—
The thread that links a hundred towns and towers!
And looking deeper in my dream, I see
A mighty city covering the isle
They call Manhattan, equal in her state
To all the older capitals of earth,—
The gateway city of a golden world,—
A city girt with masts, and crowned with spires,
And swarming with a host of busy men,
While to her open door across the bay
The ships of all the nations flock like doves.
My name will be remembered there, for men
Will say, "This river and this isle were found
By Henry Hudson, on his way to seek
The Northwest Passage into Farthest Inde."

BYRON RUFUS NEWTON

Byron Rufus Newton (1861–1938) was born in upstate New York, served as a war correspondent for Associated Press during the Spanish-American War, and, after writing for the *New York Herald*, became the city's tax commissioner—and so knew well of "mammon," which in his *Devil's Dictionary*, Ambrose Bierce defines as "the god of the world's leading religion. His chief temple is the holy city of New York."

OWED TO NEW YORK

Vulgar of manner, overfed.
Overdressed and underbred,
Heartless, Godless, hell's delight,
Rude by day and lewd by night;
Bedwarfed the man, o'ergrown the brute,
Ruled by boss and prostitute;
Purple-robed and pauper clad,
Raving, rotting, money-mad;
A squirming herd in Mammon's mesh,
A wilderness of human flesh;
Crazed by avarice, lust and rum,
New York, thy name's "Delirium."

RICHARD HOVEY

Born in Illinois, son of a Civil War general, inspired by Whitman, and the youngest student ever to enter Dartmouth, Richard Hovey (1864–1900) is best known for his "vagabond" poems celebrating friendships and the open road—*Songs of the Vagabondia* (1894). He translated the poems of Verlaine and Mallarmé, composed verse plays based on Arthurian legends, settled in New York in 1896, and taught briefly at Barnard College before his death at thirty-five.

NEW YORK

The low line of the walls that lie outspread
Miles on long miles, the fog and smoke and slime,
The wharves and ships with flags of every clime,
The domes and steeples rising overhead!
It is not these. Rather is it the tread
Of the million heavy feet that keep sad time
To heavy thoughts, the want that mothers crime,
The weary toiling for a bitter bread,
The perishing of poets for renown,
The shriek of shame from the concealing waves.
Ah me! how many heart-beats day by day
Go to make up the life of the vast town!
O myriad dead in unremembered graves!
O torrent of the living down Broadway!

LOUISE MORGAN SILL

Born in Honolulu during her father's consulship there, Louise Morgan Sill (1868–1961) was an editor at *Harper's Magazine*. In 1906 her poetry collection *In Sun and Shade* was released. She moved to Paris early in the twentieth century, where she remained the rest of her life. Maiden Lane was a footpath just above Wall Street from Nassau Street to the East River where young women once washed clothes. Nearby, of course, was Dandy Lane, though this has since been paved over.

MAIDEN LANE

Down Maiden Lane, where clover grew,
  Sweet-scented in the early air,
Where sparkling rills went shining through
  Their grassy banks, so green, so fair,
Blithe little maids from Holland land
  Went tripping, laughing each to each,

To bathe the flax, or spread a band
 Of linen in the sun to bleach.

More than two centuries ago
 They wore this path—a maiden's lane—
Where now such waves of commerce flow
 As never dazed a burgher's brain.
Two hundred years ago and more
 Those thrifty damsels, one by one,
With plump, round arms their linen bore
 To dry in Mana-ha-ta's sun.

But now! Behold the altered view;
 No tender sward, no bubbling stream,
No laughter,—was it really true,
 Or but the fancy of a dream?
Were these harsh walls a byway sweet,
 This floor of stone a grassy plain?
Pray vanish, modern city street,
 And let us stroll down Maiden Lane.

JAMES WELDON JOHNSON

Just short of his thirtieth birthday, James Weldon Johnson (1871–1938) came to New York in 1902 to form the musical trio Cole and the Johnson Brothers. He moved to Harlem in 1914, edited the black weekly newspaper *The New York Age*, was one of the elder statesmen of the Harlem Renaissance and a professor of literature at NYU. His 1912 novel, *The Autobiography of an Ex-Colored Man*, tells of his arrival in New York City, and this tender sonnet expresses his love for "the most fatally fascinating thing in America."

MY CITY

When I come down to sleep death's endless night,
The threshold of the unknown dark to cross,

What to me then will be the keenest loss,
When this bright world blurs on my fading sight?
Will it be that no more I shall see the trees
Or smell the flowers or hear the singing birds
Or watch the flashing streams or patient herds?
No. I am sure it will be none of these.

But, ah! Manhattan's sights and sounds, her smells,
Her crowds, her throbbing force, the thrill that comes
From being of her a part, her subtle spells,
Her shining towers, her avenues, her slums—
O God! the stark, unutterable pity,
To be dead, and never again behold my city.

GEORGE CABOT LODGE

George Cabot Lodge (1873–1909) was born in Boston, the son of statesman Henry Cabot Lodge, and educated first at Harvard University, where he studied Romance languages, and later at the University of Paris. His second volume of poetry, *The Great Adventure*, was dedicated to Walt Whitman.

LOWER NEW YORK

I

BEFORE DAWN

Time has no spectacle more stern and strange;
  Life has no sleep so dense as that which lies
  On the walls and windows, blank as sightless eyes,
  On court and prison, warehouse and exchange.
Earth has no silence such as fills the range
  Of streets left bare beneath the haughty skies:—
  Of unremembered human miseries
  Churned without purpose in the trough of change.
For here where day by day the tide-race rolls

Of sordid greed and passions mean and blind,
Here is a vast necropolis of souls!
And life, that waits as with suspended breath,
Weary and still, here seems more dead than death,
Aimless and empty as an idiot's head.

II

AT DAWN

Here is the dawn a hopeless thing to see:
Sordid and pale as is the face of one
Who sinks exhausted in oblivion
After a night of deep debauchery.
Here, as the light reveals relentlessly
All that the soul has lost and greed has won,
Scarce we believe that somewhere now the sun
Dawns overseas in stainless majesty.
Yet the day comes!—ghastly and harsh and thin
Down the cold street; and now, from far away,
We hear a vast and sullen rumor run,
As of the tides of ocean turning in . . .
And know, for yet another human day,
The world's dull, dreadful labor is begun!

AMY LOWELL

Born to a wealthy and influential Boston family (cousin to Robert Lowell, distant relative to the poet James Russell Lowell) dating back to the Massachusetts Bay Colony of 1639, Amy Lowell (1874–1925) was denied a college education by that family since it was improper for a woman. But she was an avid reader, publishing her first collection of poems in 1912 and later posthumously winning the Pulitzer Prize for *What's O' Clock* (1926). An acclaimed Keats scholar, she lived at the St. Regis at Fifth Avenue and Fifty-fifth Street, then, in the 1920s, at the Belmont on Lexington Avenue.

NEW YORK AT NIGHT

A neat horizon whose sharp jags
  Cut brutally into a sky
Of leaden heaviness, and crags
Of houses lift their masonry
  Ugly and foul, and chimneys lie
And snort, outlined against the gray
  Of lowhung cloud. I hear the sigh
The goaded city gives, not day
Nor night can ease her heart, her anguished labours stay.

Below, straight streets, monotonous,
  From north and south, from east and west,
Stretch glittering; and luminous
  Above, one tower tops the rest
  And holds aloft man's constant quest:
Time! Joyless emblem of the greed
  Of millions, robber of the best
Which earth can give, the vulgar creed
Has seared upon the night its flaming ruthless screed.

O Night! Whose soothing presence brings
  The quiet shining of the stars.
O Night! Whose cloak of darkness clings
  So intimately close that scars
  Are hid from our own eyes. Beggars
By day, our wealth is having night
  To burn our souls before alters
Dim and tree-shadowed, where the light
Is shed from a young moon, mysteriously bright.

Where art thou hiding, where thy peace?
  This is the hour, but thou art not.
Will waking tumult ever cease?
  Hast thou thy votary forgot?
  Nature forsakes this man-begot

And festering wilderness, and now
The long still hours are here, no jot
Of dear communing do I know;
Instead the glaring, man-filled city groans below!

ANNA HEMPSTEAD BRANCH

Born in New London, Connecticut, Anne Hempstead Branch (1875–1937) studied at the American Academy of Dramatic Arts in New York. For many years she worked in a settlement house on the Lower East Side in neighborhoods so crowded that had the rest of the city the same population density, New York would have had 78 million people. Still, this delicate sonnet preserves the morning's beauty even in a dense and desperate part of town.

NEW YORK AT SUNRISE

When with her clouds the early dawn illumes
Our doubtful streets, wistful they grow and mild;
As if a sleeping soul grew happy and smiled,
The whole city radiantly blooms.
Pale spires lift their hands above the glooms
Like a resurrection, delicately wild,
And flushed with slumber like a little child,
Under a mist, shines forth the innocent Tombs. ☆
Thus have I seen it from a casement high,
As unsubstantial as a dream it grows.
Is this Manhattan, virginal and shy,
That in a cloud so rapturously glows?
Ethereal, frail, and like an opening rose,
I see my city with an enlightened eye.

CHARLES COLEMAN STODDARD

Charles Coleman Stoddard (1876–1961) was born in Cedar Rapids, Iowa; he worked in the field of geology, then later as an editor and an advertising manager. He was both librarian and editor for the *Staten Island Historian*, the journal of that borough's historical society. Here, through an imaginative leap backward in time, he strolls along New York's most famous street.

WHEN BROADWAY WAS A COUNTRY ROAD ☆

No rushing cars, nor tramping feet
 Disturbed the peaceful summer days
That shone as now upon the street
 That knows our busy noisy ways.
 And blushing girls and awkward jays
Strolled slowly home, and cattle lowed
 As fell the purple twilight haze,
When Broadway was a country road.

No tailored dandies, trim and neat;
 No damsels of the latest craze
Of form and fashion; no conceit
 To catch the fancy or amaze,
 No buildings met the skyward gaze;
Nor myriad lights that nightly glowed
 To set the midnight hour ablaze—
When Broadway was a country road.

Then shady lanes with blossoms sweet
 Led gently down to quiet bays
Or to the sheltered, hedged retreat
 Some falling mansion now betrays.
 The stage-coach here no longer pays
Its daily call, nor farmer's goad
 Their oxen as in olden days
When Broadway was a country road.

Little indeed to meet the praise
Of modern times the picture showed.
And yet the fancy fondly strays
To Broadway as a country road.

CHARLES HANSON TOWNE

Born in Louisville, Kentucky, then moving to New York with his family when he was three, Charles Hanson Towne (1877–1949) was an editor for *Cosmopolitan*, *Smart Set*, and, later, *Harper's Bazaar*. His long poem *Manhattan: A Poem* (1909) won him recognition and praise, and he contributed a regular literary column to the *New York American*. This poem sings a familiar song of New Yorkers who feel truly home nowhere else in the world.

MANHATTAN

When, sick of all the sorrow and distress
That flourished in the City like foul weeds,
I sought blue rivers and green, opulent meads,
And leagues of unregarded loneliness
Whereon no foot of man had seemed to press,
I did not know how great had been my needs,
How wise the woodland's gospels and her creeds,
How good her faith to one long comfortless.

But in the silence came a Voice to me;
In every wind it murmured, and I knew
It would not cease, though far my heart might roam.
It called me in the sunrise and the dew,
At noon and twilight, sadly, hungrily,
The jealous City, whispering always—"Home!"

CARL SANDBURG

Born in Galesburg, Illinois, and having remained one of America's most popular poets, Chicagoan Carl Sandburg (1878–1967) won the Pulitzer Prize not only for *Complete Poems* (1950) but also for his multivolume biography of Abraham Lincoln. Here, in powerfully rendered images, he writes of the Great White Way that has long been the supreme image of either success or failure in New York.

BROADWAY

I shall never forget you, Broadway
Your golden and calling lights.

I'll remember you long,
Tall-walled river of rush and play.

Hearts that know you hate you
And lips that have given you laughter
Have gone to their ashes of life and its roses,
Cursing the dreams that were lost
In the dust of your harsh and trampled stones.

VACHEL LINDSAY

Born in Springfield, Illinois, Vachel Lindsay (1879–1931) came to New York in 1905 to study at the Art Students League, though he soon focused primarily on poetry, infusing it, as Langston Hughes would do, with the syncopated rhythms of jazz. In time he became something of a modern troubadour, walking the country and exchanging his poems for bed and board. *The Congo and Other Poems* appeared in 1914.

A RHYME ABOUT AN ELECTRICAL ADVERTISING SIGN

I look on the specious electrical light
Blatant, mechanical, crawling and white,
Wickedly red or malignantly green
Like the beads of a young Senegambian queen.
Showing, while millions of souls hurry on,
The virtues of collars, from sunset till dawn,
By dart or by tumble of whirl within whirl,
Starting new fads for the shame-weary girl,
By maggoty motions in sickening line
Proclaiming a hat or a soup or a wine,
While there far above the steep cliffs of the street
The stars sing a message elusive and sweet.

Now man cannot rest in his pleasure and toil
His clumsy contraptions of coil upon coil
Till the thing he invents, in its use and its range,
Leads on to the marvelous CHANGE BEYOND CHANGE.
Some day this old Broadway shall climb to the skies,
As a ribbon of cloud on a soul-wind shall rise,
And we shall be lifted, rejoicing by night,
Till we join with the planets who choir their delight.
The signs in the streets and the signs in the skies
Shall make a new Zodiac, guiding the wise,
And Broadway make one with that marvellous stair
That is climbed by the rainbow-clad spirits of prayer.

JAMES OPPENHEIM

Born in St. Paul, Minnesota, and later studying at Columbia University, editor, story writer, novelist, and poet James Oppenheim (1882–1932) lived a while with other literary notables (Theodore Dreiser, Stephen Crane, Willa Cather, John Dos Passos) at Madame

Branchard's Rooming House at 61 Washington Square South. An ardent fighter for workers' rights, he wrote "Bread and Roses" (1911), the poem providing the slogan for striking textile workers carrying banners asking for fair wages and basic human dignities: bread and roses. He was founder and editor of *The Seven Arts* magazine until he was blacklisted for his opposition to World War I.

NEW YORK, FROM A SKYSCRAPER

Up in the heights of the evening skies I see my City of cities float
In sunset's golden and crimson dyes: I look, and a great joy
 clutches my throat!
Plateau of roofs by canyons crossed: windows by thousands fire-
 unfurled
O gazing, how the heart is lost in the Deepest City in the World!

O sprawling City! Worlds in a world! Housing each strange type
 that is human—
Yonder a Little Italy curled—here the haunt of the Scarlet
 Woman—
The night's white Bacchanals of Broadway—the Ghetto
 pushcarts ringed with faces—
Wall Street's roar and the Plaza's play—a weltering focus of all
 Earth's races!

Walking your Night's many-nationed byways—brushing
 Sicilians and Jews and Greeks—
Meeting gaunt Bread Lines on your highways—watching night-
 clerks in your flaming peaks—
Marking your Theatres' outpour of splendour—pausing on
 doorsteps with resting Mothers—
I marvelled at Christs with their messages tender, their daring
 dream of a World of Brothers!

Brothers? What means Irish to Greek? What the Ghetto to
 Morningside?
How shall we weld the strong and the weak while millions
 struggle with light denied?

Yet, but to follow these Souls where they roam—ripping off
housetops, the city's mask—
At Night I should find each one in a Home, at Morn I should find
each one at a Task!

Labour and Love, four-million divided—surely the millions at
last are a-move—
Surely the Brotherhood-slant is decided—the Social Labour, the
Social Love!
Surely four millions of Souls close-gathered in this one spot could
stagger the world—
O City, Earth's Future is Mothered and Fathered where your
great streets feel the Man-tides hurled!

For the Souls in one car where they hang on the straps could send
this City a-wing through the starred—
Each man is a tiny Faucet that taps the infinite reservoir of
God!—
What if they turned the Faucet full stream? What if our millions
to-night were aware?
What if to-morrow they built to their Dream the City of Brothers
in laughter and prayer?

WILLIAM CARLOS WILLIAMS

Born in New Jersey, a practicing pediatrician all his adult life (he was an intern in the rough Manhattan neighborhood of Hell's Kitchen and wrote poems between appointments), and part of the bohemian life in Greenwich Village after WWI, William Carlos Williams (1883–1963) influenced the Black Mountain Poets, Frank O'Hara (who believed that only Williams, along with Whitman and Crane, is better than the movies), as well as Allen Ginsberg and the Beats with his dictum, "No ideas but in things." This poem inspired Charles Demuth's painting "I Saw the Figure Five in Gold" (1928), which hangs in the Metropolitan Museum of Art.

THE GREAT FIGURE

Among the rain
and lights
I saw the figure 5
in gold
on a red
firetruck
moving
tense
unheeded
to gong clangs
siren howls
and wheels rumbling
through the dark city.

SARA TEASDALE

Delicate and reclusive Sara Teasdale (1884–1933) moved to New York from St. Louis in 1916. An early voice for women's rights, she edited one of the first anthologies of women's poetry, *The Answering Voice* in 1917. Although her collection *Love Songs* won the Columbia (later Pulitzer) Prize, she lived to see her type of poetry pass out of fashion before she committed suicide in her apartment at 1 Fifth Avenue. This poem is a thrilling recollection of first walking the "terrible height" of the great sixty story building downtown, completed in 1913.

FROM THE WOOLWORTH TOWER ☆

Vivid with love, eager for greater beauty
Out of the night we came
Into the corridor, brilliant and warm.
A metal door slides open,
And the lift receives us.

Swiftly, with sharp unswerving flight
The car shoots upward,
And the air, swirling and angry,
Howls like a hundred devils.
Past the maze of trim bronze doors,
Steadily we ascend
I cling to you
Conscious of the chasm under us,
And a terrible whirring deafens my ears.

The flight is ended.

We pass through a door leading onto the ledge—
Wind, night and space!
Oh terrible height
Why have we sought you?
Oh bitter wind with icy invisible wings
Why do you beat us?
Why would you bear us away?
We look through the miles of air,
The cold blue miles between us and the city,
Over the edge of eternity we look
On all the lights,
A thousand times more numerous than the stars;
Oh lines and loops of light in unwound chains
That mark for miles and miles
The vast black mazy cobweb of the streets;
Near us clusters and splashes of living gold
That change far off to bluish steel
Where the fragile lights on the Jersey shore
Tremble like drops of wind-stirred dew.
The strident noises of the city
Floating up to us
Are hallowed into whispers.
Ferries cross through the darkness
Weaving a golden thread into the night,
Their whistles weird shadows of sound.

We feel the millions of humanity beneath us,—
The warm millions, moving under the roofs,
Consumed by their own desires;
Preparing food,
Sobbing alone in a garret,
With burning eyes bending over a needle,
Aimlessly reading the evening paper,
Dancing in the naked light of the café,
Laying out the dead,
Bringing a child to birth—
The sorrow, the torpor, the bitterness, the frail joy
Come up to us
Like a cold fog wrapping us round,
Oh in a hundred years
Not one of these blood-warm bodies
But will be worthless as clay.
The anguish, the torpor, the toil
Will have passed to other millions
Consumed by the same desires.
Ages will come and go,
Darkness will blot the lights
And the tower will be laid on the earth.
The sea will remain
Black and unchanging,
The stars will look down
Brilliant and unconcerned.

Beloved,
Tho' sorrow, futility, defeat
Surround us,
They cannot bear us down.
Here on the abyss of eternity
Love has crowned us
For a moment
Victors.

MOISHE LEIB HALPERN

Born in Zlochov (in eastern Galicia, under Austro-Hungarian rule), Moishe Leib Halpern (1886–1932) moved to New York in 1908, soon associating himself with the group of Yiddish poets who referred to themselves as Di Yunge (The Young). He was a waiter, a sign painter, a pants presser, and an accomplished painter. His first book, *In New York* (1919), established him as a major Yiddish-language poet in America and tells in first-person narrative the disillusionment and loss of hope of the immigrant Jew.

SONG: WEEKEND'S OVER

There is the shadowy, dank hall
Right alongside the ground-floor stair—
A weeping girl, attended by
A grimy hand in the mussed-up hair.
—A little love in big Manhattan.

The hair—a whiff of some cheap rinse
The hand—hard, stiff and leathery
Two equal lovers, for whom this is
As good as it'll ever be.
—A little love in big Manhattan.

It's strange to listen to two people
Standing there in the dark, unheard;
Why doesn't Sammy say a word?
Why doesn't Bessie say a word?
—A little love in big Manhattan.

They may be talking, but it's all
Blanketed by the howl, instead,
From a million iron fire escapes
And all the dark ceilings overhead.
—A little love in big Manhattan.

Ceilings on ceilings and beds over beds;
Steamy air, wrapped in smoking shrouds;
From the top floor down, a chasm falls;
From above, acres open to the clouds.
—A little love in big Manhattan.

O huge night city, such grim strangeness
Wraps you up in the darkness here!
Man and wife sleep by the million
Like drunks all bloated up with beer.
—A little love in big Manhattan.

Like monkeys in the trees, the children
Hang in their fire escapes, asleep;
Soot drifts down from above their heads,
Dropped by the moon, a chimney sweep.
—A little love in big Manhattan.

And the girl Bessie knows "from nothing"
And Sammy, too, with his mouth open,
And Monday swims up before your eyes,
A desert of dead miles toward the south.
—A little love in big Manhattan.

And even Bessie's poor old mother
No longer asks, "Where is that kid?"
It doesn't matter that black hair
Has all been bleached to blond and red.
—A little love in big Manhattan.

It isn't that he's ill, the sad one
Who contemplates these sad things at night;
But sick of his own sadness only,
He lies and broods, his pipe alight.
—A little love in big Manhattan.

TRANS. JOHN HOLLANDER

SIEGFRIED SASSOON

British-born Siegfried Sassoon (1886–1967) was awarded the Military Cross for bravery in WWI, though he gradually grew disillusioned with the war, which he had once believed was for "defence and liberation" instead of "aggression and conquest." One of the great poets of the Great War (*The Old Huntsman* in 1917 and *Counter-Attack* a year later), he uses striking, muscular images to heroically describe the city after WWI.

STORM ON FIFTH AVENUE

A sallow waiter brings me six huge oysters . . .
Gloom shutters up the sunset with a plaque
Of unpropitious twilight jagged asunder
By flashlight demonstrations. *Gee, what a peach*
Of a climate! (Pardon slang: these sultry storms
Afflict me with neurosis: rumbling thunder
Shakes my belief in academic forms.)

An oyster-coloured atmospheric rumpus
Beats up to blot the sunken daylight's gildings.
Against the looming cloud-bank, ivory-pale,
Stand twenty-storied blocks of office-buildings.
Snatched upward on a gust, lost news-sheets sail
Forlorn in lone arena of mid-air;
Flapping like melancholy kites, they scare
My gaze, a note of wildness in the scene.

Out on the pattering side-walk, people hurry
For shelter, while the tempest swoops to scurry
Across to Brooklyn. Bellying figures clutch
At wide-brimmed hats and bend to meet the weather,
Alarmed for fresh-worn silks and flurried feather.
Then hissing deluge splashes down to beat
The darkly glistening flatness of the street.
Only the cars nose on through rain-lashed twilight:

Only the Sherman Statue, angel-guided, ☆
Maintains its mock-heroic martial gesture.

A sallow waiter brings me beans and pork . . .
Outside there's fury in the firmament.
Ice-cream, of course, will follow; and I'm content.
O Babylon! O Carthage! O New York!

MARIANNE MOORE

Born near St. Louis, Missouri, Marianne Moore (1887–1972) moved to New York in 1918, later settling in Brooklyn where she had a special fondness for the Brooklyn Dodgers (though in 1968 she threw out the first ball on opening day at Yankee Stadium). One of the central poets in Greenwich Village after WWI, she published in and later edited *Dial*, perhaps the most important journal of the arts in its day. Her *Collected Poems* (1951) won the Pulitzer Prize. When she crossed into Manhattan from Brooklyn she always took the Manhattan Bridge so as to get a better view of the Brooklyn Bridge, "synonymous with endurance," she wrote, "united by stress."

GRANITE AND STEEL ☆

Enfranchising cable, silvered by the sea,
  of woven wire, grayed by the mist,
  and Liberty dominate the Bay—
  her feet as one on shattered chains,
  once whole links wrought by Tyranny.

Caged Circe of steel and stone,
her parent German ingenuity.
"O catenary curve" from tower to pier,
implacable enemy of the mind's deformity,
of man's uncompunctious greed
his crass love of crass priority
  just recently

obstructing acquiescent feet
about to step ashore when darkness fell
 without a cause,
as if probity had not joined our cities
 in the sea.

"O path amid the stars
crossed by the seagull's wings!"
"O radiance that doth inherit me!"
—affirming inter-acting harmony!

Untried experiment, untried; then tried;
way out; way in; romantic passageway
first seen by the eye of the mind,
then by the eye. O steel! O stone!
Climatic ornament, double rainbow,
as if inverted by French perspicacity,
 John Roebling's monument,
 German tenacity's also;
 composite span—an actuality.

DOCK RATS

There are human beings who seem to regard the place as craftily
 as we do—who seem to feel that it is a good place to come
 home to. On what a river; wide—twinkling like a chopped sea
 under some
 of the finest shipping in the

world; the square-rigged four-rigged four-master, the liner, the
 battleship like
 the two-
 thirds submerged section of an iceberg; the tug
 dipping and pushing, the bell striking as it comes; the steam
 yacht, lying
 like a new made arrow on the

stream; the ferry-boat—a head assigned, one to each
compartment, making
a row of chessmen set for play. When the wind is from the east,
the smell is of apples, of hay; the aroma increased and decreased
as the wind changes;

of rope, of mountain leaves for florists; as from the west,
it is aromatic of salt. Occasionally a parakeet
from Brazil, arrives clasping and clawing; or a monkey—
tail and feet
in readiness for an over-

ture; all arms and tail; how delightful! There is the sea, moving
the bulk-
head with its horse strength; and the multiplicity of rudders
and propellers; the signals, shrill, questioning, peremptory,
diverse;
the wharf cats and the barge dogs; it

is easy to overestimate the value of such things. One does
not live in such a place from motives of expediency
but because to one who has been accustomed to it,
shipping is the
most interesting thing in the world.

H. LEYVIK

H. Leyvik is the pseudonym of Leyvik Halpern (1888–1962), born in Ihumen, a small town in Byelorussia. He was sentenced to four years of forced labor and exiled for life to Siberia where he wrote his first dramatic poem, "The Chains of Messiah." After escaping to New York in the summer of 1913, he, as did many Jews before and since, celebrated this most tolerant and wondrous city. The first and last parts of the poem are presented here.

HERE LIVES THE JEWISH PEOPLE

The towering life of the towering city
Is burning in white fires.
And in the streets of the Jewish East Side
The whiteness of the fires burns even whiter.

I like to stroll in the burning frenzy of the Jewish East Side,
Squeezing through the crammed stands and pushcarts,
Breathing the smell and saltiness
Of a hot naked life.
And whenever, in the whiteness, before my eyes emerge
Bearded Jews, covered from head to toe
With long hanging gowns for girls and women;
Men or women with sick birds,
Looking up with craving, begging eyes
For a buyer, to offer him a lucky ticket;
Jews in wheel chairs,
Blind cripples, sunk deep in their own shoulders,
Who can see with their shoulders the color and size
Of a flung coin—
Then a hidden nostalgia awakens in me,
A nostalgia buried since childhood:
To be transformed into the limping beggar
Who used to hop from street to street in my hometown
(Luria was his name)
And knock with his crutch on sidewalks and thresholds
Who knows, whether in this wheelchair before my eyes
Does not sit the beggar of my childhood nostalgia
Watching my amazement through blind eyelids?—
Then the world had no towers,
Yet was white as now,
Fiery and white as now.

I walk for hours in the streets of the Jewish East Side
And imagine in the fiery whiteness before my eyes
Fantastic gates, soaring columns,
Rising from all the dilapidated stands

Upward, to the far and empty New York sky.
Gates—on all their cornices
Glowing, sparkling signs, inscribed:
Here lives the Jewish people.

Silence. Midnight.
My childhood nostalgia cries in me.

TRANS. BENJAMIN AND BARBARA HARSHAV

CLAUDE MCKAY

Born in Jamaica, viewed by many as the precursor of the Harlem Renaissance, Claude McKay (1889–1948) moved to Harlem in 1914. A poet and radical spokesman, editor of the *Liberator* and world traveler, he wrote of Harlem both in poems (his 1922 collection *Harlem Shadows* is considered by some as the first great book of the Harlem Renaissance) and in his 1928 novel, told in the lyrical dialect of the neighborhood, *Home to Harlem*, the first work of fiction by an African American to make the best-seller list.

HARLEM SHADOWS

I hear the halting footsteps of a lass
   In Negro Harlem when the night lets fall
Its veil. I see the shapes of girls who pass
   To bend and barter at desire's call.
Ah, little dark girls who in slippered feet
Go prowling through the night from street to street!

Through the long night until the silver break
   Of day the little gray feet know no rest;
Through the lone night until the last snow-flake
   Has dropped from heaven upon the earth's white breast,
The dusky, half-clad girls of tired feet
Are trudging, thinly shod, from street to street.

Ah, stern harsh world, that in the wretched way
Of poverty, dishonor and disgrace,
Has pushed the timid little feet of clay,
The sacred brown feet of my fallen race!
Ah, heart of me, the weary, weary feet
In Harlem wandering from street to street.

CHRISTOPHER MORLEY

Born in Haverford, Pennsylvania, a New York news reporter, and one of the founders of the *Saturday Review of Literature*, Christopher Morley (1890–1957) was the author of more than fifty books of poems and novels, and he revised and expanded Bartlett's *Familiar Quotations*. He lived across the street from Gotham Book Mart when it was at 41 W. Forty-seventh Street and, as part of the "Three Hours Lunch Club," was significant in turning that small treasure of a bookstore in the diamond district into a hangout for writers of his day. This poem tells a familiar story of pandering, irresistible New York.

BALLAD OF NEW YORK, NEW YORK ☆

Around the bend of Harbor Hill
Comes Number 33,
Says: Board the cars, my bonny boy,
And ride to Town with me.

A Town that has no ceiling price,
A Town of double-talk;
A Town so big men name her twice,
Like so: N'Yawk, N'Yawk.

Then spake the old Belittlin' Witch:
"Beware the crowded trains;
Of all towns she's the Biggest Bitch—
Bide here, and save your brains.

"What though she numbers boroughs five
With many a noble spot,
Her thought is mostly gin and jive,
Her repartee, So What?"

Himself replied: "Old Gloomy Spook,
I fear no blatherskites,
I'll blow my nickel in the juke
Behind the neon lights.

"Or I might even show 'em
At Sardi's or The Stork—
I feel to write a poem
About New York, New York."

The Witch:—

She's Run-around, and In-and-Out,
And futile To-and-Fro,
And then what it was All About
You will not even know.

She'll ring you mad by telephone
And foul your wits with ink;
Men's tricks to get their products shown
I will not say. They stink!

Across the fifty nations
Her yokel accents go,
Her mispronunciations
Broadcast by radio.

When ever did New York requite
The glamor poets lent her?
Her soul is café-socialite,
A simian garment-center.

Himself:—

The Town is what you make it
  Of glory and of pain;
I've earned the right to take it
  As Comédie Humaine.

For I have watched her faces
  To educate my soul,
Been drunk in public places
  With bliss, not alcohol.

Yes, I have known a crosstown street
  In sunset parallel
Where lovers lay in peace so sweet
  They never heard the El.

And I have stood, alone, alone,
  Where ships blew hoarse for sea
And armored planes were crowded on
  Like blackbirds on a tree.

The worm is on her portal?
  The Dollar is her joss?
Her sin is, being mortal?
  I enter: *Nolle Pros.*

The Witch:—

Okay. Then learn the answers,
  Eternally crack wise,
And be among the dancers
  With belladonna eyes.

Okay. All doors cry Welcome
  (If only Name you bring)
To swamis who talk talcum
  Or poets who can't sing.

Okay. Her mind still plays with blocks,
And, reckoned in brain-hours,
When she outgrows her bobbysocks
She starts on whiskey sours.

O consommé of gas-balloons,
Whoopsdearie of them all!
A town of seven million goons
Behind the octave ball.

Of what avail her towers high
If in them men devote
Their minds to trivial things? But I
Should worry! (End of quote).

Himself:—

Avaunt, old bag! (Himself replied)
Pipe down, and cut the squawk.
Your remarks are much too snide
About N'Yawk, N'Yawk.

You bet, her tastes are corny:
The public's always are;
And I may end my journey
In some unritzy bar,

But, in the final ember,
Discriminate am I;
From boyhood I remember
Diana in the sky,

When life was all for learning
(The top of human time!)
And mind was full of morning,
And language burst with rhyme.

Now, when my hours are shortened,
 Fresh music I would bring;
She gives me, when disheartened,
 Magnificence to sing—

The song of smart connivers,
 Of crowded subway stops,
Of tough old taxi-drivers
 And much-enduring cops,

The ancient Down Town Fever,
 The smell of ferry slips,
And always and forever
 The pageant of her ships.

Unroll me then this mappamond
 Of all the life men know,
Grotesque and arabesque beyond
 The Tales of Edgar Poe.

And though she tear my mind in two
 In joy and pity split,
I love her; and so Nuts to You—
 It's *my* mind, isn't it?

New York, New York!—Two moods betwixt,
 Half fearful and half fain
(O love, O anger, always mixed!)
 He got aboard the train

EDNA ST. VINCENT MILLAY

Born in Maine but settling in Greenwich Village, famous for her bohemian lifestyle, Edna St. Vincent Millay (1892–1950) was the first woman to receive the Pulitzer Prize (*The Harp-Weaver, and*

Other Poems, 1923). She was active in the Provincetown Playhouse (still on MacDougal Street) and her poem "First Fig" ("my candle burns at both ends . . .") became the motto of her restless generation. Her poem here captures the tranquil beauty of a morning in Washington Square Park, where Fifth Avenue begins.

ENGLISH SPARROWS (WASHINGTON SQUARE) ☆

How sweet the sound in the city an hour before sunrise,
When the park is empty and grey and the light clear and so lovely
I must sit on the floor before my open window for an hour with
 my arms on the sill
And my cheek on my arm, watching the spring's sky
Soft suffusion from the roofed horizon upward with palest rose,
Doting on the charming sight with eyes
Open, eyes closed;
Breathing with quiet pleasure the cool air cleansed by the night,
 lacking all will
To let such happiness go, nor thinking the least thing ill
In me for such indulgence, pleased with the day and with myself.
 How sweet
The noisy chirping of the urchin sparrows from crevice and shelf
Under my window, and from down there in the street,
Announcing the advance of the roaring competitive day with
 city bird-song.

A bumbling bus
Goes under the arch. A man bareheaded and alone
Walks to a bench and sits down.
He breathes the morning with me; his thoughts are his own.
Together we watch the first magnanimous
Rays of the sun on the tops of greening trees and on houses of
 red brick and of stone.

VLADIMIR MAYAKOVSKY

Known as Russia's poet of the revolution, influential in the public's acceptance of avant-garde art, Vladimir Mayakovsky (1893–1930) imagined himself another Whitman when he visited New York in 1925. Although the bridge he loved and wrote about here actually crosses the East River and connects Manhattan to Brooklyn, the poet mistakenly (though perhaps symbolically) placed the bridge over the Hudson River, connecting Manhattan to the mainland of America.

BROOKLYN BRIDGE

Give, Coolidge,
a shout of joy!

I too will spare no words
about good things.
Blush
at my praise,
go red as our flag,
however
united-states
-of
-america you may be.
As a crazed believer
enters
a church,
retreats
into a monastery cell,
austere and plain;
so I,
in graying evening
haze,
humbly set foot
on Brooklyn Bridge.
As a conqueror presses

into a city
all shattered,
on cannon with muzzles
craning high as a giraffe—
so, drunk with glory,
eager to live,
I clamber,
in pride,
upon Brooklyn Bridge.
As a foolish painter
plunges his eye,
sharp and loving,
into a museum madonna,
so I
from the near skies
bestrewn with stars,
gaze
at New York
through the Brooklyn Bridge.
New York,
heavy and stifling
till night,
has forgotten
its hardships
and height;
and only
the household ghosts
ascend
in the lucid glow of its windows.
Here
the elevateds
drone softly.
And only
their gentle
droning
tell us:
here trains
are crawling and rattling

like dishes
being cleared into a cupboard.
While
a shopkeeper fetched sugar
from a mill
that seemed to project
out of the water—
the masts
passing under the bridge
looked
no larger than pins.
I am proud
of just this
mile of steel;
upon it,
my visions come to life, erect—

here's a fight
for construction
instead of style,
an austere disposition
of bolts
and steel.
If
the end of the world
befall—
and chaos
smash our planet
to bits,
and what remains
will be
this
bridge, rearing above the dust of destruction;
then,
as huge ancient lizards
are rebuilt
from bones
finer than needles,

to tower in museums,
so,
from this bridge,
a geologist of the centuries
will succeed
in recreating
our contemporary world.
He will say:
—Yonder paw
of steel
once joined
the seas and the prairies;
from this spot,
Europe
rushed to the West,
scattering
to the wind
Indian feathers.
This rib
reminds us
of a machine—
just imagine,
would there be hands enough,
after planting
a steel foot
in Manhattan,
to yank
Brooklyn to oneself
by the lip?
By the cables
of electric strands,
I recognize
the era succeeding
the steam age—
here
men
had ranted
on radio.

Here
men
had ascended
in planes.
For some,
life
here
had no worries;
for others,
it was a prolonged
and hungry howl.
From this spot,
jobless men
leapt
headlong
into the Hudson.
Now
my canvas
is unobstructed
as it stretches on cables of string
to the feet of the stars.
I see:
here
stood Mayakovsky,
stood,
composing verse, syllable by syllable.
I stare
as an Eskimo gapes at a train,
I seize on it
as a tick fastens to an ear.
Brooklyn Bridge—
yes . . .
That's a quite a thing!

TRANS. MAX HAYWARD AND GEORGE REAVEY

MAXWELL BODENHEIM

Part of the bohemian scene in Greenwich Village after World War I, Maxwell Bodenheim (1893–1954) came to New York in 1915 from Hermanville, Mississippi, worked with the Provincetown Players, and published his first collection, *Minna and Myself*, in 1918 (Minna was his first wife). After writing two New York novels, *Ninth Avenue* (1926) and *New York Madness* (1933), he slipped into alcoholism and poverty, eventually selling poems on the street for drinks. He was murdered in a flophouse near the Bowery by a fellow drunk found to be insane. In this poem he contrasts the ugliness of day to the danger and beauty of the city's night.

NEW YORK CITY

New York, it would be easy to revile
The flatly carnal beggar in your smile,
And flagellate, with a superior bliss,
The gasping routines of your avarice.
Loud men reward you with an obvious ax,
Or piteous laurel-wreath, and their attacks
And eulogies blend to a common sin.
New York, perhaps an intellectual grin
That brings its bright cohesion to the warm
Confusion of the heart, can mold your swarm
Of huge, drab blunders into smaller grace . . .
With old words I shall gamble for your face.

The evening kneels between your filthy brick,
Darkly indifferent to each scheme and trick
With which your men insult and smudge their day.
When evenings metaphysically pray
Above the weakening dance of men, they find
That every eye that looks at them is blind.
And yet, New York, I say that evenings free
An insolently mystic majesty
From your parades of automatic greed.

For one dark moment all your narrow speed
Receives the fighting blackness of a soul,
And every nervous lie swings to a whole—
A pilgrim, blurred yet proud, who finds in black
An arrogance that fills his straining lack.

Between your undistinguished crates of stone
And wood, the wounded dwarfs who walked alone—
The chorus-girls, who indiscretions hang
Between the scavengers of rouge and slang;
The women moulding painfully a fresh
Excuse for pliant treacheries of flesh;
The men who raise the tin sword of a creed,
Convinced that it can kill the lunge of greed;
The thieves whose poisoned vanity purloins
A fancied victory from ringing coins;
The staidly bloated men whose minds have sold
Their quickness to an old, metallic Scold;
The neatly cultured men whose hopes and fears
Dwell in soft prisons honored by past years;
The men who tortured youth bends to the task
Of hardening offal to a swaggering mask—
The night, with black hands, gathers each mistake
And strokes a mystic challenge from each ache.
The night, New York, sardonic and alert,
Offers a soul to your reluctant dirt.

MELECH RAVITCH

Born Zekharye-Khone Bergner in Rodymno, Galicia, Melech Ravitch (1893–1976) was at the very center of Yiddish life in Warsaw and served for many years as the secretary of the Jewish Writers Association. Here he celebrates the wonder, glory, and freedom of this most exciting and tolerant of cities.

SHADOW OF A VISION OF AN ODE TO NEW YORK

—Hey, you messenger boy of the universe!
Hand me a pen of bright lightning!

—What?

Turn over the Chrysler Tower, ☆
Pierce, shove it into the granite
By its sharp spike,

Fill it like an inkstand with ink,
With black thunder, lightning and wind.
In ink
Fused
Must I write today.

—A poem?

And you, you chief butler of the universe,
Hand me some such hard drink.
And transform into metal my tongue—
And here is out of my mind
The pile of rage, worry!
—Stop!
Stop!

—Are we already in New York?

—The heart—the h-e-a-r-t—
—What about heart
—Between the ribs
—A dynamo machine
We shall set—in there!

—Sense is nonsense and nonsense is sense!
Accompaniment
To the poem

Twenty million hands play
In keys of black and white granite.

The epic of New York,
Of the city of cities, of cities, of cities,
With no morn at dawn, with no delay in lateness.
Timeless,
Here is the city
The devil chases after God
And God chases after the devil.
Here God is reviled, while absorbed in devil worship.
And the devil is reviled, while absorbed in God worship.
The day does not arrive and the night does not descend.
There are no sinners here, since there are no just;
No weeping, since there is no laughter.
All are present—since this is the city of being!
The chant of New York streets!
Streets lengthwise.
Streets breadthwise.
Streets upwards.
Streets like ribbons.
Bridges like streets,
Over the span of rivers,
Over the breadth of the sea.
Streets under river
Streets under sea
Streets through ground, streets through granite,
Streets over your head, streets through the midst of your own
heart,
Streets through your days and your nights,
Streets through your years, streets through your life—
The granite chant,
No rhythm, rhythm, pure rhythm, asphalt, concrete,
Of New York streets.

The chant of New York,
Chant of light,

Light over you, through you, within you,
Light out of you—light meeting you,
Light in stone, concrete and asphalt,
On the tenth,
Hundredth,
Thousandth image.
In seven hues,
Ten rainbows, seventy pigmentations,
A thousand rainbows, seven thousand colorings!
Lights like butterflies—born today—dying today.
Eternal lights, sun, star systems.
Lamps, not lamps, ultra-Edisons,
Hundreds of lights, tens of thousands, millions!
Lamps that are born ignited,
Like meteors.
The sun is but their reflection-lamp to the play, exemplary lamp
Of heavenly impotence.
Lights they are!
Lights that may compel a blind man to see,
And may a seeing one blind.
You can jump into them
As into a sea of lights.
Immerse in them—
And in one minute
There will in your veins flow light instead of blood,
The lights of New York.

The epic of New York,
City of towers, of stone and metal.
Who would say they are placed on the ground?
They are placed in the universe,
Placed in sharpest zigzag—
The great skyline,
Border gate in cosmic space,
Between worlds two—the past of truth,
And today's of dreams.
Border between millennium two and millennium three.
The wall of the walls, of the walls, of the walls,

And the hundred towers is Super-God's house, New York,
Where ten million hearts beat
In a unified prayer together.

Abyss of abysses,
City with no cover above
And no bottom below,
Whoever once passed through you,
City, abyss of abysses,
Has lost his God within you.
Now he yells:
—Once more we want to find God!
And the echo reverberates from end to end
—Find—God!
And the God of New York has no name as yet
And even thought of Him is not yet born.

But on pinnacles of the sky towers
You may readily see the glow of the coming,
Like the glow of the oncoming of the sun of Genesis,
When God has not bestowed a name on her. . . .

Hey, you! quill-giver of the universe,
Another dip of the quill is lightning,
For the last verse!
The song of New Yorkers, the latest man.
A song of intoxication, of the rise of a new race,
Quintuple-colored blood cocktail,
White, black, red, brown, yellow . . .

—You! Have you lost your mind?
—You write of Me? and I am
The man of New York!
—Now
Arrived at Mecca from universal people-wanderings,
I am the last of a millennium.
All the bloods in my blood, all cultures absorbed in my spirit,
My speech, seventy tongues,

I am the first of millennium the third,
Violent, drunk cocktail,
My blood white, black, red, brown, yellow,
My heart—human heart—
White, red, brown, black,
Rushing, striving, fervent.
Red, brown, white,
At last rose against foe, death;
Brown death,
The five golden spikes of the crown,
The skin is brown—
Robust
Son composite of all races—
New York becomes star-thousand rays, thousand streets,
The last, the great Place d'Etoile;
To the entire globe—to the universe—
Get out, you people, to the streets of New York
From the star-thousand rays,
For the new man from here shall come—
To the new universe.

TRANS. JEHIEL B. COOPERMAN AND
SARAH H. COOPERMAN

E. E. CUMMINGS

Born in Massachusetts, Edward Estlin Cummings (1894–1962) was a volunteer ambulance driver in France during WWI, an expatriate, and one of the twentieth century's most innovative and experimental poets. He was part of the generation that settled in Greenwich Village after returning from Paris (subject of Malcolm Cowley's *Exile's Return*). In 1923 he moved to his much-loved Patchin Place off W. Tenth Street and Sixth Avenue.

"AT THE FEROCIOUS PHENOMENON"

at the ferocious phenomenon of 5 o'clock i find myself gently decomposing in the mouth of New York. Between its supple financial teeth delir iously sprouting from complacent gums,a morsel prettily wanders buoyed on the murderous saliva of industry. the morsel is i.

Vast cheeks enclose me.

a gigantic uvula with imperceptible gesticulations threatens the tubular downward blackness occasionally from which detaching itself bumps clumsily into the throat. A meticulous vulgarity:

a sodden fastidious normal explosion;a square murmur,a winsome flatulence—

In the soft midst of the tongue sits the Woolworth building a serene pastille-shaped insipid kinesis or frail swooping lozenge. a ruglike sentience whose papillae expertly drink the docile perpendicular taste of this squirming cube of undiminished silence,supports while devouring the firm tumult of exquisitely insecure sharp algebraic music.
For the first time in sorting from this vast nonchalant inward walk of volume the flat minute gallop of careful hugeness i am conjugated by the sensual mysticism of entire vertrical being ,i am skillfully construed by a delicately experimenting colossus whose irrefutable spiral antics involve me with the soothings of plastic hypnotism .i am accurately parsed by this gorgeous rush of upward lips. . . .

cleverly

perching on the sudden extremity of one immense tooth myself surveys safely the complete important profane frantic inconsequential gastronomic mystery of mysteries

,life

Far below myself the lunging leer horizontal large distinct ecstasy wags and.rages Laughters jostle grins nudge smiles push—. deep into the edgeless gloaming gladness hammers incessant putrid spikes of madness (at

Myself 's height these various innocent ferocities are superseded by
the sole prostituted ferocity of silence,it is) still 5 o'clock

I stare only always into the tremendous canyon the
,tremendous canyon always only exhales a climbing dark exact walloping human noise of digestible millions whose rich slovenly obscene procession always floats through the thin amorous enormous only lips of the evening

And it is 5 o'clock

in the oblong air,from which a singular ribbon of common sunset is hanging,

snow speaks slowly

CHARLES REZNIKOFF

Son of Russian immigrants, Charles Reznikoff (1894–1976) was born in Brooklyn and received a law degree from New York University but quickly abandoned law for poetry. An editor at the *Jewish Daily Forward* known for taking long walks through Brooklyn and Manhattan, he writes about the life of typical Jews struggling in the New World, as in his 1929 collection *By the Waters of Manhattan.*

from BY THE WELL OF THE LIVING AND SEEING

[115]

When I came for my laundry, I found a shirt missing.

The laundryman—a Jew—considered the situation:
"There are four ways of losing a shirt," he said thoughtfully;
"in the first place, it may never have been delivered by the steam
laundry;
and in the second place, it may be lying around here, unpacked;
in the third place, it may have been delivered and packed in
someone else's bundle;
and in the fourth place it may be really lost.
Come in again at the end of the week and I'll know what has
happened."
And his wife, recognizing a fellow Jew,
smiled and spoke up in Yiddish,
"We won't have to go to the rabbi about it, will we?"

[116]

The new janitor is a Puerto Rican;
still a young man and he has four small children.
He has been hired because he is cheap—
not because he is the handy man
a good janitor is supposed to be.
I doubt if he ever saw any plumbing
before he came to this country,
to say nothing of a boiler and radiators.
Anyway, he was soon overwhelmed by requests from the tenants
to do this and fix that.
He does his best and spends hours at simple jobs,
and seldom does them well—or can do them at all.

He was in my flat once
to do something or other and, when he was through,
asked me if he might sit down.
"Of course," I said and offered him a drink,
but he would not take it.
"It is so quiet here," he explained.
And then he began to talk about a man who lived in the house and
taught Spanish.

"He talks to me in Spanish," the janitor said,
"but I do not understand.
You see, I am not an educated man."
His eye caught the print of a water-color by Winslow Homer
which I have hanging: a palm tree in the Bahamas.
"That is my country," he said,
and kept looking at the print
as one might look at a photograph of one's mother
long dead

[118]

The dark subway-station was almost empty at a little after ten
that summer morning. The man who sold tokens for the turnstiles
was going back to his booth with a broad smile on his face.
I suppose he had been engaged in an amusing conversation
with the Negro alone on the platform.
The black man's face was wrinkled. As he stood there,
stooped over a stick, he kept on talking:
"I cuss my mother in her grave," he was saying in a loud angry
voice,
"because she borned me!"
What a line for a "Mammy" song, I thought.
By this time there were two or three other passengers on the
platform
and we stood at a distance from the Negro and watched him,
though we pretended not to. He turned to us and said,
"I wonder how it feels to be white."

Just then the train came in and we went inside
hoping that the Negro with his disturbance
would not enter the brightly-lit car.

[123]

In the street, nine stories below, the horn of an automobile out of
order
began sounding its loudest

steadily—without having to stop for breath.
We tried to keep on talking
In spite of that unceasing scream;
raised our voices somewhat, no longer calm and serene.
Our civilization was somewhat out of order, it seemed.

But, just as we began to knit out brows,
tighten our jaws, twist our lips,
the noise stopped;
and we dipped our heads,
like ducks on a stream, into the cool silence,
and talked again quietly, smiling at each other

NAFTALI GROSS

Born in Kolomea, Galicia, and emigrating to New York in 1913, Naftali Gross (1896–1956) worked as a typesetter, as a teacher in Yiddish schools, as a translator of one of the great Yiddish versions of the Bible, and on the staff of the *Jewish Daily Forward*. The cemetery in the poem's title, now deep in Chinatown, is the first cemetery of the Spanish and Portuguese Synagogue, built in 1682, the oldest surviving manmade artifact in Manhattan, where the grave of Benjamin Bueno de Mezquita has the city's oldest tombstone.

THE CEMETERY AT CHATHAM SQUARE ☆

At Chatham Square, shaded and obscured,
In the shadow of the Bowery and East Broadway,
Lies between narrow houses secured,
Hidden from people's eyes, strange and faraway,
The first Jewish cemetery in the U.S.A.

The effaced tombstones row by row
Lie spread out, hearken and hearken to
The noise of the Square and the rushalong
Of people and trains all day long,

And overhead at night the course of the stars too.
They lie spread out as though they hear
Deep underneath the times long passed away
When from the hillocks to the valley they
Could look down and see the open bay,
The green water and the sailboats,
And dream of that time and farness
When open, free, there was the shore
For the people alien and homeless,
Who, just like these, deep beneath them lay;
Persecuted, came over the deeps
To be able to start a life once more.

TRANS. JEHIEL B.COOPERMAN AND
SARAH A. COOPERMAN

ELIEZER GREENBERG

Born in Russia, a translator and editor of Yiddish literature, Eliezer Greenberg (1896–1977) was dedicated to bringing Yiddish literature to American readers. He writes here of Second Avenue from E. Fourteenth Street south to Houston Street, the central artery of the East Village and, for a while, at the heart of Jewish life.

VISITING SECOND AVENUE ☆

I seldom come to see you, these days,
And except for a used-up old building
They have managed to leave alone—
Like some old souvenir—
I'd never recognize this neighborhood;
You have changed so much, Second Avenue!
But even these trinkets abandoned by the past
Remind me of the treasure here that was ours!

O closest of all these neighboring streets!
I said good-by to you long ago

And try to keep out of your way
—It's painful, now, to come across you,
For when I tread your ground
It's as though I were walking
On my nearest ones' graves.

But must we talk of loss,
Plunging hearts into mourning?
Whoever forgets these things
Has never remembered,
Nor ever shared our joy,
Nor sips of our sorrow now!

But if the woes of sacrifice are vast
They command neither memory nor imagination:
A true treasure can never be wasted!
There is a Great, One-Shot Festival
That burns all the weekdays in eternal flames.

More than just that one time
Its awakening breath
Can make dry bones live,
Raising them from the valley of death,
Giving them life, winged with faith, and hope.

TRANS. JOHN HOLLANDER

FEDERICO GARCIA LORCA

A major twentieth-century poet, Spanish-born Federico Garcia Lorca (1898–1936) wrote *Poems of the Deep Song*, his first major work, in 1921, but another decade passed before it was published. He first came to New York in 1929, and though an admirer of Whitman he did not like what New York did to its minorities, for he had, he once said, "a sympathetic understanding of those who are persecuted—the Gypsy, the black, the Jew." His *Poeta en Nueva York* (*Poet in New York*) appeared in 1930 while he was a student at Columbia University and describes the "bitter root" that he experienced in the city .

NEW YORK

(Office and Attack)

TO FERNANDO VELA

Beneath all the statistics
there is a drop of duck's blood.
Beneath all the columns
there is a drop of sailor's blood.
Beneath all the totals, a river of warm blood;
a river that goes singing
past the bedrooms of the suburbs,
and the river is silver, cement, or wind
in the lying daybreak of New York.
The mountains exist, I know that.
And the lenses ground for wisdom,
I know that. But I have not come to see the sky.
I have come to see the stormy blood,
the blood that sweeps the machines to the waterfalls,
and the spirit on to the cobra's tongue.
Every day they kill in New York
ducks, four million,
pigs, five million,
pigeons, two thousand, for the enjoyment of dying men,
cows, one million,
roosters, two million
who turn the sky to small splinters.
You may as well sob filing a razor blade
or assassinate dogs in the hallucinated foxhunts,
as try to stop in the dawnlight
the endless trains carrying milk,
the endless trains carrying blood,
and the trains carrying roses in chains
for those in the field of perfume.
The ducks and the pigeons

and the hogs and the lambs
lay their drops of blood down
underneath all the statistics;
and the terrible bawling of the packed-in cattle
fills the valley with suffering
where the Hudson is getting drunk on its oil.
I attack all those persons
who know nothing of the other half,
the half who cannot be saved,
who raise their cement mountains
in which the hearts of the small
animals no one thinks are beating,
and from which we will all fall
during the final holiday of the drills.
I spit in your face.
The other half hears me,
as they go on eating, urinating, flying in their purity
like the children of the janitors
who carry delicate sticks
to the holes where the antennas
of the insects are rusting.
This is not hell, it is a street.
This is not death, it is a fruit-stand.
There is a whole world of crushed rivers and unachievable
distances
In the paw of a cat crushed by a car,
and I hear the song of the worm
in the heart of so many girls.
Rust, rotting, trembling earth.
And you are earth, swimming through the figures of the office.
What shall I do, set my landscapes in order?
Set in place the lovers who will afterwards be photographs,
who will be bits of wood and mouthfuls of blood?
No, I won't; I attack,
I attack the conspiring
of these empty offices
that will not broadcast the sufferings,
that rub out the plans of the forest,

and I offer myself to be eaten by the packed-up cattle
when their mooing fills the valley
where the Hudson is getting drunk on its oil.

TRANS. ROBERT BLY

HART CRANE

Hart Crane (1899–1932) hoped his eight-part epic poem *The Bridge*, written in the late 1920s, had both Whitman's all-embracing spirit of America as well as the epic modernism of Eliot's *Waste Land*, published a few years earlier. To write this poem, the poet moved to 110 Columbia Heights, the former apartment of Washington Roebling, who, despite the crippling effects of caisson's disease sustained while working on the bridge, had finished what his father began fourteen years before. Included here is part 7, a journey beneath the city.

THE TUNNEL

To Find the Western path
Right thro' the Gates of Wrath.
—BLAKE

PERFORMANCES, assortments, résumés—
Up Times Square to Columbus Circle lights ☆
Channel the congresses, nightly sessions,
Refractions of the thousand theatres, faces—
Mysterious kitchens. . . . You shall search them all.
Someday by heart you'll learn each famous sight
And watch the curtain lift in hell's despite;
You'll find the garden in the third act dead,
Finger your knees—and wish yourself in bed
With tabloid crime-sheets perched in easy sight.

Then let you reach your hat
and go.
As usual, let you—also

walking down—exclaim
to twelve upward leaving
a subscription praise
for what time slays.

Or can't you quite make up your mind to ride;
A walk is better underneath the L a brisk
Ten blocks or so before? But you find yourself
Preparing penguin flexions of the arms,—
As usual you will meet the scuttle yawn:
The subway yawns the quickest promise home.

Be minimum, then, to swim the hiving swarms
Out of the Square, the Circle burning bright—
Avoid the glass doors gyring at your right,
Where boxed alone a second, eyes take fright
—Quite unprepared rush naked back to light:
And down beside the turnstile press the coin
Into the slot. The gongs already rattle.

And so
of cities you bespeak
subways, rivered under streets
and rivers. . . . In the car
the overtone of motion
underground, the monotone
of motion is the sound
of other faces, also underground—

"Let's have a pencil Jimmy—living now
at Floral Park
Flatbush—on the fourth of July—
like a pigeon's muddy dream—potatoes
to dig in the field—travlin the town—too—
night after night—the Culver line—the
girls all shaping up—it used to be—"

Our tongues recant like beaten weather vanes.

This answer lives like verdigris, like hair
Beyond extinction, surcease of the bone;
And repetition freezes—"What

"what do you want? getting weak on the links?
fandaddle daddy don't ask for change—IS THIS
FOURTEENTH? it's half past six she said—if
you don't like my gate why did you
swing on it, why *didja*
swing on it
anyhow—"

And somehow anyhow swing—

The phonographs of hades in the brain
Are tunnels that re-wind themselves, and love
A burnt match skating in a urinal—
Somewhere above Fourteenth TAKE THE EXPRESS
To brush some new presentiment of pain—

"But I want service in this office SERVICE
I said—after
the show she cried a little afterwards but—"

Whose head is swinging from the swollen strap?
Whose body smokes along the bitten rails,
Bursts from a smoldering bundle far behind
In back forks of the chasms of the brain,—
Puffs from a riven stump far out behind
In interborough fissures of the mind . . . ?

And why do I often meet your visage here,
Your eyes like agate lanterns—on and on
Below the toothpaste and the dandruff ads?
—And did their riding eyes right through your side,
And did their eyes like unwashed platters ride?
And Death, aloft,—gigantically down
Probing through you—toward me, O evermore!

And when they dragged your retching flesh,
Your trembling hands that night through Baltimore—
That last night on the ballot rounds, did you
Shaking, did you deny the ticket, Poe?

For Gravesend Manor change at Chambers Street.
The platform hurries along to a dead stop.

The intent escalator lifts a serenade
Stilly
Of shoes, umbrellas, each eye attending its shoe, then
Bolting outright somewhere above where streets
Burst suddenly in rain. . . . The gongs recur:
Elbows and levers, guard and hissing door.
Thunder is galvothermic here below. . . . The car
Wheels off. The train rounds, bending to a scream,
Taking the final level for the dive
Under the river—
And somewhat emptier than before,
Demented, for a hitching second, humps; then
Lets go. . . . Toward corners of the floor
Newspapers wing, revolve and wing.
Blank windows gargle signals through the roar.

And does the Dæmon take you home, also,
Wop washerwoman, with the bandaged hair?
After the corridors are swept, the cuspidors—
The gaunt sky-barracks cleanly now, and bare,
O Genoese, do you bring mother eyes and hands
Back home to children and to golden hair?

Dæmon, demurring and eventful yawn!
Whose hideous laughter is a bellows mirth
—Or the muffled slaughter of a day in birth—
O cruelly to inoculate the brinking dawn
With antennæ toward worlds that glow and sink;—
To spoon us out more liquid than the dim

Locution of the eldest star, and pack
The conscience navelled in the plunging wind,
Umbilical to call—and straightway die!

O caught like pennies beneath soot and steam,
Kiss of our agony thou gatherest;
Condensed, thou takest all—shrill ganglia
Impassioned with some song we fail to keep.
And yet, like Lazarus, to feel the slope,
The sod and billow breaking,—lifting ground,
—A sound of waters bending astride the sky
Unceasing with some Word that will not die . . . !

A tugboat, wheezing wreaths of steam,
Lunged past, with one galvanic blare stove up the River.
I counted the echoes assembling, one after one,
Searching, thumbing the midnight on the piers.
Lights, coasting, left the oily tympanum of waters;
The blackness somewhere gouged glass on a sky.

And this thy harbor, O my City, I have driven under,
Tossed from the coil of ticking towers. . . . Tomorrow,
And to be. . . . Here by the River that is East—
Here at the waters' edge the hands drop memory;
Shadowless in that abyss they unaccounting lie.
How far away the star has pooled the sea—
Or shall the hands be drawn away, to die?

Kiss of our agony Thou gatherest,
O Hand of Fire
gatherest—

AARON ZEITLIN

Born in the Ukraine, son of the noted Yiddish writer Hillel Zeitlin, Aaron Zeitlin (1899–1974) wrote essays and plays as well as poetry. Coming to New York in 1939 for the production of his play *Esterke*, he was saved from the fate that overtook his wife and family under Hitler's Europe. In this poem he writes of New Amsterdam's first director general who refused, unsuccessfully, to admit the town's first Jews.

PETER STUYVESANT ☆

Scornful was the church in the Old World,
And frigid.
I was irked,
By its heavy bells and its God-the-wounded upon the Cross.
Churches here are wonderful, cheerful, American,
Affect me not with wounds exposed.
The church with the clock steeple
Opposite my chamber
Signals gentlemanly, "Hello, how do you do?"
I glance at it—
And in my balance shake
My restless grief.
My torments are smiling.
An old verse of Scripture is recalled:
"Thus have I seen the wicked buried."
For he lies here, right across,
Right here, on the church grounds rests he:
The peg-legged captain
Who roared a roar of wrath
At my brothers from Brazil.

Into his New Amsterdam, the fisher village,
It did not suit him to admit
The guest who the world builds and is loathed,
Jerusalem's straying children.
Well, now
You rise and stamp your peg leg,
Peter Stuyvesant!
This time you'll have to stamp, captain,

Not on twenty-odd men
But on millions, two and one half.

Do not wonder
That I, a newcomer,
Write this verse in a bright, big land
Just across your grave, wooden sinner.
It is inscribed on the walls
Of all Babylons
And on tablets
Of all histories:
Jew is element.
Could you destroy an element?

TRANS. JEHIEL B. COOPERMAN AND
SARAH A. COOPERMAN

JORGE LUIS BORGES

Born in Buenos Aires, Jorge Luis Borges (1899–1986) remained nearly unknown until winning the Prix Formentor, the International Publishers Prize, in 1961. Recognized mostly for his prose, Borges was influenced early in his life by Whitman, whose work he translated for an Argentinian audience. In this poem, the poet is mesmerized by the Cloisters, a replica of a medieval monastery and home to the Metropolitan Museum of Art's Romanesque and Gothic collection at the northwest edge of Manhattan.

THE CLOISTERS ☆

From a place in the kingdom of France
they brought the stained glass and the stones
to build on the island of Manhattan
these concave cloisters.
They are not apocryphal.
They are faithful monuments to a nostalgia.

An American voice tells us
to pay what we like,
because this whole structure is an illusion,
and the money as it leaves our hand
will turn into old currency or smoke.
This abbey is more terrible
than the pyramid at Giza
or the labyrinth of Knossos
because it is also a dream.
We hear the whisper of the fountain
but that fountain is in the Patio of the Orange Trees
or the epic of *Der Asra*.
We hear clear Latin voices
but those voices echoed in Aquitaine
when Islam was just over the border.
We see in the tapestries
the resurrection and the death
of the doomed white unicorn
because the time of this place
does not obey an order.
The laurels I touch will flower
when Leif Eriksson sights the sands of America.
I feel a touch of vertigo.
I am not used to eternity.

TRANS. W. S. MERWIN

KENNETH FEARING

Born in Oak Park, Illinois, Kenneth Fearing (1902–1961) moved to New York in 1924 and worked for the WPA, *Time* magazine, and the United Jewish Appeal, and he also wrote semipornographic novels to support himself. When asked during the McCarthy hearings if he was a Communist, the poet replied, "Not yet." His *Stranger at Coney Island and Other Poems*, such as this terrifying panorama of the city, appeared in 1948.

MANHATTAN

Deep city,
Tall city, worn city, switchboard weaving what ghost horizons
(who commands this cable, who escapes from this net, who
shudders in this web?), cold furnace in the sky,

Guardian of this man's youth, graveyard of the other's, jailer of
mine,
Harassed city, city knowing and naïve, gay in the theaters, wary
in the offices, starved in the tenements,
City ageless in the hospital delivery rooms and always too old or
too young in the echoing morgues—

City for sale, for rent:
Five rooms, the former tenant's mattress, still warm, is leaving on
the van downstairs;
Move in;
Here are the keys to the mailbox, the apartment, and the
outside door,
It is yours, all yours, this city, this street, this house designed by a
famous architect, you would know the name at once,
This house where the suicide lived, perhaps this floor, this room
that reflects the drugstore's neon light;
Here, where the Wall Street clerk, the engineer, the socialist, the
music teacher all lived by turns,
Move in,
Move in, arrange the furniture and live, live, go in the morning to
return at night,
Relax, plan, struggle, succeed, watch the snow fall and hear the
rain beat, know the liner's voice, see the evening plane, a
star among stars, go west at the schedule hour,
Make so many phone calls in the foyer again, have so many
business talks in the livingroom, there will be cocktails,
cards, and the radio, adultery again (downtown), vomit
(again) in the bath,
Scenes, hysterics, peace,

Live, live, live, and then move out,
Go with the worn cabinets and rugs all piled on the curb while the
city passes and the incoming tenant (unknown to you) awaits,
Yes, go,
But remember, remember that, that year, that season—

Do you, do you, do you,
City within city, sealed fortress within sealed fortress, island
within enchanted island,
Do you, there outside the stationer's shop, still hear gunfire and
instant death on winter nights,
Still see, on bright Spring afternoons, a thin gray figure crumple
to the walk in the park
(Who stared, who struggled and went home, who stayed and
shivered until the ambulance arrived?—
Let the spirit go free, ship the body west),
Do you remember that, do you,
Do you remember the missing judge, the bigshot spender and the
hundred dollar bills (did he do three years?)
The ballgame of ballgames (the fourth in the series, or was that
the sixth?)
The reform party and the gambling clean-up (a ten-day laugh),
the returning champion (what about it?), the abortion (so
what?), the rape (who cares?),
The paralyzed newsboy, the taxi-driver who studied dramatics,
the honest counterman, the salesman in love
with the aviator's wife, the day at the zoo, the evening in the park,
the perfect girl, the funny little guy with the funny little
face—

City, city, city,
Eye without vision, light without warmth, voice without mind,
pulse without flesh,
Mirror and gateway, mirage, cloud against the sun,
Do you remember that, that year, that day, that hour, that name,
that face,
Do you remember:

Only the day, fulfilled, as it burns in the million windows of the
west,
Only the promise of the day, returning, as if flames on the roofs
and spires and steeples of the east.

LANGSTON HUGHES

"More than Paris," wrote Missouri-born Langston Hughes (1902–1967) before his first visit to New York in 1921, "I wanted to see Harlem." After attending Columbia while staying at the YMCA on 135th Street, he was on the editorial staff of *Fire*, intended to be a Negro literary quarterly though only one issue was published, in 1926, the same year as his first collection, *The Weary Blues*. Perhaps the most noted Harlem Renaissance writer (he was known as "the bard of Harlem"), Hughes celebrates first the great migration that occurred within America to Harlem and then the heart of that black capital of the world.

GOOD MORNING

Good morning, daddy!
I was born here, he said,
watched Harlem grow
until colored folks spread
from river to river
across the middle of Manhattan
out of Penn Station
dark tenth of a nation,
planes from Puerto Rico,
and holds of boats, chico,
up from Cuba Haiti Jamaica,
in buses marked New York
from Georgia Florida Louisiana
to Harlem Brooklyn the Bronx
but most of all to Harlem
dusky sash across Manhattan

I've seen them come dark
    wondering
    wide-eyed
    dreaming
out of Penn Station—
but the trains are late.
The gates open—
Yet there're bars
at each gate.

    What happens
    to a dream deferred?

Daddy, ain't you heard?

THE HEART OF HARLEM ☆

The buildings in Harlem are brick and stone
And the streets are long and wide,
But Harlem's much more than these alone,
Harlem is what's inside—
It's a song with a minor refrain,
It's a dream you keep dreaming again.
It's a tear you turn into a smile.
It's the sunrise you know is coming after a while.
It's the shoes that you get half-soled twice.
It's the kid you hope will grow up nice.
It's the hand that's working all day long.
It's a prayer that keeps you going along—
    That's the Heart of Harlem!

It's Joe Louis and Dr. W. E. B.,
A stevedore, a porter, Marian Anderson, and me.
It's Father Divine and the music of Earl Hines,
Adam Powell in Congress, our drivers on bus lines.
It's Dorothy Maynor and it's Billie Holiday,
The lectures at the Schomburg and the Apollo down the way.
It's Father Shelton Bishop and shouting Mother Horne.

It's the Rennie and the Savoy where new dances are born.
It's Canada Lee's penthouse at Five-Fifty-Five.
It's Small's Paradise and Jimmy's little dive.
It's 409 Edgecombe or a cold-water walk-up flat—
But it's where I live and it's where my love is at
　　Deep in the Heart of Harlem!

It's the pride all Americans know.
It's the faith God gave us long ago.
It's the strength to make our dreams come true.
It's a feeling warm and friendly given to you.
It's that girl with the rhythmical walk.
It's my boy with the jive in his talk.
It's the man with the muscles of steel.
It's the right to be free a people never will yield.
A dream . . . a song . . . half-soled shoes . . . dancing shoes
A tear . . . a smile . . . the blues . . . sometimes the blues
Mixed with the memory . . . and forgiveness . . . of our wrong.
But more than that, it's freedom—
Guarded for the kids who came along—
　　Folks, that's the Heart of Harlem!

OGDEN NASH

One of America's most popular and often quoted poets, Ogden Nash (1902–1971) from Rye, New York, was for a while a bond salesman, a writer of streetcar ads, then a member of the editorial staff at *The New Yorker*. Like most of his poems, this love poem to New York is filled with his inventive, flexible rhyme, and though in 1931 he wrote, "Bronx, no thonx," over thirty years later he changed his attitude: "I wrote those lines, 'The Bronx? No thonx.'/ I shudder to confess them. / Now I'm an older, wiser man I cry, / 'The Bronx? God bless them!' "

I WANT NEW YORK

I think those people are utterly unreliable
Who say they'd be happy on a desert island with a copy of the Biable
And Hamlet (by Shakespeare) and Don Quixote (by Cervantes)
And poems by Homer and Virgil and perhaps a thing or two of Dante's.
And furthermore, I have a feeling that if they were marooned till the millennium's dawn
Very few of us would notice that they were gone.
Perhaps they don't like my opinions any better than I like theirs,
But who cares?
If I were going to be marooned and could take only one thing along
I'd be perfectly happy if I could take the thing which is the subject of this song.
I don't mean anything that was brought either by the postman or the stork.
I mean the City of New York.
For New York is a wonder city, a veritable fairyland
With many sights not to be seen in Massachusetts or Maryland.
It is situated on the island of Manhattan
Which I prefer to such islands as Welfare or Staten. ☆
And it is far superior
To the cities of the interior.
What if it has a heterogeneous populace?
That is one of the privileges of being a metropulace
And heterogeneous people don't go around bothering each other
And you can be reasonably sure that everything you do won't get right back to your dear old mother.
In New York beautiful girls can become more beautiful by going to Elizabeth Arden
And getting stuff put on their faces and waiting for it to harden
And poor girls with nothing to their names but a letter or two can get rich and joyous
From a brief trip to their loyous.

And anybody with a relative of whose will he is the beneficiary
Can do pretty well in the judiciary.
So I can say with impunity
That New York is a city of opportunity.
It also has many fine theaters and hotels,
And a lot of taxis, buses, subways and els,
Best of all, if you don't show up at the office or at a tea nobody
will bother their head
They will just think you are dead.
That's why I really think New York is exquisite.
It isn't all right just for a visit
But by God's Grace
I'd live in it and like it even better if you gave me the place.

PHYLLIS MCGINLEY

Born in Ontario, Oregon, Phyllis McGinley (1905–1978) moved to New York in 1929. Poetry editor for *Town and Country*, she modestly referred to herself as a writer of light verse despite winning the Pulitzer Prize in 1961 for *Times Three*. Her collection *One More Manhattan* appeared in 1937, shortly before this love poem appeared in *The New Yorker*.

VALENTINE FOR NEW YORK ☆

Moscow is Red, Pittsburgh is gritty.
I know a nicer kind of city.
It's on the Hudson, not the Rhine.
Manhattan, be my valentine.

Tumultuous town, absurd and thunderful,
I think you're wonderful—
Sleeping or waking, frivolous or stable,
Down at the heel, or opulent in sable,
I like your voices, single or together.

I even like your weather
(Your rains, your wind that down the river blows,
Your heat, your fogs, your perishable snows).
I like your pomp and civic ceremony.
I like you real. I love you when you're phony.
In other words, no matter where I gad about,
You're what I'm mad about.

Then stay with me and be my dear,
Accept this honest flattery,
And I will sing your praises, clear
From Harlem to the Battery.

I sing the Empire State that magnates dwell in.
I sing Sixth Avenue without the "L" in,
Bedraggled square and screaming boulevard,
And Mr. Morgan's elegant back yard.
I sing St. Thomas's, which sponsors marriages.
I sing your parks equipped with lads and wenches,
With dogs on leashes, and with tots in carriages
And men on wooden benches.
I sing the penthouse, harboring your élite,
And four-flight walkups snug on Barrow Street;
Your native cops, more virile than the bobby,
And Powers models and the Astor lobby.

I sing your Automats,
Your gentle tearooms, wary of the scallion;
The Colony, where wend the risible hats,
And tables d'hôte excessively Italian;
And ferryboats and boogie-woogie bands
And Nedick Orange stands.

Metropolis, aloud I praise
Your febrile nights, your clamorous days.
Not even the sales tax, trying hard,
Can cut in two my deep regard.

Be mine, be mine:
Shop, subway, danceteria, picket line;
The Planetarium, replete with stars;
Buses and banks and débutante bazaars;
And traffic lights reflected, when it rains,
In all the pavements; and the skiing trains;
Orchids by Schling and men in areaways
Selling bouquets;
The show that sells out and the one that closes;
Auctions, and all the deeds of Mr. Moses,
And Sunday bells, and pretty secretaries
Eating their lunches at soda stands or dairies;
Progressive schools that cope with Freudian symbols,
And monasteries selling cheap at Gimbels;
Jaywalkers, and St. Patrick's Day parades;
And part-time maids,
And art museums, where I take my aunts;
And Mott Street, and the Ballroom Renaissance,
Where sound the brasses that the dancers spin to;
And El Morocco, which I've never been to;
And kitchenettes and pubs,
And Kansas clubs;
The elms at Radio City, spreading tall;
Foghorns, and pigeons—yes, and Tammany Hall.

Let others, finding flaw or pointing fault,
Accept you with their cautious grains of salt.
Egregious city, facing toward the sea,
Abide with me.

Boston's well bred, and Philadelphia's Blue.
Borough of Manhattan, I love you.

LÉOPOLD SÉDAR SENGHOR

Born in Joal, Senegal, Léopold Sédar Senghor (1906–2001) served in the French colonial troops, was a prisoner of war, a French resistance fighter, the 1963 winner of the International Grand Prize for Poetry, and president of the Republic of Senegal from 1960 until 1980. Deeply influenced by the poetry of Claude McKay, the poet expresses here, with a jazz accompaniment, the tantalizing beauty and treachery of New York.

NEW YORK

Jazz orchestra; solo trumpet

I

New York! At first your beauty confused me, and your great
 long-legged, golden girls.
I was so timid at first under your blue metallic eyes, your frosty
 smile,
So timid. And the disquiet in the depth of your skyscraper streets
Lifting up owl eyes in the sun's eclipse.
Your sulphurous light and the livid shafts (their heads
 dumbfounding the sky)
Skyscrapers defying cyclones on their muscles of steel and their
 weathered stone skins.
But a fortnight on the bald sidewalks of Manhattan
—At the end of the third week the fever takes you with the
 pounce of a jaguar
A fortnight with no well or pasture, all birds of the air
Fall suddenly dead under the high ashes of the terraces.
No child's laugher blossoms, his hand in my fresh hand
No mother's breast. Legs in nylon. Legs and breasts with no
 sweat and no smell.
No tender word for mouths are lipless. Hard cash buys artificial
 hearts.
No book where wisdom is read. The painter's palette flowers with
 crystals of coral.

Insomniac nights O nights of Manhattan, tormented by fatuous fires, while the klaxons cry through the empty hours
And dark waters bear away hygienic loves, like the bodies of children on a river in flood.

II

It is the time of signs and reckonings
New York! It is the time of manna and hyssop.
Only listen to God's trombones, your heart beating to the rhythm of blood your blood.
I have seen Harlem humming with sounds and solemn colour and flamboyant smells
—(It is tea-time for the man who delivers pharmaceutical products)
I have seen them preparing at flight of day, the festival of the Night. I proclaim there is more truth in the Night than in the day.
It is the pure hour when God sets the life before memory germinating in the streets
All the amphibious elements shining like suns.
Harlem Harlem! I have seen Harlem Harlem! A breeze green with corn springing from the pavements ploughed by the bare feet of dancers In
Crests and waves of silk and breasts of spearheads, ballet of lilies and fabulous masks
The mangoes of love roll from the low houses under the police horses' hooves.
I have seen down the sidewalks streams of white rum and streams of black milk in the blue haze of cigars.
I have seen the sky at evening snowing cotton flowers and wings of seraphim and wizard's plumes.
Listen, New York, listen to your brazen male voice your vibrant oboe voice, the muted anguish of your tears falling in great clots of blood
Listen to the far beating of your nocturnal heart, rhythm and blood of the drum, blood and drum and blood.

III

New York! I say to New York, let the black blood flow into
your blood
Cleaning the rust from your steel articulations, like an oil of life
Giving your bridges the curve of the hills, the liana's suppleness.
See, the ancient times come again, unity is rediscovered the
reconciliation of the Lion the Bull and the Tree
The idea is linked to the act the ear to the heart the sign to
the sense.
See your rivers murmuring with musky caymans, manatees with
eyes of mirage. There is no need to invent the Mermaids.
It is enough to open your eyes to the April rainbow
And the ears, above all the ears to God who with a burst of
saxophone laughter created the heavens and the earth in
six days,
And on the seventh day, he slept a great negro sleep.

TRANS. JOHN REED AND CLIVE WAKE

EDOUARD RODITI

Edouard Roditi (1910–1992) was born in Paris, educated in Europe, and served as an interpreter for the Nuremberg War Crime trials. He taught literary criticism and art history at the University of California and Brown University. Though written early in WWII, this poem has a hip, streetwise tone of today.

MANHATTAN NOVELETTES

I.

The Lorelei with the spaghetti hair
Queens it at the raw-meat piano
While her heliotropic audience pays
A thousand looks for every note.

Desperate beneath her platformed feet,
Her rubber lover sweats pure oil;
He's jealous of his snoring neighbor,
The Hairy Ainu with a dyed mink face.

Both men now think her heels are round,
Since each in turn has been her beau
Though neither long enough to know
That art's her love and love her art.

II.

Nursing his beer until it boils,
The boy whose fall cost but a dime
Watches the blonde with parrot voice
And hopes she'll whisper love at last.

This pretty polly knows her stuff.
She's no sad sister: hard as nails,
She'll trail her man through fog or fen
And turn her dollar, come what may.

And come who may, by hook or crook,
He'll think this houri's worth her price;
He'll never find, concealed beneath
The feathers smooth, bird-claw, bird-beak.

III.

The subway cowboy with a midnight tan
Texas of sex will nightly roam;
He'll sell his body to any devil
For a greenback dollar bill.

For a greenback dollar bill or two
He'd sell his soul. But who will pay
Visible coin for invisible wares,
Temporal for eternal, who?

All for a greenback dollar bill,
What Wests can we discover yet
Who roam Manhattan's midnight range
From neonrise to neonset?

NEW YORK, 1942

DELMORE SCHWARTZ

Brooklyn-born Delmore Schwartz (1913–1966) published his most famous work, the story "In Dreams Begin Responsibilities" in 1937 but never achieved the greatness that story promised. He taught at Harvard and Syracuse and was an editor at *Partisan Review* and a famous customer at the White Horse Tavern in Greenwich Village. Portrayed as Von Humboldt Fleischer in Saul Bellow's novel *Humboldt's Gift*, he writes here of the city's power with a bravado inspired by Whitman.

AMERICA, AMERICA!

I am a poet of the Hudson River and the heights above it,
the lights, the stars, and the bridges
I am also by self-appointment the laureate of the Atlantic
—of the peoples' hearts, crossing it
to new America.

I am burdened with the truck and chimera, hope,
acquired in the sweating sick-excited passage
in steerage, strange and estranged
Hence I must descry and describe the kingdom of emotion.

For I am a poet of the kindergarten (in the city)
and the cemetery (in the city)
And rapture and ragtime and also the secret city in the heart and
mind.
This is the song of the natural city self in the 20th century.

It is true but only partly true that a city is a "tyranny of numbers"
(This is the chant of the urban metropolitan and metaphysical self
After the first two World Wars of the 20th century)

—This is the city self, looking from window to lighted window
When the squares and checks of faintly yellow light
Shine at night, upon a huge dim board and slab-like tombs,
Hiding many lives. It is the city consciousness
Which sees and says: more: more and more: always more.

(1954)

MURIEL RUKEYSER

Born in New York City and a graduate of Columbia University, Muriel Rukeyser (1913–1980) won the Yale Series of Young Poets with her first book *Theory of Flight* (1935). She was newspaper editor and campaigner for civil liberties—especially for women, Jews, and minorities—and she was active in anti–Vietnam War rallies, translator of the poems of Octavio Paz, and instrumental in dedicating the wall of poetry at the Poet's Corner in New York's Cathedral of St. John the Divine. In this poem she turns a humorous, heart-breaking eye to Harlem.

THE BALLAD OF ORANGE AND GRAPE

After you finish your work
after you do your day
after you've read your reading
after you've written your say—
you go down the street to the hot dog stand,
one block down and across the way.
On a blistering afternoon in East Harlem in the twentieth century.

Most of the windows are boarded up,
the rats run out of a sack—
sticking out of the crummy garage

one shiny long Cadillac;
at the glass door of the drug-addiction center,
and man who'd like to break your back.
But here's a brown woman with a little girl dressed in rose and
pink, too.

Frankfurters frankfurters sizzle on the steel
where the hot-dog-man leans—
nothing else on the counter
but the usual two machines,
the grape one, empty, and the orange one, empty,
I face him in between.
A black boy comes along, looks at the hot dogs, goes on walking.

I watch the man as he stands and pours
in the familiar shape
bright purple in the one marked ORANGE
orange in the one marked GRAPE,
the grape drink in the machine marked ORANGE
and orange drink in the GRAPE.
Just the one word large and clear, unmistakable, on each machine.

I ask him : How can we go on reading
and make sense out of what we read?—
How can they write and believe what they're writing,
the young ones across the street,
while you go on pouring grape into ORANGE
and orange into the one marked GRAPE—?
(How are we going to believe what we read and we write and we
hear and we say and we do?)

He looks at the two machines and he smiles
and he shrugs and smile and pours again.
It could be violence and nonviolence
it could be white and black women and men
it could be war and peace or any
binary system, love and hate, enemy, friend.
Yes and no, be and not-be, what we do and what we don't do.

On a corner in East Harlem
garbage, reading, a deep smile, rape,
forgetfulness, a hot street of murder,
misery, withered hope,
a man keeps pouring grape into ORANGE
and orange into the one marked GRAPE,
pouring orange into GRAPE and grape into ORANGE forever.

MAY SWENSON

May Swenson (1913–1989) was born in Logan, Utah, daughter of Swedish immigrants. She attended Utah State University then moved to New York in 1936. For a while she worked with the Federal Writers' Project, and from 1959 to 1966, she was an editor at New Directions. She served as chancellor of the Academy of American Poets from 1980 until her death. Celebrating what other poets in this collection disparage, she takes a life-affirming ride on the city's most famous subway line. ☆

RIDING THE A

I ride
the "A" train
and feel
like a ball-
bearing in a roller skate.
I have on a gray
rain-
coat. The hollow
of the car
is gray.
My face
a negative in the slate
window,
I sit
in a lit

corridor that races
through a dark
one. Strok-
ing steel,
what a smooth rasp—it feels
like the newest of knives
slicing
along
a long
black crusty loaf
from West 4th to 168th.
Wheels
and rails
in their prime
collide,
make love in a glide
of slickness
and friction.
It is an elation
I wish to pro-
long.
The station
is reached
too soon.

OCTAVIO PAZ

Noble Prize winner Octavio Paz (1914–1998) was born in Mexico City and first came to New York as part of the Mexican foreign service. His epic poem "I Speak of the City"—though set in Mexico City—embraces all aspects of a great city, as Whitman's poetry did, but also shows urban life's numbing conformity as in Eliot's *The Waste Land* and the greed and excess described in Ginsberg's "The Charnel Ground." This poem opened the catalog to the Pierre Alechinsky retrospective held at the Guggenheim Museum in February 1987.

CENTRAL PARK

Green and black thickets, bare spots,
leafy river knotting into itself:
it runs motionless through the leaden buildings
and there, where light turns to doubt
and stone wants to be a shadow, it vanishes.
Don't cross Central Park at night.

Day falls, night flares up,
Alechinsky draws a magnetic rectangle,
a trap of lines, a corral of ink:
inside there is a fallen beast,
two eyes and a twisting rage.
Don't cross Central Park at night.

There are no exits or entrances,
enclosed in a ring of light
the grass beast sleeps with eyes open,
the moon exhumes razors,
the water in the shadows has become green fire.
Don't cross Central Park at night.

There are no entrances but everyone,
in the middle of a phrase dangling from the telephone,
from the top of the fountain of silence or laughter,
from the glass cage of the eye that watches us,
everyone, all of us falling in the mirror.
Don't cross Central Park at night.

The mirror is made of stone and the stone now is shadow,
there are two eyes the color of anger,
a ring of cold, a belt of blood,
there is a wind that scatters the reflections
of Alice, dismembered in the pond.
Don't cross Central Park at night.

☆

Open your eyes: now you are inside yourself,
you sail in a boat of monosyllables
across the mirror-pond, you disembark
at the Cobra dock: it is a yellow taxi
that carries you to the land of flames
across Central Park at night.

TRANS. ELIOT WEINBERG

THOMAS MERTON

Born in France, educated in Cambridge and later Columbia, Thomas Merton (1915–1968) worked in a Harlem settlement house before converting to Catholicism and, in 1941, entering a Trappist monastery in Gethsemani, Kentucky, where he lived the rest of his life. His best-selling autobiography, *The Seven Storey Mountain* (1948), raised public awareness of racism, economic injustice, and militarism before his death in Bangkok while attending an ecumenical conference of Buddhist and Christian monks.

HYMN OF NOT MUCH PRAISE FOR NEW YORK CITY

When the windows of the West Side clash like cymbals in the
    setting sunlight,
And when wind wails amid the East Side's aerials,
And when, both north and south of thirty-fourth street,
In all the dizzy buildings,
The elevators clack their teeth and rattle the bars of their cages,
Then the children of the city,
Leaving the monkey-houses
    of their office-buildings and apartments,
With the greatest difficulty open their mouths, and sing:
"Queen among the cities of the Earth: New York!
Rich as a cake, common as a doughnut,
Expensive as a fur and crazy as cocaine,

We love to hear you shake
Your big face like a shining bank
Letting the mad world know you're full of dimes!

"This is your night to make maraccas out of all that metal money
Paris is in the prison-house, and London dies of cancer.
This is the time for you to whirl,
Queen of our hopped-up peace,
And let the excitement of your somewhat crippled congas
Supersede the waltzes of more shining
Capitals that have been bombed.

"Meanwhile we, your children,
Weeping in our seasick zoo of windows while you dance,
Will gobble aspirins,
And try to keep our cage from caving in.
All the while our minds will fill with these petitions,
Flowering quietly in between our gongs of pulse.
These will have to serve as prayers:

" 'O lock us in the safe jails of thy movies!
Confine us to the semiprivate wards and white asylums
Of the unbearable cocktail parties, O New York!
Sentence us for life to the penitentiaries of thy bars and
nightclubs,
And leave us stupefied forever by the blue, objective lights
That fill the pale infirmaries of thy restaurants,
And the clinics of thy schools and offices,
And the operating-rooms of thy dance-halls.

" 'But never give us any explanations, even when we ask,
Why all our food tastes of iodoform,
And even the freshest flowers smell of funerals.
No, never let us look about us long enough to wonder
Which of the rich men, shivering in the overheated office,
And which of the poor men, sleeping face-down on the
Daily Mirror,
Are still alive, and which are dead.' "

JOHN CIARDI

Son of Italian immigrants, John Ciardi (1916–1986) wrote *How Does a Poem Mean?* which became a standard text for poetry classes. He translated Dante's *Divine Comedy*, and his attempts to interest his own children in reading produced the collection *I Met a Man Who Sang the Sillies* (1961). Here he writes of the world's busiest bridge and what modernist architect Le Corbusier believed to be not only the most beautiful one in the world but "the only seat of grace in the disordered city."

GEORGE WASHINGTON BRIDGE ☆

The buttresses of morning lift the sun
Across an arc of steel and flying piers.
The twin cadenzas of the cable run
Like landless gulls across the hemispheres.

Out of a step of mist the caisson root
Spires from the consonant rock to the vowel of the sky,
The highway rings the morning underfoot
Scoring the traffic for a symphony.

And arc and piers and highway soar from steel
Into a swinging web of flying sound.
A gull's geometry, a flashing keel,
A flowering ceremony of the ground.

The men who climbed like birds to trap that wire,
Like birds were born to know what song and flight meant:
The tempo of an arc, curve of a choir,
The eye's adagio and the blood's excitement.

ROBERT LOWELL

Born in Boston, a conscientious objector during WWII (subject of his poem "Memories of West Street and Lepke"), and twice winner of the Pulitzer Prize for *Lord Weary's Castle* (1947) and for *The Dolphin* in 1974, Robert Lowell (1917–1977) covered a great range of styles and content in his work, often seeing the failure of mankind, as in this poem, written in 1966 when the park—and much of the city— struggled through hard times.

CENTRAL PARK

Scaling small rocks, exhaling smog,
gasping at game-scents like a dog,
now light as pollen, now as white
and winded as a grounded kite—
I watched the lovers occupy
every inch of earth and sky:
one figure of geometry,
multiplied to infinity,
straps down, and sunning openly . . .
each precious, public, pubic tangle
an equilateral triangle,
lost in the park, half covered by
the shade of some low stone or tree.
The stain of fear and poverty
spread through each trapped anatomy,
and darkened every mote of dust.
All wished to leave this drying crust,
borne on the delicate wings of lust
like bees, and cast their fertile drop
into the overwhelming cup.

Drugged and humbled by the smell
of zoo-straw mixed with animal,
the lion prowled his slummy cell,
serving his life-term in jail—
glaring, grinding, on his heel,

with tingling step and testicle . . .
Behind a dripping rock, I found
a one-day kitten on the ground—
deprived, weak, ignorant and blind,
squeaking, tubular, left behind—
dying with its deserter's rich
Welfare lying out of reach:
milk cartons, kidney heaped to spoil,
two plates sheathed with silver foil.

Shadows had stained the afternoon;
high in an elm, a snagged balloon
wooed the attraction of the moon.
Scurrying from the mouth of night,
a single, fluttery, paper kite
grazed Cleopatra's Needle, and sailed ☆
where the light of the sun had failed.
Then night, the night—the jungle hour,
the rich in his slit-windowed tower . . .
Old Pharaohs starving in your foxholes,
with painted banquets on the walls,
fists knotted in your captives' hair,
tyrants with little food to spare—
all your embalming left you mortal,
glazed, black, and hideously eternal,
all your plunder and gold leaf
only served to draw the thief . . .
We beg delinquents for our life.
Behind each bush, perhaps a knife;
each landscaped crag, each flowering shrub,
hides a policeman with a club.

M. L. ROSENTHAL

Born in Washington, D.C., Macha Louis Rosenthal (1917–1996) received his Ph.D. from New York University in 1949, later to be professor emeritus there. He edited *The New Modern Poetry: An Anthology of American and British Poetry Since World War II*, as well as *The William Carlos Williams Reader*. Here, in quiet details, the poet dramatizes the conflict between nature and the city, and what occurs when the two blend harmoniously.

GEOMETRIES OF MANHATTAN: MORNING

Foggy morning. The mist-held horizons
move closer, being broken now
by hulks without grace or thrust, not skyscrapers,
not experiments—dumped crates, deadweights
dropped by monsters on strike against the sun.
They block a mile of river, mile of sky.

Still stately, serene,
the thwarted Hudson poises them in its frame
while, weary, soiled, the massed clouds brace them. The aching eye
presses, past clouds and water, to the ruined Jersey shore whose
mysterious, unfocused distances alone sustain
lost promises as mute as Leonardo's far-off forest green.

And now
the relenting eye returns, the river brightens. One gull, two,
invite the dreamer back toward the wakening city. A raindrop-
pool
ripples on a factory rooftop. A tiny cardboard carton
drifts from some crevice in the glittering heights,
a box-kite to the lucky watcher. Turning, turning,
past this hotel window, downward to older Manhattan
drifting and turning, towards the unseeing multitudes, the cars,
the shadows, the shafts of sunlight, the life below.

JANE MAYHALL

Jane Mayhall, born in Louisville, Kentucky, in 1918, attended Black Mountain College and has taught at the New School for Social Research in New York City. Her most recent collection is *Sleeping Late on Judgment Day* (2004). This poem captures a small, treasured piece of the city's past, before plastic Metrocards replaced the brass tokens that first appeared in 1953 when the dime ride went up to fifteen cents. (Tokens are now used as common ornaments for bracelets and cufflinks.)

TOKEN

In the bottom of my shoulder bag
I found a subway token from about eight tokens
back, that makes it long ago,
a monumental oldie. What's it made of?
Bronze-copper beveled and a dull sterling inside glow.
The "NYC" insignia like a secret fraternity embellish.
Brings to mind! Lively morning stench,
hot steel rails, the crowds
I used to sink in.

I could get up and down subway steps, I wasn't
dying. I loved dirt and torn-up newspapers, I was
able to walk. I wrote, it was like a church, like a god-
less tabernacle was God. That was
young. Whirling past the Coney Island darkness,
into flared faces on the platform, the token
rides my hand in the crush.

The old New York system. I remember
a black guy in a baseball cap, two legs gone, coming
through aisles, on a platform on skate wheels,
dignified and with a beautiful
voice. People dropped quarters and tokens
in his basket. He wasn't sanctimonious or drugged on
crime, or we didn't know it.

A token of the incommensurate.
(Even if wrong) I wasn't dying then and could
afford to think in
big words.

HILDA MORLEY

Hilda Morley (1919–1998) was born in New York City and educated at Wellesley College and New York University. She published five books of poetry and writes here of a most common, equalizing factor in the lives of many New Yorkers, showing a side of the city's character too often overshadowed by its seeming indifference.

NEW YORK SUBWAY

The beauty of people in the subway
that evening, Saturday, holding the door for whoever
was slower or
left behind
                    (even with
                    all that Saturday-night
                    excitement)
& the high-school boys from Queens, boasting,
joking together
proudly in their expectations
& power,   young frolicsome
bulls,
        & the three office-girls
each strangely beautiful,   the Indian
with dark skin & the girl with her haircut
very short and fringed, like Joan
at the stake,   the corners
of her mouth laughing
                              & the black girl delicate
as a doe, dark-brown in pale-brown clothes
& the tall woman in a long caftan, the other day,

serene & serious   & the Puerto Rican
holding the door for more than 3 minutes for
the feeble, crippled, hunched little man who
could not raise his head,
        whose hand I held, to
help him into the subway-car—
          so we were
joined in helping him   & someone,
seeing us, gives up his seat,
         learning
from us what we had learned from each other.

LAWRENCE FERLINGHETTI

Lawrence Ferlinghetti was born in Yonkers just north of the Bronx in 1919, the son of an Italian who arrived WOP (with out papers) to become an auctioneer in Brooklyn. The poet was a major voice in the Beat movement and cofounder of San Francisco's famous City Lights Books, the first to publish Allen Ginsberg's *Howl* in 1956. His poem here refers to a beauty contest renewed in 2004 after thirty years as part of the transit system's centennial celebration.

MEET MISS SUBWAYS ☆

Meet Miss Subways
of 1957
See Miss Subways
of 1957
riding the Times Square Shuttle
back and forth
at four in the morning

Meet Miss Subways
of 1957
with fiftycentsize cotton plugs
in her flat black nose

shuttling back and forth
on the Times Square Shuttle
at four in the morning
and hanging on
to heaven's iron rings
with cut-up golden arms
a black weed in a black hand

You can meet Miss Subways
You can see Miss Subways
of 1957
wearing sad slacks
and matching handbag
and cruising thru the cars
and hanging on
with beat black arms
a black butt in a black hand

And the iron cars
shunting on forever
into death and darkness

o lost Ubangi

staggering thru
the 'successive ogives' of Hell
down Dante's final
fire escape

REED WHITTEMORE

Born in 1919, formerly a teacher at the University of Maryland, Reed Whittemore was literary editor for the *New Republic* and twice the poetry consultant for the Library of Congress. Written in 1974 when, like many cities in the country, New York was going through hard times, this poem is a scathing satire of the city all the way—in a Brooklyn accent— to the poem's last "word."

ODE TO NEW YORK

Let me not be unfair Lord to New York that sink that sewer
Where the best the worst and the middle
Of our land and all others go in their days of hope to be
made over
Into granite careerists
Let me not be unfair to that town whose residents
Not content to subside in their own stench
Drag down the heavens met me not be unfair because I
have known
An incorruptible New Yorker (he was a saint)
Also NY has produced at least three books
Two plays
A dozen fine dresses meals shirts taxidrivers
Not to mention jack (Steve?) Brodie ☆
And Mayor LaGuardia why should it matter
That the rest is garbage?

No let me be fair
And mention wonders like East 9th Street
Why should anybody care that NY is ⅔ of our country's ills
(And Washington ⅓, and Muncie Dallas Birmingham and
LA the rest)
When it has crooks so rich and powerful that when they
drive to town
They can park?
Let us not forget that TV is in New York and
the worst slums
the largest fortunes
the most essential inhumanity
Since Nero or maybe Attila as well as
Hospitals that admit no patient without a $1000 deposit if I
were a local

I'd take the express to Rahway but let me just say
That I don't like New York much
All that corrupt stone
All those dishonest girders decadent manholes diseased telephones
New York reminds me of when I had jaundice
New York is sick in the inner soul
Of its gut but we'll be dead of it
Before it is and so New York
You wonderful fun town
Who inspireth my animus
And leadeth two hundred million other Americans to wish they
had not been born under the spell of free enterprise but in a
Martian restroom
New York
I know that when I speak of you I speak of me
I speak of us
I speak of selves who resolved at the age of four to convert
themselves into currency
Because at the age of four they (I, we) had already learned
That no food clothing housing
Existed other than currency
And no faith hope charity
Other than currency
good waterproof dollars
And if there were labor that could not be turned into currency
They (I, we) knew not to do it
And if there were thoughts that could not be turned into currency
They (I, we) knew not to have them
So here we are in the latter day of our wisdom
Yesterday sweetness and light reached a new low
In heavy trading
Even porn is in trouble
what can be done?
In a decade a dozen of our holiest ones
Will own the island
But rats will be running the island

In a decade not a minute of a working man's day will belong to a
working man
All subway riders will pay dues to the Limousine Club

Rats will be running the island
There is no surer route to the grave than through NY
And all American routes go through NY
NY lurks in the corners of our churches paintings novels
NY infests our playing fields newspapers trade unions
There is not a square foot of American sidewalk without the
mark of a NY entrepreneur
Whenever you drive he will cut in front of you
he will get there first

Rats on the island
Ravenous rats
Bred by the banks and the stock exchange
Fed by the eighteen percenters
World that will end
But when?

Lord
you have sent us prophets
They have prattled about revolution and pocketed the proceeds
They have made it
by an infallible law of New York
In direct proportion to the extravagance and falsehood of their
announced visions
They have built the hysteria of constant and drastic social change
into each breakfast
They have taught our children how to stop war on Monday
poverty on Tuesday racism on Wednesday sexism on
Thursday and final exams on Friday

Yet nothing changes

And wherever one drives the prophets are out in front
they get there first

Rats on the island

On New York let me be fair you hell town
I was born to the north of you have lived to the west of you
I have sneaked up on you by land air and sea and been robbed in
        your clip joints
I have left you hundreds of times in the dream that I *could*
Leave you
                but always you sit there
Sinking
            my dearest my sweet
Would you buy these woids?

AMY CLAMPITT

Born in Iowa, Amy Clampitt (1920–1994) attended Columbia University, served as reference secretary for the National Audubon Society in New York, and received a fellowship for distinguished poetic achievement from the Academy of American Poets. This poem dramatizes, with unsettling beauty, nature's subtle, continuous, and inevitable deterioration of the city's infrastructure.

TIMES SQUARE WATER MUSIC

By way of a leak
in the brickwork
beside a stairway
in the Times Square
subway, midway
between the IR
and the BM T, weeks
of sneaking seepage
had smuggled in,
that morning,
a centimeter
of standing water.

To ward off the herd
we tend to turn into,
turned loose on
the tiered terrain
of the Times Square
subway, somebody
had tried, with
a half-hearted
barricade or tether
of twine,
to cordon off
the stairway—

as though anyone
could tie up seepage
into a package—
down which the
water, a dripping
escapee, was surrep-
titiously proceeding
with the intent,
albeit inadvertent,
in time, at an
inferior level,
to make a lake.

Having gone round
the pond thus far
accumulated, bound
for the third, infra-
infernal hollow
of the underground,
where the N, RR,
and QB cars are
wont to travel,
in mid-descent I
stopped, abruptly way-
laid by a sound.

Alongside the iron-
runged nethermost
stairway, under
the banister,
a hurrying skein
of moisture had begun,
on its way down,
to unravel
into the trickle
of a musical
minuscule
waterfall.

Think of spleen-
wort, of moss
and maiden-
hair fernwork,
think of water
pipits, of ouzels
and wagtails
dipping into
the course of it
as the music
of it oozes
from the walls!

Think of it
undermining
the computer's
cheep, the time
clock's hiccup,
the tectonic
inchings of it
toward some
general crackup!

Think of it, think of
water running, running,
running till it
                        falls!

BARBARA GUEST

Often associated with the New York school of poets, Barbara Guest (1920–2006) was born in North Carolina and moved to New York shortly after graduating from the University of California at Berkeley. She fell in love with the downtown painter/poet scene of the 1950s, and for a while was poetry editor at the *Partisan Review* and associate editor at *Art News*. A private person, she believed "it is the poem, not the poet, whose autobiography matters."

THE LOCATION OF THINGS

Why from this window am I watching leaves?
Why do halls and steps seem narrower?
Why at this desk am I listening for the sound of the fall
of color, the pitch of the wooden floor
and feet going faster?
Am I to understand change, whether remarkable
or hidden, am I to find a lake under the table
or a mountain beside my chair
and will I know the minute water produces lilies
or a family of mountaineers scales the peak?

Recognitions

On Madison Avenue I am having a drink, someone
with dark hair balances a carton on his shoulders
and a painter enters the bar. It reminds me
of pictures in restaurants, the exchange of hunger
for thirst, art for decoration, and in a hospital

love for pain suffered beside the glistening rhododendron
under the crucifix. The street, the street bears light
and shade on its shoulders, walks without crying,
turns itself into another and continues, even
cantilevers this barroom atmosphere into a forest
and shed its leaves on my table
carelessly as if it wanted to travel somewhere else
and would like to get rid of its luggage
which has become in this exquisite pointed rain
a bunch of umbrellas. An exchange!

That head against the window
how many times one has seen it. Afternoons
of smoke and wet nostrils,
the perilous make-up on her face and on his,
numerous corteges. The water's lace creates funerals
it makes us see someone we love in an acre of grass.

The regard of dramatic afternoons

through this floodlit window
or from a pontoon on this theatrical lake,
you demand your old clown's paint and I hand you
from my prompter's arms this shako,
wandering as I am into clouds and air
rushing into darkness as corridors
who do not fear the melancholy of the stair.

HAYDEN CARRUTH

Born in Waterbury, Connecticut, in 1921, Hayden Carruth has been editor of *Poetry* magazine and poetry editor of *Harper's*. He lives in Johnson, Vermont, home of his Crow's Mark Press. The setting of this poem of natural beauty with echoes of an archaic world occurs along perhaps the city's most beautiful esplanade, in Brooklyn Heights.

THE HYACINTH GARDEN IN BROOKLYN

A year ago friends
    took me walking
on the esplanade
    in Brooklyn. I've
no idea where it
    was, I could never
find it on my own.
    And as we walked,
looking out over
    the water, a sweet
aroma came to us,
    heavy and rich,
of a hyacinth
    garden set
on the landward side
    among apartment
houses, a quite large
    garden with flowers
of every size and color,
    and the famous
perfume filled the air.
    It surrounded me,
dazed me, as I stood
    by the rail looking
down. There vaguely
    among the blooms
I saw Hyacinthus,
    the lovely African
boy beloved by Apollo,
    lying there, dying,
the dark body already
    rotting, melting
among flowers, bleeding
    in Brooklyn, in
Paradise, struck down
    by the quoit thrown

by the grief-stricken god,
　an African boy
chosen for beauty, for love,
　for death, fragrance
beside the water
　on the esplanade
somewhere in Brooklyn,
　in Paradise.

JACK KEROUAC

A major figure in the Beat Generation, Jack Kerouac (1922–1969) from Lowell, Massachusetts, attended Columbia University on a football scholarship. While there he met William Burroughs and Allen Ginsberg before sailing the Atlantic and Mediterranean as a merchant seaman. He wrote his first novel, *The Town and the City* (1950), mostly about Times Square; described the "Paradise Alley" neighborhood of East Eleventh Street in *The Subterraneans* (although the book is set in San Francisco); and wrote *On the Road* (1951) in his apartment at 454 W. Twentieth Street.

from MACDOUGAL STREET BLUES ☆

"Canto Uno"

The goofy foolish
　human parade
Passing on Sunday
　art streets
Of Greenwich Village

Pitiful drawings of
　images on an
　iron fence
　ranged there

by self believing
artists
with no hair
and black berets
showing green seas
eating at rock
and Pleiades
of Time.

Pestiferating at moon squid
Salt flat tip fly toe
tat sand traps
With cigar smoking interesteds
puffing at the
stroll
I mean sincerely
naive sailors buying prints
Women with red banjos
On their handbags
And arts handicrafty
Slow shuffling
art-ers of Washington Square
Passing in what they think
Is a happy June afternoon
Good God the Sorrow
They dont even listen to me when
I try to tell them they will die

They say "Of course I know
I'll die, why should you mention
It now—Why should I worry
About it –It ll happen
It ll happen—Now
I want a good time—
Excuse me—
It's a beautiful happy June
Afternoon I want to walk in—

Why are you so tragic & gloomy?
And in the corner at the
    Pony Stables
On Sixth Ave & 4th
Sits Bodhisattva Meditating
In Hobo Rags
  Praying at Joe Gould's chair
For the Emancipation

Of the shufflers passing by,
Immovable in Meditation
He offers his hands & feet
 To the passers by
And nobody believes
 That there's nothing to believe in.
Listen to Me.
There is no sidewalk artshow
    No strollers are there

No poem here, no June
    afternoon of Oh
But only Imagelessness
Unrepresented on the iron fence
Of bald artists
With black berets
 Passing by
 One moment less than this
Is future Nothingness Already

The Chess men are silent, assembling
 Ready for funny war—
 Voices of Washington Square Blues
 Rise to my Bodhisattva Poem
   Window
I will describe them:—
  Ey t k ey e e
  Sa la o s o
  F r u p t u r t

Etc.
No need, no words to
describe
The sound of ignorance—
They are strolling to
their death
Watching the Pictures of Hell
Eating Ice Cream
of Ignorance
On wood sticks
That were once sincere
in trees—
But I cant write, poetry,
just prose
* * *
I mean
This is prose
Not poetry
But I want
To be sincere

HOWARD MOSS

Born in New York City, Howard Moss (1922–1987) grew up in Rockaway Beach in Queens. After graduate work at Columbia, he became poetry editor in 1950 for *The New Yorker*, a position he held for a quarter of a century. His collection Buried City (1975) is set in New York and tells of change, loss, and the passing of time. In 1980 he edited the anthology *New York: Poems*.

THE ROOF GARDEN

A nervous hose is dribbling on the tar
This morning on this rooftop where I'm watching you
Move among your sparse, pinchpenny flowers,
Poor metronomes of color one month long

That pull the sun's rays in as best they can
And suck life up from one mere inch of dirt.
There's water in the sky but it won't come down.
Once we counted the skyline's water towers,
Barrels made of shingle, fat and high,
An African village suspended above
The needle hardness of New York that needs
More light than God provides to make it soft,
That needs the water in the water towers
To snake through pipe past all the elevators
To open up in bowls and baths and showers.
Soon our silence will dissolve in talk,
In talk that needs some water and some sun,
Or it will go the same way as before:
Dry repetitions of the ill we bear
Each other, the baited poles of light
Angling through the way the sun today
Fishes among the clouds.
Now you are through
Watering geraniums, and now you go
To the roof edge to survey the real estate
Of architectural air—tense forms wrought up,
Torn down, replaced, to be torn down again . . .
So much like us. Your head against the sky
Is topped by a tower clock, blocks away,
Whose two black hands are closing on the hour,
And I look down into the street below,
Rinsed fresh this morning by a water truck,
Down which a girl, perky in high heels,
Clops by, serenely unaware of us,
Of the cables, gas lines, telephone wires,
And water mains, writhing underfoot

JOHN LOGAN

Born in Red Oak, Iowa, John Logan (1923–1987) served as poetry editor for the *Nation*, and perhaps his degree in zoology contributed to his ability to notice generally unobserved details of life, such as in this poem where, like a tourist, he explores the city's wonders.

MANHATTAN MOVEMENTS ☆

I

My friend Daniela met us in her Subaru
after we had found our way through a crowd or two
at legendary LaGuardia,
and Tim and I went off on a prearranged sojourn
to Mother Cabrini's tomb in Fort Tryon Park—
one hundred and ninetieth street
way out the line on the A train.
We visited her bones in their black habit with wax mask,
her skeleton which for certain will rise up again,
for that is what it means to be a saint. We knelt,
and I prayed for my family
and the new found friendship with Tim,
who is Christ's age at thirty-three.
Then we touched each other's fingers
with the holy water and walked off into the park
in the October sun. I felt young
and smiled at the aging faces
of couples sunning themselves on benches on the walks.
I am fifty-eight, but this day
was a respite from my age.
Tim and I stood by the wall and watched the passing ships
like those visions of Fellini
on the gorgeous blue-black Hudson.
We didn't talk much, both of us wrapped up in our thoughts
as we approached The Cloisters, medieval branch
of the Metropolitan Museum, monastery

carted over stone by stone from Spain
and then reconstructed around a small central court.
It is easy to be overwhelmed here where they store
what is thought to be the true chalice of Jesus Christ,
where the polychromed and gilded
wood Pieta strikes to the heart with its anguished
faces of the pierced Christ and the grieving Virgin and friends,
and where the melancholy white unicorn is penned
in a field of bright flowers bleeding from a neck wound,
its beard and tail both majestically curved, heroic.
And the crazed, craven faces of the hunters, their dogs
yelping and nipping from the threads of the tapestries.
One thanks God for the Gregorian chant which sounds there
so beautifully filling the air of the Cloisters.
Tim and I left, caught the subway,
and descended into the frenetic city again.

II

On the next day, we went to the Light Gallery
to look at the photographs of Harry Callahan.
The naked picture of his wife
Eleanor holding the hand of their small nude daughter
particularly struck me with its beauty. The two
are stepping up onto a sill
fully into the sunlight, the child just visible,
and the wife's thigh and torso are quite handsomely turned.
This photograph is the amazing color of flesh!
And who would believe the ten brilliant red tomatoes
ripening there in another scene on a blue sill?
But this frame has black behind it.
What puts the tomatoes and the nudes both on a sill
but the genius camera eye and hand of Callahan.
And the mannequin—her long forefinger gesturing
beneath her chin! Then in *Venice*
1957 an old man strides in a single
flash of light in a dark chasm
of buildings and blackened canals.

"I wish," writes Callahan, "that more people felt as I:
Photography is an adventure, and the same as life."
We left the gallery and went on to drink champagne
in the loft of the rich boyfriend
of a lovely member of our party. He was gone
to LA and turned the loft over to us for the day.
What a scene: two floors of paintings reached by a spiral
staircase, a greenhouse and an open porch looking out
over lower Manhattan—Wall Street, World Trade Center,
the East River and the Lady—
all drenched by sun as the bright edge
of the Brooklyn Bridge whose cables hummed in the afternoon.
There was much pleasant talk, some of it inane,
as we friends sipped champagne and began to reel a bit,
so that some of us flopped onto the twenty-foot couch.
Tim and I went off to dinner
at Daniela's in Brooklyn Heights
where we had stayed the night before.

I remembered the time well because I woke up once
to find I had flung my left arm over his belly
in our sleep, and as he breathed, his diaphragm rose and
fell with the young life he keeps so well.
Tim played on the piano his song "Mannequin's Dream."
Then after fettucine, wine, and good talk, we were off
to listen to the astounding musical statue
and all his gifted friends in Mozart's *Don Giovanni*
our last night in the city.

JAMES SCHUYLER

Born in Chicago in 1923, James Schuyler moved to New York in the early 1950s, edited *Art News*, and, along with John Ashbery, Kenneth Koch, Frank O'Hara, and others, formed the New York school of poets. His collection *Morning of the Poem* won the 1980 Pulitzer Prize. Of these two poems, "The Morning" occurs in the

Chelsea Hotel, the most famous hotel in American literature, art, and music, and the poet's home (room 625) from 1979 until his death in 1991.

THE MORNING

breaks in splendor on
the window glass of
the French doors to
the shallow balcony
of my room with a
cast iron balustrade
in a design of flowers,
mechanical and coarse
and painted black:
sunburst of a coolish
morning in July. I
almost accept the fact
that I am not in
the country, where I
long to be, but in
this place of glass
and stone—and metal,
let's not forget
metal—where traffic sounds and the day
is well begun. So
be it, morning.

BACK

from the Frick. the weather ☆
cruel as Henry Clay himself.
Who put this collection together?
Duveen? I forget. It was nice
to see the masterpieces again,
covered with the strikers' blood.
What's with art anyway, that
we give it such precedence?

I love the paintings, that's for sure.
What I really loved today
was New York, its street and
men selling flowers and hot dogs
in them. Mysterious town houses,
the gritty wind. I used to live
around here but it's changed some.
Why? That was only thirty years ago.

DENISE LEVERTOV

Born in England, where she served as a nurse in WWII, Denise Levertov (1923–1997), an activist and reformer whose poetry was influenced by William Carlos Williams and the Black Mountain Poets, arrived in New York in 1948 and was poetry editor for the *Nation* as well as a teacher at City College of New York. "I believe in writing about what lies under the hand," she said, as in this poem set in a most familiar city icon but seen with a most uncommon eye.

THE CABDRIVER'S SMILE

Tough guy. Star of David
and something in Hebrew—a motto—
hang where Catholics used to dangle
St. Christopher (now discredited).
No smile. White hair. American-born,
I'd say, maybe the Bronx.
When another cab pulls alongside
at a light near the Midtown Tunnel, and its driver
rolls down his window and greets this guy
with a big happy face and a first-name greeting,
he bows like a king, a formal acknowledgement,
and to me remarks,
                                        deadpan,
            "Seems to think he knows me."

"You mean you don't know him?"–I lean forward laughing,
close to the money-window.
"Never seen him before in my life."
Something like spun steel floats invisible, until
questions strike it,
all around him, the way light gleams webs among
grass in fall.

And on we skim
in silence past the cemeteries, into
the airport, ahead of time. He's beat
the afternoon traffic. I tip him well.
A cool acceptance. Cool? It's
cold as ice.
Yet I've seen,
squinting to read his license,
how he smiled—timidly?—anyway,
smiled, as if hoping to please,
at the camera. My heart
stabs me. Somewhere this elderly
close-mouthed skeptic hides
longing and hope. Wanted
—immortalized for the cops, for his fares, for the world—
to be looking his best.

TULI KUPFERBERG

Born on New York's Lower East Side in 1923, Tuli Kupferberg graduated from Brooklyn College; was part of the Beat Generation, which he wrote about in his 1961 book *The Beatniks; Or the War Against the Beats*; and, with poet Ed Sanders, formed the rock group The Fugs. Here, in a rollicking series of references and juxtapositions, he captures Greenwich Village at a most energetic and memorable time.

GREENWICH VILLAGE OF MY DREAMS ☆

A rose in a stone.
Chariots on the West Side Highway.
Blues in the Soviet Union.
Onions in times square.
A Japanese in Chinatown.
A soup sandwich.
A Hudson terraplane.
Chess in a Catskill bungalow.
Awnings in Atlanta.
Lewisohn stadium in the blackout.
Brooklyn beneath the East River
  the waves passover.
The Battery in startling sunlight.
Kleins in Ohrbachs.
Love on the dole. Roosevelt not elected.
Hoover under the 3rd Avenue El.
Joe Gould kissing Maxwell Bodenheim
  & puffing on his pipe
Edna Millay feeling Edmund Wilson
Charlie Parker & Ted Joans talking
  in Sheridan Sq Park & its cold man!
The Cedar St Bar with Cedars in it
  & authors crashing against the cedars
The Chase Manhattan Bank closed
  down for repairs. To open as the
  new Waldorf Cafeteria.
Lionel Trilling kissing Allen Ginsberg
  after great Reading in the Gaslight
The Limelight changes its name to
  the Electric Light & features
  Charlie Chaplin as a s(w)inging
  waiter
Edgar Allan Poe becoming the dentist
  in the Waverly dispensary & giving
  everyone free nitrous oxide high

Louis getting thrown out of Louis'
San Remo stepping up to the bar &
  asking for a wet Martini
The Charleston on Charles St
  featuring my Sister Eileen
  & the Kronstadt sailors.
Max Eastman & John Reed
  buying Gungawala hashish candy
  at the German Delicatessen on 6th
  Ave & West 4th Street.
Tourists bringing pictures to sell
  to artists in their annual disposition.
Civilians telling cops to move on
Coffeehouses that sell brandy
  in their coffee cups
Eugene O'Neill insisting on coffee
John Barrymore in offbroadway Hamlet
Walt Whitman cruising on MacDougal
Ike & Mamie drunk in Minettas
Khrushchev singing peat bog soldiers
  in the circle (with a balalaika)
Everybody kissing & hugging squeezing
Khrushchev & Eisenhower a big fat kiss
The world an art
Life a joy
The village comes to life again
I wake up singing
I that dwell in New York
Sweet song bless my mouth
Beauty bless my eyes

Song of the world
Fly forth from dreams!

How beautiful is love
And the fruit thereof
Holy holy holy
A kiss and a star

EDWARD FIELD

Born in Brooklyn in 1924, Edward Field attended New York University before becoming a second lieutenant in the Air Force during WWII and flying twenty-five missions over Europe. A translator of Eskimo stories and songs, he also wrote the 1965 Academy Award–winning short documentary *To Be Alive*. His most recent book is the literary memoir *The Man Who Would Marry Susan Sontag, and Other Intimate Literary Portraits of the Bohemian Era*. Like others in this collection, Field writes of his love affair with a city that others despise, then looks back with candor and melancholy at his—and the city's— past.

NEW YORK

I live in a beautiful place, a city
people claim to be astonished
when you say you live there.
They talk of junkies, muggings, dirt, and noise,
missing the point completely.

I tell them where they live it is hell,
a land of frozen people.
They never think of people.

Home, I am astonished by this environment
that is also a form of nature
like those paradises of trees and grass
but this is a people paradise
where we are the creatures mostly
though thank God for dogs, cats, sparrows, and roaches.

This vertical place is no more an accident
than the Himalayas are.
The city needs all those tall buildings
to contain the tremendous energy here.
The landscape is in a state of balance.

We do God's will whether we know it or not:
Where I live the streets end in a river of sunlight.

Nowhere else in the country do people
show just what they feel—
we don't put on any act.
Look at the way New Yorkers
walk down the street. It says,
I don't care. What nerve,
to dare to live their dreams, or nightmares,
and no one bothers to look.

True, you have to be an expert to live here.
Part of the trick is not to go anywhere, lounge about,
go slowly in the midst of the rush for novelty.
Anyway, besides the eats the big event here
is the streets which are full of love—
we hug and kiss a lot. You can't say that
for anywhere else around. For some
it is the sex they care about and get—
there's all the opportunity in the world if you want it.
For me it is different:
Out walking, my soul seeks its food.
It knows what it wants.
Instantly it recognizes its mate, our eyes meet,
and our beings exchange a vital energy,
the universe goes on Charge
and we pass by without holding.

THE LAST BOHEMIANS

for Rosetta Reitz

We meet in a cheap diner and I think, God,
this continuity, I mean, imagine
our still being here together
from the old days of the Village
when you had the bookshop on Greenwich Avenue

and Jimmy Baldwin and Jimmy Merrill used to drop in.
Toying with your gooey chicken, you remind me
how disappointed I was with you for moving
to Eighth Street and adding gifts and art cards,
but little magazines, you explain, couldn't pay the rent.
Don't apologize, I want to say, it's been forty years!

Neither of us, without clinging to our old apartments,
could pay Village rents nowadays,
where nobody comes "to be an artist" anymore.
Living marginally still, we are shabby as ever,
though shabby was attractive on us once—those years
when the latest Williams or Stevens or Moore was sold
in maybe five bookstores, and the Horton
biography of Hart Crane an impossible find.
Continuity! We're still talking of our problems
with writing, finding a publisher,
as though that was the most important thing in the world—
sweetheart, we are as out of it as old lefties.

Someone came into my apartment recently and exclaimed
"Why, it's bohemian!" as if she had discovered the last
of a near-extinct breed. Lady, I wanted to protest,
I don't have clamshell ashtrays, or chianti bottles
encrusted with candle wax, or Wilhelm Reich,
Henry Miller and D. H. Lawrence,
much less Kahlil Gibran and Havelock Ellis,
on my bricks-and-boards bookshelves.
But it's not just the Salvation Army junk she saw,
or the mattress and pillows on the floor—
my living style represented for her the aesthetic
of an earlier generation, the economics, even,
of a time, our time, Rosetta, before she was born.

The youth still come weekends, though not to "see
a drag show" or "bull daggers fighting in the gutters,"
or to "pick up a queer or artist's model."
But there is something expectant in them

for something supposed to be here, once called,
(shiver) bohemian. Now it's I who shiver
as I pass them, fearing their rage against
an old guy with the sad face of a loser.
Daytime, it's safer, with couples in from the suburbs
browsing the antique shops.
I find it all so boring, but am stuck here,
a ghost in a haunted house.

At a movie about a war criminal whose American
lawyer daughter blindly defends him—blasted by the critics
because it is serious and has a message—
the audience is full of old Villagers, drawn to see it
because it's serious and has a message,
the women, no longer in dirndls and sandals,
but with something telltale about the handcrafted jewelry,
the men not in berets, but the kind that would wear them—
couples for whom being young, meant being radical,
meant free love. Anyway,
something about them says Villager,
maybe the remnants of intellect, idealism—
which has begun to look odd on American faces.

Nowadays, there's nothing radical left, certainly not
in the Village, no Left Bank to flee to, no justification
for artistic poverty, nothing for the young to believe in,
except their careers, and the fun of flaunting
their youth and freaky hairstyles in trendy enclaves.

Leftovers from the old Village, we spot each other
drifting through the ghostly
high rental picturesque streets, ears echoing
with typewriters clacking and scales and arpeggios
heard no more, and meet furtive in coffee shops,
partly out of friendship, but also, as we get shabbier and rarer,
from a sense of continuity—like, hey we're historic!—
and an appreciation, even if we never quite got there,
of what our generation set out to do.

HARVEY SHAPIRO

Born in Chicago in 1924 from Kiev immigrants, Harvey Shapiro moved to New York with his parents when he was a child. A radio gunner during WWII , he flew thirty-five missions over Germany and Austria, earning the Distinguished Flying Cross. While in service he read Whitman and Hart Crane, then entered Columbia University where he received an M.A. For a while a fiction editor at *The New Yorker*, then an editor at the *New York Times Magazine*, he also was part of the inception of the *Village Voice*.

THROUGH THE BOROUGHS

I hear the music from the street
Every night. Sequestered at my desk,
My luminous hand finding the dark words.
Hard, very hard. And the music
From car radios is so effortless.
And so I strive to join my music
To that music. So that
The air will carry my voice down
The block, across the bridge,
Through the boroughs where people I love
Can hear my voice, saying to them
Through the music that their lives
Are speaking to them now, as mine to me.

BROOKLYN HEIGHTS ☆

1

I'm on Water Street in Brooklyn,
between the Brooklyn Bridge
and the Manhattan Bridge,
the high charge of their traffic
filling the empty street.
Abandoned warehouses
on either side.
In the shadowed doorways, shades

of Melville and Murder Incorporated.
Five o'clock October light.
Jets and gulls in the fleecy sky.
Climbing the hill to Columbia Heights,
I turn to see the cordage
of the Brooklyn Bridge, and behind it
the battle-gray Manhattan.

2

This room shelved high with books
echoes with my midnights. Pages
of useless lines swim in it. Only
now and then a voice cuts through
saying something right: No sound
is dissonant which tells of life.
The gaudy ensigns of this life
flash in the streets; a December light,
whipped by wind, is at the windows.
Even now the English poets are in the street,
Keats and Coleridge on Hicks Street,
heading for the Bridge. Swayed aloft there,
the lower bay before them, they can
bring me back my City line by line.

KENNETH KOCH

Kenneth Koch (1925–2002) was born in Cincinnati, Ohio, received a Ph.D. from Columbia, and was a teacher, a writer about poetry, and a member of the influential and self-effacing New York school of poets of the 1950s. This excerpt from his rollicking, heavily autobiographic work captures one of the great times in New York's past, when poets and painters were intimately involved with each other and acutely aware of themselves in the art capital of the world.

from A TIME ZONE ☆

Frank and I are writing very long poems
Long is really the operative word for these poems
His is called Second Avenue mine When the Sun Tries to Go On
I don't know where I got the title
I'm working on it every afternoon the words seem to me arriving
like stampeding cattle
It's not at all clear but for the first time in my life the words seem
completely accurate
If I write for three hours I allow myself a cigarette
I'm smoking it's a little too much I'm not sure I can get through
it alone
Frank and I read each other segments of these long works daily
on the phone
Janice finds it funny now that I've dropped this bunch of pages
That I can't get them back in the right order well I do but
it's by stages
It is April I have a job at the Hunter College Library
I come down to the Cedar on a bus hoping to see O'Hara and
Ashbery
Astonishingly on the bus I don't know why it's the only occasion
I write a poem Where Am I Kenneth? It's on some torn-out
notebook pages
The Cedar and the Five Spot each is a usable place
A celebrated comment Interviewer What do you think of space?
De Kooning Fuck space!
In any case Frank is there he says he likes Where Am I Kenneth?
I carry this news home pleasantly and the poem it mentions her to
Janice
John's poem Europe is full of avant-garde ardor
I am thinking it's making an order out of a great disorder
I wonder at what stage in life does this get harder
The Cedar Bar one hardly thinks of it is what may be called a
scene
However one closed to the public since no one goes there
to be seen

It is a meeting place for the briefest romances
And here is Norman Bluhm at the bar saying Who cares about
those nances?
And here he is shoving and here is de Kooning and there is a beer
Being flung at someone Arnold Weinstein or me through the
smoke-talky atmosphere
Of this corner booth
Voici Guston and Mitchell and Smith and here on top of
everything is Ruth
Kligman being bedazzling without stop
She writes a poem with the line At the bar you've got to be on top
Meanwhile tonight Boris Pasternak
Is awarded the Nobel Prize and is forced to give it back
Frank O'Hara is angry there seems both a flash and a blur
in his eyes
Kenneth we've got to do something about Pasternak and the
Nobel Prize
What? well we ought to let him know
That we support him Off flies a cable into the perpetual snow
Dear Boris Pasternak We completely support you and we also
love your early work
Signed puzzlingly for him in the morning's glare if he ever
receives it Frank O'Hara and Kenneth Koch
Staging George Washington Crossing the Delaware
Alex Katz comes up looking like a pear
He has some white plywood boards with him he says where
Shall I put this stuff and a big bare
Wall is the side of their emplacement No chair
For Alex painting and cutting And now they're there
The seven soldiers one cherry tree one Delaware crossing boat
Hey hey Ken cries Alex I've done it
I've made you a set for George Washington Crossing the
Delaware
The British and American armies face each other on wooden feet
I write this play in our apartment on Commerce Street
I am working in the early afternoon and stay up late
Dawn is peeling oranges on top of the skyscrapers
On the stage a wall goes up and then it's taken down

And under the Mirabeau Bridge flows the Seine
Today Larry and Frank are putting together "Stones"
It's a series of lithographs
Larry puts down blotches violently they look like the grapes of
wrath
Frank is smoking and looking his best ideas come in transit
I walk the nine blocks to the studio he says Come in
New York today is white dirty and loud like a snow-clogged
engine
Huge men in undershirts scream at each other in trucks near
Second Avenue and Tenth Street
De Kooning's landscapey woman is full of double-exposure
perfections
Bob Goodnough is making some small flat red corrections
Jane is concentrating she's frowning she has a look of happy
distress
She's painting her own portrait in a long-sleeved dark pink dress
I'm excited I'm writing at my typewriter it doesn't make too
much sense

DONALD JUSTICE

Winner of the Pulitzer Prize for *Selected Poems* (1979), Donald Justice was born in Miami in 1925. He received a Ph.D. from the University of Iowa's Writing Workshop and was an educator, a painter, and the editor of *The Collected Poems of Weldon Kees*. Justice possessed a musicality in his work from his extensive background as a pianist. Although invited in 2003 to be poet laureate of the Library of Congress, he was suffering too much from Parkinson's disease to accept, dying but a year later.

MANHATTAN DAWN (1945)

There is a smoke of memory
That curls about these chimneys

And then uncurls; that lifts,
Diaphanous, from sleep

To lead us down some alleyway
Still vaguely riverward;
And so at length disperses
Into the wisps and tatters

That garland fire escapes.
—And we have found ourselves again
Watching, beside a misty platform,
The first trucks idling to unload

(New England's frost still
Unstippling down their sides).
Or turned
To catch blue truant eyes upon us

Through steam that rose up suddenly from a grate . . .
Grinning—
And the grin slid off across the storefronts.
Dawn always seemed to overtake us, though,
Down Hudson somewhere, or Horatio.
—And we have seen it bend
The long stripes of the awnings down
Toward gutters where discarded flowers
Lay washing in the night's small rain—
Hints, glimmering of a world
Not ours.
And office towers
Coast among lost stars.

SAMUEL MENASHE

Samuel Menashe, born in New York in 1925, fought in the Battle of the Bulge in WWII, studied in Paris after that, and recently won the first Neglected Poets Award. His first collection, *The Many Named Beloved*, appeared in 1961, and *New and Selected Poems* was published by the Library of America.

OLD AS THE HILLS ☆

The lilt of a slope
Under the city
Flow of the land
With streets in tow
Where houses stand
Row upon row

SHEEP MEADOW

French spoken
across the snow
on Sheep Meadow
evokes a very rich hour
of the Duke of Berry . . .
three men traversing
a field of snow—
one of them alone—
hedged by trees
on the south side
where the towers
of the city rise . . .
one of those hours
in early afternoon
when nothing happens
but time makes room

STANLEY MOSS

Born in New York City in 1925, educated at Trinity College and then Yale University, awarded the Silver Star and a Purple Heart from the U.S. Navy during World War II, Stanley Moss is an international art dealer, a founder of Sheep Meadow Press, and author of three books of poetry, most recently *Asleep in the Garden: New and Selected Poems*. This poem partakes of what is a visual delight to some New Yorkers but the stain of urban blight to others.

SM

With spray can paint,
I illuminate my name
on the subway cars and hand ball courts,
in the public school yards of New York,
S M
written in sky-above-Harlem blue,
surrounded by a valentine splash
of red and white, not for Spiritus Mundi,
like the back of the headboard of my bed,
part al fresco, part catacomb—I spray my name
for the ghetto populations of my city
with those who stand for public art
that doesn't ignore our sacred lives.
In secret if I must
and wearing sneakers, I sign with those
who have signed for me.

GERALD STERN

Born in Pittsburgh in 1925, Gerald Stern received an M.A. from Columbia University and won the 1998 National Book Award for *This Time: New and Selected Poems*. Like many writing of New York, the poet finds, even amid the many unsettling images of the city, beauty and peace, in this case in the solid and overwhelming presence of the Cathedral of St. John the Divine.

THE POEM OF LIBERATION

The smell of piss is what we have in the city
to remind us of the country and its dark ammonia.
In the subway it's like a patch of new lilac
or viburnum in the air or like that pocket
of cold water you swim in at Batsto ☆
or that other pocket of water at Amagansett.
In the telephones it sinks in the metal plates
like the smell in a rug or a rotten sofa,
a stain you run away from in grief and anger.

Sometimes I walk in the East Side past the brownstones
on Fifty-second Street or the long sleek canopies
that almost cover the sidewalks from Fifth to Madison.
Then it's like remembering the stone walls in Italy
or the tiny alleys behind the bazaars in Africa.
Then I know, walking in front of Park East
or the Hampton House or the Penguin,
that New York will be the first city to go,
and we will no longer live like English,
hating the sight of sweet bananas and thick-armed
women smashing dice against the boards.

Across the street from St. John's there is a large
vegetable garden planted in the rubble
of a wrecked apartment house, as if to claim
the spirit back before it could be buried
in another investment of glass and cement.
There are thin maples and pieces of orange brick
and weeds and garbage as well as little rows
of beans and lettuce and hills of squash and melons.
It is a confused garden but I think the
soul of New York is there in the vague balance
of shape against shape and in the lush presence
of objects, from the blue cement fish pond
to the curved brick walk to the outdoor grille and chair;

a boxed-in mulch pit, iron candelabra, deep
irrigation ditches, delicate flower beds,
everything crowded into the smallest space.

I stand on the steps in front of the straining prophet,
looking across at the other two buildings, saved
by the squatters in 1970. I look at the splintered
doors and the pile of rubbish outside the windows
and make my own philosophical connections.
Behind the church, totally hidden from the streets,
is another garden, planted by the women
of St. John's, this one a biblical
fantasy of trees and herbs and flowers,
from Matthew and John and Samuel, laid out in perfect
clusters, poplar from Genesis, reeds from Kings,
nettles from Job, lovely carob from Luke,
completely different from the other garden,
but not a mirror image of it
and not a sacred version of the profane,
one a vile parody of the other,
although these ideas flooded through my mind.

I fall asleep under the olive trees
thinking of Jezebel and Elijah.
I want to like one garden and hate the other
but I find myself loving both, both ideas,
both deeply thought out, both passionate.
I talk to the fat Englishman—the curator
of the church museum—about the two gardens
and the squatters and the church's benign role
and get his views on property, and mercy,
and study his tiny feet and row of books.
Finally I walk across the street again
to look at the People's Garden and plan my
little corner next to the climbing roses,
maybe a hosta or a bleeding heart.

My last hour is spent reading the poem
of liberation—in Spanish and English—
nailed up on the wire fence
and walking through the Plaza Caribe
under the slogans and the brown faces.
—At first I think it's hope again, hope played out
on a two-stringed instrument or a soggy drum.
Hebrew melancholy and Moorish wailing
under a fringed lamp, in a ruined chair,
but then I realize it's hope mixed in with memory
and not that other bitter stupid dream again,
stuck to the face like a drop of baby dew.

I love memory too, the weeping mouth
that will not let you go, the sweet smell drifting
through the alleys, the hum at the high window;
and I love the fact that, this time, no one will stand
with his straw hat in his hand in the marble courtroom
singing, "I love you, Kate Smith. I love you, I love you,
I love you, *presidente*, I love you, *señor* mayor."
I dig a hole in the ground
and pour in my mixture of meal and water.
I spread the roots out in three directions
and pack them in with dirt.
I leave by the southern gate
across the street from the Hungarian pastry
and walk down 111th like a Bedouin farmer,
like a Polish shepherd,
like a Korean rope master,
my small steel shovel
humming and singing in the blue dust.

FRANK O'HARA

Originally from Baltimore, Frank O'Hara (1926–1966) arrived in New York in the early 1950s when the city reached creative heights never seen before. His love for New York recalls Whitman, whom O'Hara referred to as "my great predecessor." Developing a new type of diarylike, "personal" poem that influenced his contemporaries and poets to follow, part of the self-effacing New York school of poets, he walked the city during his lunch break as a curator at the Museum of Modern Art (he began there selling postcards), recording action and feeling in his *Lunch Poems* (1965), some of the most joyous bursts of love ever written to the city.

STEPS

How funny you are today New York
like Ginger Rogers in *Swingtime*
and St. Bridget's steeple leaning a little to the left ☆

here I have just jumped out of a bed full of V-days
(I got tired of D-days) and blue you there still
accepts me foolish and free
all I want is a room up there
and you in it
and even the traffic halt so thick is a way
for people to rub up against each other
and when their surgical appliances lock
they stay together
for the rest of the day (what a day)
I go by to check a slide and I say
that painting's not so blue

where's Lana Turner
she's out eating
and Garbo's backstage at the Met
everyone's taking their coat off
so they can show a rib-cage to the rib-watchers
and the park's full of dancers with their tights and shoes
in little bags
who are often mistaken for worker-outers at the West Side Y
why not
the Pittsburgh Pirates shout because they won

and in a sense we're all winning
we're alive

the apartment was vacated by a gay couple
who moved to the country for fun
they moved a day too soon
even the stabbings are helping the population explosion
though in the wrong country
and all the those liars have left the UN
the Seagram Building's no longer rivalled in interest
not that we need liquor (we just like it)

and the little box is out on the sidewalk
next to the delicatessen
so the old man can sit on it and drink beer
and get knocked off it by his wife later in the day
while the sun is still shining

oh god it's wonderful
to get out of bed
and drink too much coffee
and smoke too many cigarettes
and love you so much

A STEP AWAY FROM THEM ☆

It's my lunch hour, so I go
for a walk among the hum-colored
cabs. First, down the sidewalk
where laborers feed their dirty
glistening torsos sandwiches
and Coca-Cola, with yellow helmets
on. They protect them from falling
bricks, I guess. Then onto the
avenue where skirts are flapping
above heels and blow up over
grates. The sun is hot, but the
cabs stir up the air. I look

at bargains in wristwatches. There
are cats playing in sawdust.

On
to Times Square, where the sign
blows smoke over my head, and higher
the waterfall pours lightly. A
Negro stands in a doorway with a
toothpick, languorously agitating.
A blonde chorus girl clicks: he
smiles and rubs his chin. Everything
suddenly honks: it is 12:40 of
a Thursday.

Neon in daylight is a
great pleasure, as Edwin Denby would
write, as are light bulbs in daylight.
I stop for a cheeseburger at JULIET'S
CORNER. Giulietta Masina, wife of
Federico Fellini, *è bell' attrice*.
And chocolate malted. A lady in
foxes on such a day puts her poodle
in a cab.

There are several Puerto
Ricans on the avenue today, which
makes it beautiful and warm. First
Bunny died, then John Latouche,
then Jackson Pollack. But is the
earth as full as life was full, of them?
And one has eaten, and one walks,
past the magazines and nudes
and the posters for BULLFIGHT and
the Manhattan Storage Warehouse,
which they'll soon tear down. I
used to think they had the Armory
Show there.

A glass of papaya juice
and back to work. My heart is in my
pocket, it is Poems of Pierre Reverdy.

PAUL BLACKBURN

Born in Vermont, Black Mountain poet Paul Blackburn (1926–1971) translated medieval troubadour poetry and organized readings by Beats and other poets in New York during the 1950s and 1960s at such legendary cafes as Les Deux Mégots on East Seventh Street and Le Metro on Second Avenue. His *Brooklyn-Manhattan Transit* (1960) is an ironic, elegiac collection of poems of city life, as in this piece about the small treasure, once troubled and now revived, behind the New York Public Library.

BRYANT PARK ☆

I think it
is its
location—
between 40th & 42nd—
gives it its princely
quality, by contrast

At the top of the steps in the spring dusk
the sun gone behind
Crompton Velvet & Union Dime, the massive stone
grace of the Public Library at one's back, the
loungers of varying quality on the stone benches
and about one on the steps, across the stairs stretched out
like so many Etruscan statues, old bums, the youngmen, the
college girls with their long legs under short skirts, curled
there on the steps in the fading light . and below one
the lawn stretching out dark-green velvet all the way to
the fountain near Sixth Avenue, one can almost hear
the sound of falling water between the red and green
light interstices of evening traffic, plash, and at
regular intervals on this edge of lawn, between the
flower beds running an equal length, three signs
KEEP OFF KEEP OFF KEEP OFF
simple enough . The trees
in lines, doubled at the far sides, have sent

the spring sap up and leaves, the first-broken buds
and moves of green have startled the streetlamps as they
open and see the blood has started up in the dusk, and
there the small leaves are
tender as the legs of girls
opening equally to night and
warm air . The flower beds
splay and tighten the tulips
the hands of men from the Park Department have planted there
in, patterns of triangles, white intersecting the pink and
further down, pink intersecting red isosceles
cut to the side with sun . The other bed,
being shade-side, shows only green, the spikes, with
green spikes rising will be flowers tomorrow, next week,
a few white blossoms al-
ready out some halfway down toward the avenue
where buildings rise their own flowers of light, the ugliness
hidden in the new dark . I stand

arms parallel to the lines of the balustrades, forward, out
stretching as though I were dusk or stone, above the girls,
the men
as though my hands were those of the Park Department men,
pressing
bulbs into the dark earth months ago, fall of the year,
my stone hands warm with sun, wet and dark with earth, o-
pening, closing, like the flowers all that action will become
tonight for me, now, this evening moment of new leaves and
grass.

The lawn stretches out its moment of princely peace .
From the bottom of the steps one
cannot see the bare spots on it, it
stretches out perfect to the eye .
There are those signs . For the moment I am
that tired monarch, that prince after a long day's riding

out for birds or boar or stag . I move my legs
lazily
        twice, and stand
                                at the edge of the grass.

JOHN HOLMES

John Clellon Holmes (1926–1988) and Jack Kerouac are credited (by Kerouac) with coming up with the term "Beat" as a name for their generation. Holmes's 1952 novel, *Go*, inspired Kerouac to write *On the Road*, and it was Holmes's essay "This Is the Beat Generation" in *New York* magazine that gave his generation greater exposure and notoriety. His insightful collection of essays and memoirs, *Nothing More to Declare* (1967), describes New York as the art capital of the world—and the young artists and poets who came here knew it.

FROM BROOKLYN

I came there the first time late at night by
Loud subway, wet streets, long stairs to a room
Hung for all I knew in nowhere, in Brooklyn,
Walled with black windows and books in bloom.
Morning was tall in the windows when I woke,
Sounds not my morning sounds marked time.
I saw from the pillow up and outdoors such sky
As never blew by my windows waking at home.

Where? Why? Look! And I looked at Manhattan
Over across the full gray river, far and framed
Like history going on, and too much of it
To look at once, too much of it to be named.

Begin with the near sounds, tugboats, gulls,
I said, under the heaven covering New York

Silent above this century, this high morning's
Harbor, patient with the Egyptian work of
Nobody I know with grains and grains of sand
Hurrying up and down the beautiful towers.
The far sound is a hum, a huge hollow dreaming
Murmur, a sprawled confidence of power, power.

Before me man's old animal that never sleeps
Smiled in a dream of bloody murder in his cave,
Woke to the music of museums, strode, flourished
His women in flower, to be living ruthless love
Of ships slow up the East River, planes rising fast,
Trains in from Chicago, trouble and trade and rain
Blown in from the northeast, west, southwest,
To stir tender and terrible meanings in his brain.
Magnificent world, inexhaustible energy, there are
No words for it. It is. The hours of my day
Were tide, smoke, noon on a staggered skyline
Massive and meaningful and furious and far away.

Behind me the streets were doorways, baseball,
Leafshadow on sunwarm brick, and high school pride,
Millions of store-fronts, bus-stops, signs, names,
Brightened and blurred in an all-day taxi ride.
History is a book I read a chapter of in Brooklyn,
Wondering out a window how to read plain words.
Time is the windy heaven changing over Brooklyn,
Cloud going, light coming, the drift of sea-birds.

JAMES MERRILL

Son of Charles Merrill, founder of the powerful Wall Street firm Merrill Lynch, James Merrill (1926–1995) was born in New York City and believed he was as "American as chiffon pie."☆ Known as the "Ouija poet" for his poems recording sessions with spirits conjured up on a Ouija board, he won the 1977 Pulitzer Prize for *Divine Comedies*.

164 EAST 72ND STREET

These city apartment windows—my grandmother's once—
Must be replaced come Fall at great expense.
Pre-war sun shone through them on many a Saturday
Lunch unconsumed while frantic adolescence
Wheedled an old lady into hat and lipstick,
Into her mink, the taxi, the packed lobby,
Into our seats. Whereupon gold curtains parted
On Lakmè's silvery, not yet broken-hearted

Version of things as they were. But what remains
Exactly as it was except those panes?
Today's memo from the Tenants' Committee deplores
Even the ongoing deterioration
Of the *widows* in our building. Well. On the bright side,
Heating costs and street noise will be cut.
Sirens at present like intergalactic gay
Bars in full swing whoop past us night and day.

Sometimes, shocked wide awake, I've tried to reckon
How many lives—fifty, a hundred thousand?—
Are being shortened by that din of crosstown
Ruby flares, wherever blinds don't quite . . .
And shortened by how much? Ten minutes each?
Reaching the Emergency Room alive, the victim
Would still have to live *years*, just to repair
The sonic fallout of a single scare.

"Do you ever wonder where you'll—" Oh my dear,
Asleep somewhere, or at the wheel. Not here.
Within months of the bathroom ceiling's cave-in,
Which missed my grandmother by a white hair,
She moved back South. The point's to live in style,

Not to drop dead in it. On a carpet of flowers
Nine levels above ground, like Purgatory,
Our life is turning into a whole new story:
Juices, blue cornbread, afternoons at the gym—
Imagine who remembers how to swim!
Evenings of study, or intensive care
For one another. Early to bed. And later,
If the mirror's drowsy eye perceives a slight
But brilliant altercation between curtains
Healed by the leaden hand of—one of us?
A white-haired ghost? or the homunculus.

A gentle alchemist behind them trains
To put in order these nocturnal scenes—
Two heads already featureless in gloom
Have fallen back to sleep. Tomorrow finds me
Contentedly playing peekaboo with sylphlike
Quirk in the old glass, making the brickwork
On the street's far (bright) side ripple. Childhood's view.
My grandmother—and easy-to-see-through

Widow by the time she died—made it my own.
Bless her good sense. Far from those parts of town
Given to high finance, or the smash hit and steak house,
Macy's or crack, Saks or quick sex, this neighborhood
Saunters blandly forth, adjusting its clothing.
Things done in purple light before we met,
Uncultured things that twitched as on a slide
If thought about, fade like dreams. Two Upper East Side

Boys again! Rereading Sir Walter Scott
Or *Through the Looking Glass*, it's impossible not
To feel how adult life, with its storms and follies,
Is letting up, leaving me ten years old,
Trustful, inventive, once more good as gold
—And counting on this to help, should a new spasm
Wake the gray sleeper, or to improve his chances
When ceilings flush with unheard ambulances.

ALLEN GINSBERG

Born in Newark, New Jersey, Allen Ginsberg (1926–1997) attended Columbia University before moving to the Lower East Side, where "you'd walk around hearing 'Rhapsody in Blue' in your head."☆ He became a leading voice of the Beat Generation both in New York and San Francisco, and his *Howl* was a poem as powerful to his generation when it appeared in 1956 as Eliot's *The Waste Land* had been to the generation before. A political activist, social guru, and East Village notable, inspired by his mentor and model Walt Whitman, as well as the "precise real images" of William Carlos Williams, but infused with jazz and "spontaneous bop prosody," Ginsberg was the first of the Beats to live in the East Village where his first apartment, at 206 E. Seventh Street, provided haven for poets, renegades, and social outcasts.

from MUGGING

I

Tonite I walked out of my red apartment door on East tenth
    street's dusk—
Walked out of my home ten years, walked out in my honking
    neighborhood
Tonite at seven walked out past garbage cans chained to concrete
    anchors
Walked under black painted fire escapes, giant castiron plate
    covering a hole in ground
—Crossed the street, traffic lite red, thirteen bus roaring by
    liquor store,
past corner pharmacy iron grated, past Coca Cola & Mylai
    posters fading scraped on brick
Past Chinese Laundry wood door'd, & broken cement stoop steps
    For Rent hall painted green & purple Puerto Rican style
Along E. 10th's glass splattered pavement, kid blacks & Spanish
    oiled hair adolescents' crowded house fronts—
Ah, tonite I walked out on my block NY City under humid
    summer sky Halloween,

thinking what happened Timothy Leary joining brain police for
a season?
thinking what's all this Weathermen, secrecy & selfrighteousness
beyond reason—F.B.I. plots?
Walked past a taxicab controlling the bottle strewn curb—
past young fellows with their umbrella handles & canes leaning
against a ravaged Buick
—and as I looked at the crowd of kids on the stoop—a boy
stepped up, put his arm around my neck
tenderly I thought for a moment, squeezed harder, his umbrella
handle against my skull,
and his friends took my arm, a young brown companion tripped
his foot 'gainst my ankle—
as I went down shouting Om Ah Hūm to gangs of lovers on the
stoop watching
slowly appreciating, why this is a raid, these strangers mean
strange business
with what—my pockets, bald head, broken-healed-bone leg, my
softshoes, my heart—
Have they knives? Om Ah Hūm—Have they sharp metal wood
to shove in eye ear ass? Om Ah Hūm
& slowly reclined on the pavement, struggling to keep my
woolen bag of poetry address calendar & Leary-lawyer
notes hung from my shoulder
dragged in my neat orlon shirt over the crossbar of a broken
metal door
dragged slowly onto the fire-soiled floor an abandoned store,
laundry candy counter 1929—
now a mess of papers & pillows & plastic car seat covers cracked
cockroach-corpsed ground—
my wallet back pocket passed over the iron foot step guard
and fell out, stole by God Muggers' lost fingers, Strange—
Couldn't tell—snakeskin wallet actually plastic, 70 dollars my
bank money for a week,
old broken wallet—and dreary plastic contents—Amex card
& Manf. Hanover Trust Credit too—business card from
Mr. Spears British Home Minister Drug Squad—my draft

card—membership ACLU & Naropa Institute Instructor's identification
Om Ah Hūm I continued chanting Om Ah Hūm
Putting my palm on the neck of an 18 year old boy fingering my back pocket crying "Where's the money"
"Om Ah Hūm there isn't any"
My card Chief Boo-Hoo Neo American Church New Jersey & Lower East Side
Om Ah Hūm—what not forgotten crowded wallet—Mobil Credit, Shell? old lovers addresses on cardboard pieces, booksellers calling cards—
—"Shut up or we'll murder you"—"Om Ah Hūm take it easy"
Lying on the floor shall I shout more loud?—the metal door closed on blackness
one boy felt my broken healed ankle, looking for hundred dollar bills behind my stocking weren't even there—a third boy untied my Seiko Hong Kong watch rough from right wrist leaving a claspprick skin tiny bruise
"Shut up and we'll get out of here"—and so they left,
as I rose from the cardboard mattress thinking Om Ah Hūm didn't stop em enough,
the tone of voice too loud—my shoulder bag with 10,000 dollars full of poetry left on the broken floor—

NOVEMBER 2, 1974

THE CHARNEL GROUND

. . . Rugged and raw situations, and having accepted them as part of your home ground, then some spark of sympathy or compassion could take place. You are not in a hurry to leave such a place immediately. You would like to face the facts, realities of that particular world . . .

CHÖGYAM TRUNGPA, RINPOCHE

Upstairs Jenny crashed her car & became a living corpse, Jake sold grass, the white-bearded potbelly leprechaun silent climbed their staircase
Ex-janitor John from Poland averted his eyes, cheeks flushed with vodka, wine who knew what

as he left his groundfloor flat, refusing to speak to the inhabitant
of Apt. 24
who'd put his boyfriend in Bellevue, calling police, while the
artistic Buddhist composer
on sixth floor lay spaced out feet swollen with water, dying slowly
of AIDS over a year—
The Chinese teacher cleaned & cooked in Apt. 23 for the
homosexual poet who pined for his gymnast
thighs & buttocks—Downstairs th' old hippie flower girl fell
drunk over the banister, smashed her jaw—
her son despite moderate fame cheated of rocknroll money,
twenty thousand people in stadiums
cheering his tattooed skinhead murderous Hare Krishna
vegetarian drum lyrics—
Mary born in the building rested on her cane, heavy-legged with
heart failure on the second landing, no more able
to vacation in Caracas & Dublin—The Russian landlady's
husband from concentration camp disappeared again—
nobody mentioned he'd died—
tenants took over her building for hot water, she couldn't add
rent & pay taxes, wore a long coat hot days
alone & thin on the street carrying groceries to her crooked
apartment silent—
One poet highschool teacher fell dead mysterious heart
dysrhythmia, konked over
in his mother's Brooklyn apartment, his first baby girl a year old,
wife stoical a few days—
their growling noisy little dog had to go, the baby cried—
Meanwhile the upstairs apartment meth head shot cocaine &
yowled up and down
East 12th Street, kicked out of Christine's Eatery till police
cornered him, 'top a hot iron steamhole ☆
near Stuyvesant Town Avenue A telephone booth calling his deaf
mother—sirens speed the way to Bellevue—
past whispering grass crack salesman jittering in circles on East
10th Street's

southwest corner where art yuppies come out of the overpriced
Japanese Sushi Bar—& they poured salt into potato soup
heart failure vats at KK's Polish restaurant
—Garbage piled up, nonbiodegradable plastic bags emptied by
diabetic sidewalk homeless
looking for returnable bottles recycled dolls radios half-eaten
hamburgers—thrown away Danish—
On 13th Street the notary public sat in his dingy storefront,
driver's lessons & tax returns prepared on old metal desks—
Sunnysides crisped in butter, fries & sugary donuts passed over
the luncheonette counter next door—
The Hispanic lady yelled at the rude African-American behind
the Post Office window
"I waited all week my welfare check you sent me notice I was
here yesterday
I want to see the supervisor bitch dont insult me refusing to
look in—"
Closed eyes of Puerto Rican wino lips cracked skin red
stretched out
on the pavement, naphtha backdoor open for the Korean family
dry cleaners at the 14th Street corner—
Con Ed workmen drilled all year to bust electric pipes 6 feet deep
in brown dirt
so cars bottlenecked wait minutes to pass the M14 bus stopped
midroad, heavy dressed senior citizens step down in
red rubble
with Reduced Fare Program cards got from grey city Aging
Department officers downtown up the second flight by
elevators don't work—
News comes on the radio, they bombed Baghdad and the Garden
of Eden again?
A million starve in Sudan, mountains of eats stacked on docks,
local gangs & U.N.'s trembling bureaucrat officers sweat
near the equator arguing over
wheat piles shoved by bulldozers—Swedish doctors ran out of
medicine— The Pakistan taxi driver

says Salman Rushdie must die, insulting the Prophet in fictions—
"No that wasn't my opinion, just a character talking like in a
poem no judgment"—
"Not till the sun rejects you do I," so give you a quarter by the
Catholic church 14th St. you stand half drunk
waving a plastic glass, flush-faced, live with your mother a
wounded look on your lips, eyes squinting,
receding lower jaw sometimes you dry out in Bellevue, most days
cadging dollars for sweet wine
by the corner where Plump Blindman shifts from foot to foot
showing his white cane, rattling coins in a white paper cup
some weeks
where girding the subway entrance construction saw-horses
painted orange guard steps underground—And across the
street the NYCE bank machine cubicle door sign reads
Not in Operation as taxis bump on potholes asphalt mounded at
the cross road when red lights change green
& I'm on my way uptown to get a CAT scan liver biopsy, visit the
cardiologist,
account for high blood pressure, kidneystones, diabetes, misty
eyes & dysesthesia—
feeling lack in feet soles, inside ankles, small of back, phallus
head, anus—
Old age sickness death again come round in the wink of an eye—
High school youth the inside skin of my thighs was silken smooth
tho nobody touched me there back then—
Across town the velvet poet takes Darvon N, Valium nightly,
sleeps all day kicking methadone
between brick walls sixth floor in a room cluttered with collages
& gold dot paper scraps covered
with words: "The whole point seems to be the idea of giving
away the giver."

AUGUST 19, 1992

GALWAY KINNELL

Born in Providence, Rhode Island, in 1927, Galway Kinnell, like the people in this remarkable poem, is the child of immigrants: an Irish mother and a Scottish father and carpenter. The Erich Maria Remarque Professor of Creative Writing as well as the Samuel F. B. Morse Professor of Fine Arts at New York University, the poet won the Pulitzer Prize for *Selected Poems* in 1983. For a few years in the late 1950s, Kinnell lived on the Lower East Side, the setting for this mosaic of sights and sounds, people and places around Avenue C, one of the oldest, most diverse, and often troubled and anachronistic neighborhoods in Manhattan.

THE AVENUE BEARING THE INITIAL OF CHRIST INTO THE NEW WORLD ☆

Was diese kleine Gass doch fur ein Reich an sich war. . .

1

pcheek pcheek pcheek pcheek pcheek
They cry. The motherbirds thieve the air
To appease them. A tug on the East River
Blasts the bass-note of its passage, lifted
From the infra-bass of the sea. A broom
Swishes over the sidewalk like feet through leaves.
Valerio's pushcart Ice Coal Kerosene
Moves clack
clack
clack
On a broken wheelrim. Ringing in its chains
The New Star Laundry horse comes down the street
Like a roofleak whucking into a pail.
At the redlight, where a horn blares,
The Golden Harvest Bakery brakes on its gears,
Squeaks, and seethes in place. A propane-
gassed bus makes its way with big, airy sighs.

Across the street a woman throws open
Her window,
She sets, terribly softly,
Two potted plants on the windowledge
                tic   tic
And bangs shut her window.

A man leaves a doorway tic toc tic toc tic toc tic hurrah toc splat
    on Avenue C tic etc and turns the corner.
Banking the same corner
A pigeon coasts 5th Street in shadows,
Looks for altitude, surmounts the rims of buildings,
And turns white.

The babybirds pipe down. It is day.

2

In sunlight on the Avenue
The Jew rocks along in a fur shtraimel,
Black rode, black knickers, black knee-stockings,
Black shoes. His beard like a sod-bottom
Hides the place where he wears no tie.
A dozen children troop after him, barbels flying,
In skullcaps. They are Reuben, Simeon, Levi, Judah, Issachar,
    Zebulun, Benjamin, Dan, Naphtali, Gad, Asher.
With the help of the Lord they will one day become
Courtiers, thugs, rulers, rabbis, asses, adders, wrestlers,
    bakers, poets, cartpushers, infantrymen.

The old man is sad-faced. He is near burial
And one son is missing. The women who bore him sons
And are past bearing, mourn for the son
And for the father, wondering if the man will go down
Into the grave of a son mourning, or if at the last
The son will put his hands on the eyes of his father.

The old man wades toward his last hour.
On 5th Street, between Avenue A and B,

In sunshine, in his private cloud, Bunko Certified Embalmer,
Cigar in his mouth, nose to the wind, leans
At the doorway of Bunko's Funeral Home & Parlour,
Glancing west toward the Ukrainians, eastward idly
Where the Jew rocks toward his last hour.

Sons, grandsons at his heel, the old man
Confronts the sun. He does not feel its rays
Through his beard, he does not understand
Fruits and vegetables live by the sun.
Like his children he is sallow-faced, he sees
A blinding signal in the sky, he smiles.

Bury me not Bunko damned Catholic I pray you in Egypt.

3

From the Station House
under demolishment on Houston
to the Power Station on 14th,
Jews, Negroes, Puerto Ricans
Walk in the spring sunlight.

The Downtown Talmud Torah
Blosztein's Cutrate Bakery
Areceba Panataria Hispano
Peanuts Dried Fruit Nuts & Canned Goods
Productos Tropicales
Appetizing Herring Candies Nuts
Nathan Kugler Chicken Store Fresh Killed Daily
Little Rose Restaurant
Rubinstein the Hatter Mens Boys Hats Caps Furnishings
J. Herrmann Dearler in All Kinds of Bottles
Natural Bloom Cigars
Blony Bubblegum
Mueren las Cucarachas Super Potente Garantizada de Matar las
        Cucarachas mas Resistentes
Wenig מעבזת
G. Schnee Stairbuilder

Everyouth la Original Loción Eterna Juventud Satisfacción
Dinero Devuelto
Happy Days Bar & Grill

Through dust-stained windows over storefronts
Curtains drawn aside, onto the Avenue
Thronged with Puerto Ricans, Negroes, Jews,
Baby carriages stuffed with groceries and babies,
The old women peer, blessed damozels
Sitting up there young forever in the cockroached rooms,
Eating fresh-killed chicken, productos, tropicales,
Appetizing herring, canned goods, nuts;
They puff out smoke from Natural Bloom cigars
And one day they puff like Blony Bubblegum.

From a rooftop a boy fishes at the sky,
Around him a flock of pigeons fountains,
Blown down and swirling up again, seeking the sky.
A red kite wriggles like a tadpole
Into the sky beyond them, crosses
The sun, lays bare its own crossed skeleton.

To fly from this place—to roll
On some bubbly blacktop in the summer,
To run under the rain of pigeon plumes, to be
Tarred, and feathered with birdshit, Icarus,

In Kugler's glass headdown dangling by yellow legs.

4

First Sun Day of the year. Tonight,
When the sun will have turned from the earth,
She will appear outside Hy's Luncheonette,
The crone who sells the *News* and the *Mirror*,
The oldest living thing on Avenue C,
Outdating much of its brick and mortar.
If you ask for the *News* she gives you the *Mirror*
And squints long at the nickel in her hand

Despising it, perhaps, for being a nickel,
And stuffs it in her apron pocket
And sucks her lips. Rain or stars, every night
She is there, squatting on the orange crate,
Issuing out only in darkness, like the cucarachas
And strange nightmares in the chambers overhead.
She can't tell one newspaper from another,
She has forgotten how Nain her dead husband looked,
She has forgotten her children's whereabouts
Or how many there were, or what the *News*
And *Mirror* tell about that we buy them with nickels.
She is sure only of the look of a nickel
And that there is a Lord in the sky overhead.
She dwells in a flesh that is of the Lord
And drifts out, therefore, only in darkness
Like the streetlamp outside the Luncheonette
Or the light in the secret chamber
In the firmament, where Yahweh himself dwells.
Like Magdalene in the Battistero of Saint John
On the carved-up continent, in the land of the sun,
She lives shadowed, under a feeble bulb
That lights her face, her crab's hands, her small bulk on the crate.

She is Pulchería mother of murderers and madmen,
She is also Alyona whose neck was a chicken leg.

Mother was it in the insufferable wind?
She sucks her lips a little further into the mousehole.
She stares among the stars, and among the streetlamps.

The mystery is hers.

5

That violent song of the twilight!
Now, in the silence, will the motherbirds
Be dead, and the infantbirds
That were in the dawn merely transparent
Unfinished things, nothing but bellies,

Will they have been shoved out
And in the course of a morning, casually,
On scrawny wings, have taken up the life?

6

In the pushcart market, on Sunday,
A crate of lemons discharges light like a battery.
Icicle-shaped carrots that through black soil
Wove away lie like flames in the sun.
Onions with their shirts ripped seek sunlight
On green skins. The sun beats
On beets dirty as boulders in cowfields,
On turnips pinched and gibbous
From budging rocks, on embery sweets,
On Idahos, Long Islands and Maines,
On horseradishes still growing weeds on the flat ends,
On cabbages lying about like sea-green brains
The skulls have been sucked from,
On tomatoes, undented plum-tomatoes, alligator-skinned
Cucumbers, that float pickled
In the wooden tubs of green skim milk—
Sky-flowers, dirt-flowers, underdirt-flowers,
Those that climbed for the sun in their lives
And those that wormed away—equally uprooted,
Maimed, lopped, shucked, and misaimed.

In the market in Damascus a goat
Came to a stall where twelve goatheads
Were lined up for sale. It sniffed them
One by one. Finally thirteen goats started
Smiling in their faintly sardonic way.

A crone buys a pickle from a crone,
It is wrapped in the *Mirror*,
At home she will open the wrapping, stained,
And stare and stare and stare at it.

And the cucumbers, and the melons,
And the leeks, and the onions, and the garlic.

7

Already the Avenue troughs the light of day.
Southwards, towards Houston and Pitt,
Where Avenue C begins, the eastern ranges
Of the wiped-out lives—punks, lushes,
Panhandlers, pushers, rumsoaks, everyone
Who took it easy when he should have been out failing at some
thing—
The pots-and-pans man pushes his cart,
Through the intersection of the light, at 3rd,
Where sunset smashes on the aluminum of it,
On the bottoms, curves, handles, metal panes,
Mirrors: of the bead-curtained cave under the falls
In Freedom, Seekonk Woods leafing the light out,
Halfway to Kingston where a road branched out suddenly,
Between Pamplonne and Les Salins two meeting paths
Over a sea the green of churchsteeple copper,
Of all places on earth inhabited by men
Why is it we find ourselves on this Avenue
Where the dusk gets worse,
And the mirrorman pushing his heaped mirrors
Into the shadows between 3rd and 2nd,
Pushes away a mess of old pots and pans?

The ancient Negro sits as usual
Outside the Happy Days Bar & Grill. He wears
Dark glasses. Every once in a while, abruptly,
He starts to sing, chanting in a hoarse, nearly breaking
Voice—

oooooooooooooo jawwwwwww
v w
u w
h w
u w
h w
din

And becomes silent
Stares into the polaroid Wilderness
Gross-Rosen, Maidanek, Flössenberg, Ravensbruck, Stutthof, Riga,
Bergen-Belsen, Mauthausen, Birkenau, Treblinka, Natzweiler,
Dachau, Buchenwald, Auschwitz—
Villages,
Pasture-bordered hamlets on the far side of the river.

8

The promise was broken too freely
To them and to their fathers, for them to care.
They survive like cedars on a cliff, roots
Hooked in any crevice they can find.
They walk Avenue C in shadows
Neither conciliating its Baalim
Nor whoring after landscapes of the senses,
Tarig bab el Amoud being in the blood
Fumigated by Puerto Rican cooking.

Among women girthed like cedar trees
Other, slender ones appear:
One yellow haired, in August,
Under shooting stars on the lake, who
Believed in promises which broke by themselves—
In a German flower garden in the Bronx
The wedding of a child and a child, one flesh
Divided in the Adirondack spring—
One who founded in the desert city of the West
The first happiness, and fled therefore—
And by a southern sea, in the pines, one loved
Until the mist rose blue in the trees
Around the spiderwebs that kept on shining,
Each day of the shortening summer.

And as rubbish burns
And the pushcarts are loaded

With fruits and vegetables and empty crates
And clank away on iron wheels over cobblestones,
And merchants infold their stores
And the carp ride motionlessly sleeplessly
In the dark tank in the fishmarket,
The figures withdraw into chambers overhead—
In the city of the mind, chambers built
Of care and necessity, where, hands lifted to the blinds,
They glimpse in mirrors backed with the blackness of the world
Awkward, cherished rooms containing the familiar selves.

9

Children set fires in ashbarrels.
Cats prowl the fires, scraps of fishes burn.

A child lay in the flames.
It was not the plan. Abraham
Stood in terror at the duplicity.
Isaac whom he loved lay in the flames.
The Lord turned away washing
His hands without soap and water
Like a common housefly.

The children laugh.
Isaac means *he laughs*.
Maybe the last instant,
The dying itself, *is* easier,
Easier anyway than the hike
From Pitt the blind gut
To the East River of Fishes,
Maybe it is as the poet said,
And the soul turns to thee
O vast and well-veiled Death
And the body gratefully nestles close to thee—

I think of Isaac reading Whitman in Chicago,
The week before he died, coming across

Such a passage and muttering, Oi!
What shit! And smiling, but not for you—I mean,

For *thee*, Sane and Sacred Death!

10

It was Gold's junkhouse, the one the clacking
Carts that little men pad after in harnesses
Picking up bedbugged mattresses, springs
The stubbornness has been loved out of,
Chairs felled by fat, lampshades lights have burned through,
Linoleum the geometry has been scuffed from,
Carriages a single woman's work has brought to wreck,
Would come to in dusk and unload before,
That the whole neighborhood came out to see
Burning in the night, flames opening out like
Eyelashes from the windows, men firing the tears in,
Searchlights smashing against the brick,
The water blooming up the walls
Like pale trees, reaching into the darkness beyond.

Nobody mourned, nobody stood around in pajamas
And a borrowed coat steaming his nose in coffee.
It was only Gold's junkhouse.
                                        But this evening
The neighborhood comes out again, everything
That may abide the fire was made to go through the fire
And it was made clean: a few twisted springs,
Charred mattresses (crawling still, naturally),
Perambulator skeletons, bicycles tied in knots—
In a great black pile at the junkhouse door,
Smelling of burnt rubber and hair. Rustwater
Hangs in icicles over the window and door,
Like frozen piss aimed at trespassers,
Combed by wind, set overnight. Carriages we were babies in,
Springs that used to resist love, that gave in
And were thrown out like whores—the black

Irreducible heap, mausoleum of what we were—
It is cold suddenly, we feel chilled,
Nobody knows for sure what is left of him.

11

The fishmarket closed, the fishes gone into flesh.
The smelts draped on each other, fat with roe,
The marble cod hacked into chunks on the counter,
Butterfishes mouths still open, still trying to eat,
Porgies with receding jaws hinged apart
In a grimace of dejection, as if like cows
They had died under the sledgehammer, perches
In grass-green armor, spotted squeteagues
In the melting ice meek-faced and croaking no more,
Mud-eating mullets buried in crushed ice,
Tilefishes with scales like bits of chickenfat.
Spanish mackerels with buttercups on the flanks,
Pot-bellied pikes, two-tone flounders
After the long contortion of pushing both eyes
To the brown side that they might look up,
Lying brown side down, like a mass laying-on of hands,
Or the oath-taking of an army.

The only things alive are the carp
That drift in the black tank in the rear,
Kept living for the usual reason, that they have not died,
And perhaps because the last meal was garbage and they might
    begin smelling
On dying, before the customer got halfway home.
They nudge each other, to be netted,
The sweet flesh to be lifted thrashing into the air,
To be slugged, and then to keep on living
While they are opened on the counter.

Fishes do not die exactly, it is more
That they go out of themselves, the visible part
Remains the same, there is little pallor,

Only the cataracted eyes which have not shut ever
Must look through the mist which crazed Homer.

These are the vegetables of the deep,
The Sheol-flowers of darkness, swimmers
Of denser darkness where the sun's rays bend for the last time
And in the sky there burns this shifty jellyfish
That degenerates and flashes and re-forms.

Fishes are nailed to the wood,
The big Jew stands like Christ, nailing them to the wood,
He scrapes the knife up the grain, the scales fly,
He unnails them, reverses them, nails them again,
Scrapes and the scales fly. He lops off the heads,
Shakes out the guts as if they did not belong in the first place,
And they are flesh for the first time in their lives.

Dear Frau ———:

Your husband, ———, died in the Camp Hospital on ———. May I express my sincere sympathy on your bereavement. ——— was admitted to the Hospital on ——— with severe symptoms of exhaustion, complaining of difficulties breathing and pains in the chest. Despite competent medication and devoted medical attention, it proved impossible, unfortunately, to keep the patient alive. The deceased voiced no final requests.

Camp Commandant, ———

On 5th Street Bunko Certified Embalmer Catholic
Leans in his doorway drawing on a Natural Bloom Cigar.
He looks up the street. Even the Puerto Ricans are Jews
And the Chinese Laundry closes on Saturday.

12

Next door, outside the pink-fronted Bodega Hispano—

(A crying: you imagine
Some baby in its crib, wailing
As if it could foresee everything.

The crying subsides: you imagine
A mother or father clasping
The damned creature in their arms.
It breaks out again,
This time in a hair-raising shriek—ah,
The alleycat, in a pleasant guise,
In the darkness outside, in the alley,
Wauling slowly in its blood.

Another, loftier shrieking
Drowns it out. It begins always
On the high note, over a clang of bells:
Hook & Ladder 11 with an explosion of mufflers
Crab-walking out of 5th Street,
Accelerating up the Avenue, siren
Sliding on the rounded distances
Returning fainter and fainter,
Like a bee looping away from where you lie in the grass.

The searchlights catch him at the topfloor window,
Trying to move, nailed in place by the shine.

The bells of Saint Brigid's
On Tompkins Square
Toll for someone who has died—
J'oïs la cloche de Serbonne,
Qui toujours à neuf heures sonne
Le Salut que l'Ange prédit . . .

Expecting the visitation
You lie on your bed,
The sounds outside
Must be outside. Here
Are only the dead spirituals
Turning back into prayers—
You rise on an elbow
To make sure they come from outside,
You hear nothing, you lay down

Your head on the pillow
Like a pick-up arm—
swing low
swing low
sweet
lowsweet—)

—Carols of the Caribbean, plinkings of guitars.

13

The garbage disposal truck
Like a huge hunched animal
That sucks in garbage in the place
Where other animals evacuate it
Whines, as the cylinder in the rear
Threshes up the trash and garbage,
Where two men in rubber suits
(It must be raining outside)
Heap it in. The groaning motor
Rises in a whine as it grinds in
The garbage, and between-times
Groans. It whines and groans again.
All about it as it moves down
5th Street is the clatter of trashcans,
The crashes of them as the sanitary engineers
Bounce them on the sidewalk.

If it is raining outside
You can only tell by looking
In puddles, under the lifted streetlamps.
It would be the spring rain.

14

Behind the Power Station on 14th, the held breath
Of light, as God is a held breath, withheld,
Spreads the East River, into which fishes leak:
The brown sink or dissolve,
The white float out in shoals and armadas,

Even the gulls pass them up, pale
Bloated socks of riverwater and rotted seed,
That swirl on the tide, punched back
To the Hell Gate narrows, and on the ebb
Steam seaward, seeding the sea.

On the Avenue, through air tinted crimson
By neon over the bars, the rain is falling.
You stood once on Houston, among panhandlers and winos
Who weave the eastern ranges, learning to be free,
To not care, to be knocked flat and to get up clear-headed
Spitting the curses out. "Now be nice,"
The proprietor threatens; "Be nice," he cajoles.
"Fuck you," the bum shouts as he is hoisted again,
"God fuck your mother." (In the empty doorway,
Hunched on the empty crate, the crone gives no sign.)

That night a wildcat cab whined crosstown on 7th.
You knew even the traffic lights were made by God,
The red splashes growing dimmer the farther away
You looked, and way up at 14th, a few green stars;
And without sequence, and nearly all at once,
The red lights blinked into green,
And just before there was one complete Avenue of green,
The little green stars in the distance blinked.

It is night, and raining. You look down
Towards Houston in the rain, the living streets,
Where instants of transcendence
Drift in oceans of loathing and fear, like lanternfishes,
Or phosphorus flashing in the sea, or the feverish light
Skin is said to give off when the swimmer drowns at night.

From the blind gut Pitt to the East River of Fishes
The Avenue cobbles a swath through the discolored air,
A roadway of refuse from the teeming shores and ghettos
And the Caribbean Paradise, into the new ghetto and the
    new paradise,

This God-forsaken Avenue bearing the initial of Christ
Through the haste and carelessness of the ages,
The sea standing in heaps, which keeps on collapsing,
Where the drowned suffer a C-change,
And remain the common poor.

Since Providence, for the realization of some unknown purpose,
has seen
fit to leave this dangerous people on the face of the earth, and did not
destroy it. . .

Listen! the swish of the blood,
The sirens down the bloodpaths of the night,
Bone tapping on the bone, nerve-nets
Singing under the breath of sleep—

We scattered over the lonely seaways,
Over the lonely deserts did we run,
In dark lanes and alleys we did hide ourselves. . .

The heart beats without windows in its night,
The lungs put out the light of the world as they
Heave and collapse, the brain turns and rattles
In its own black axlegrease—

In the nighttime
Of the blood they are laughing and saying,
Our little lane, what a kingdom it was!

oi weih, oi weih

W. S. MERWIN

Born in New York City in 1927 and educated at Princeton, W. S. Merwin—a prolific translator, and winner of the 1971 Pulitzer Prize for *The Carrier of Ladders*—here captures the often frenetic pace of life in New York even in the relative calm of his downtown apartment on the street named for the Sir Walter Scott novel.

227 WAVERLY PLACE

When I have left I imagine they will
repair the window onto the fire escape
that looks north up the avenue clear
to Columbus Circle long I have known
the lights of that valley at every hour
through that unwashed pane and have watched with no
conclusion its river flowing toward me
straight from the featureless distance coming
closer darkening swelling growing distinct
speeding up as it passed below me toward
the tunnel all that time through all that time
taking itself through its sound which became
part of my own before long the unrolling
rumble the iron solos and the sirens
all subsiding in the small hours to voices
echoing from the sidewalks a rustling
in the rushes along the banks and the loose
glass vibrated like a remembering bee
as the north wind slipped under the winter sill
at the small table by the window until
my right arm ached and stiffened and I pushed
the chair back against the bed and got up
and went out into the other room that was
filled with the east sky and the day replayed
from the windows and roofs of the Village
the room where friends came and we sat talking
and where we ate and lived together while
the blue paint flurried down from the ceiling
and we listened late with lights out to music
hearing the intercom from the hospital
across the avenue through the Mozart
Dr Kaplan wanted on the tenth floor
while reflected lights flowed backward on the walls

LEO CONNELLAN

Although born in Maine, Leo Connellan (1928–2001) lived and worked in the New York area most of his life. His collection *Another Poet in New York* appeared in 1975, and his acclaimed *Crossing America*, in 1976. Like Whitman, he is a poet of the common man, writing in large, energetic, lyric narratives. Awarded the Shelley Memorial Award from the Poetry Society of America, he writes in this poem of the subways, the most common and unifying aspect of New York City life.

HELPLESS, WE GO INTO THIS GROUND, HELPLESS

Across the bridges and under the earth,
subway trains lumber and clank.

Helpless, we go into this ground, helpless
each day packed against each other so that
we always start off irritable
at being tossed about thrown against strangers.

People who never get to know each other
but ride the train every day
without ever exchanging dreams.

The subway screeches
ear piercingly through tunnels
and rattles into the station
like an undone Accordion.

The whole subway train shudders
as it stops. The train doors
open like gasping mouths.

And we get on staggering
shadows of giants forced
to become Subway Passengers

pushing, shoving, we are made
into something else than human
in this insult cramming against each
other in our own foul exhale.
In the subway water
always falling off
station walls as though
the held-back rivers
will break through over us.

Here we are flushed out
of our anonymity.

To whom do we look good?
Villon, did you do that!

We get on the same train
every morning for years
and usually the same car.

Through the earth and on the bridges
subway trains groan. . . .

We get off the train
and go a hundred
different directions
to our daily fates.

We get on the same train
every morning, surviving
the subway each day as
prisoners do, disassociating
from what was . . . and is . . .
and will be . . .

But, Subways I
defeated you.

Overwhelming Subways I
hung on.

I climbed, climbed, climbed
your endless straight-up
stairs back out to sunshine.

Helpless, we go into this ground, helpless
onto dank dark brutally cold
impartial platform to wait
for trains that throw our insides around
until panic seizes and you gasp
in terror that you might suffocate,
with the scribblings of restrained
psychotics on everything, the walls, posts,
train windows, all over the trains in
insulting thumb noses at us vulgar orange, purple
which the rest of unstable us who somehow
cope must add to what we endure. We
let them draw on us rather than slaughter us.

But there is no such help for us,
if we suddenly blow it's Bellevue
or one of those unfortunate assassinations
by the good-guy off-duty cop who just happened
to be on his way home with a well-loaded gun ready
for us because we aren't ghetto kids
in the amnesty of invisible veiled threat to
go wild in our condition.

We go helpless down into this ground, helpless,
can you imagine getting stalled underground,
the subway train coming to a full stop down
deep in the earth in ninety-nine-degree heat,
the train stops and the sickening
scent of burning wood . . .

Off the bridges and into the earth
gouged out for it the subway train stalls.

Helpless, down in the ground, we are under
the earth now in company of people we don't
know . . . helpless into this ground, helpless.

We have resigned ourselves wrecks to them
these shattering, jarring subway trains that
we must take or not go anywhere.

MAYA ANGELOU

Born in St. Louis in 1928, Maya Angelou writes in many different media of life's most noble, enduring spirit of survival. Although telling of the black female's experience in America, her work—in her own words—"talk[s] about the human condition," as with something as common—and dreaded—as the morning commute.

AWAKING IN NEW YORK

Curtains forcing their will
against the wind,
children asleep,
exchanging dreams with
seraphim. The city
drags itself awake on
subway straps; and
I, an alarm, awake as a
rumor of war,
lay stretching into dawn,
unasked and unheeded.

IRVING FELDMAN

Born in 1928 in the Coney Island section of Brooklyn from Jewish Russian parents who emigrated to New York early in the twentieth century, Irving Feldman went first to the City College of New York, then Columbia University for graduate work. He is now the SUNY Distinguished Professor of English. His first collection, *The Pripet Marshes*, is comprised of powerful elegies to Holocaust victims and asks unsettling, unanswerable questions to God, as in his poem "To the Six Million," while his 1976 collection about New York, *Leaping Clear*, is lively and streetwise. This poem's setting is the poet's old neighborhood, though it also shows his love for handball, a game that taught him to "keep my sentences on my toes, balanced . . . ready to move . . . and to keep . . . unpredictable."

THE HANDBALL PLAYERS AT BRIGHTON BEACH ☆

TO DAVID RITZ

And then the blue world daring onward
discovers them, the indigenes, aging,
oiled, and bronzing sons of immigrants,
the handball players of the new world
on Brooklyn's bright eroding shore
who yawp, who quarrel, who shove,
who shout themselves hoarse, don't
get out of the way, grab for odds,
hustle a handicap, all crust,
all bluster, all con and gusto all
on show, tumultuous, blaring,
grunting as they lunge. True,
their manners lack grandeur, and
yes, elsewhere under the sun legs
are less bowed, bellies are less
potted, pates less bald or blanched,
backs less burned, less hairy.
So?

So what! the sun does not snub,
does not overlook them, shines,

and the fair day flares,
the blue universe booms and blooms,
the sea-space, the summer high, focuses
its great unclouded scope in ecstatic
perspection—and you see it, too,
at the edge of the crowd, edge of the sea,
between multitudes and immensity:
from gray cement ball courts under
the borough's sycamores' golden boughs,
against the odds in pure speculation
Brighton's handball heroes leap up half
a step toward heaven in burgundy, blue,
or buttercup bathing trunks, in black
sneakers still stylish after forty years,
in pigskin gloves buckled at the wrist,
to keep the ball alive, the sun up,
the eye open, the air ardent,
festive, clear, crowded with delight.

L. E. SISSMAN

Born Louis Edward Sissman (1929–1976) in Detroit, the poet wrote nearly all his poems after being diagnosed with Hodgkin's disease. His first collection, appropriately titled *Dying: An Introduction*, appeared in 1968. During the 1950s he spent "a short, unhappy stint in New York" but believed "we were not, either by temperament or experience, meant to live in paradise." His posthumously published collected poems, *Hello, Darkness* (1978) won the National Book Critics Circle Award.

THE VILLAGE: THE SEASONS

(TO SAUL TOUSTER)

I. JANUARY 22, 1932

Could a four-year-old look out of a square sedan
(A Studebaker Six in currency green
With wooden artillery wheels) and see a scene
Of snow, light lavender, landing on deepening blue
Buildings built out of red-violet bricks, and black
Passersby passing by over the widening white
Streets darkening blue, under a thickening white
Sky suddenly undergoing sheer twilight,
And the yellow but whitening streetlights coming on,
And remember it now, though the likelihood is gone
That it ever happened at all, and the Village is gone
That it ever could happen in? Memory, guttering out,
Apparently, finally flares up and banishes doubt.

II. MAY 29, 1941

Tring. Bells
On grocers' boys' bicycles ring,
Followed, on cue,
By the jaunty one-note of prayers at two
Near churches; taxi horns, a-hunt,
Come in for treble; next, the tickety bass
Of chain-driven Diamond T's, gone elephantine
And stove-enameled conifer green
Down Greenwich Avenue.
Out of the Earle ☆
I issue at half-past thirteen,
Struck, like a floral clock,
By seasonal
Manifestations: unreasonable
N.Y.U. girls out in their bobby socks
And rayon blouses; meek boys with their books

Who have already moulted mackinaws;
Desarrolimiento of
New chrome-green leaves; a rose,
Got, blooming, out of bed; and Mrs. Roos-
Evelt and Sarah Delano
Descending the front stoop of a Jamesian
House facing south against the Square, the sun—
Who, curveting, his half-course not yet run,
Infects the earth with crescence;
And the presence
Of process, seen in un-top-hatted,
Un-frock-coated burghers and their sons
And daughters, taking over
All title, right, and interest soever
In this, now their
Property, Washington Square.

III. DECEMBER 29, 1949

The Hotel Storia ascends
Above me and my new wife; ends
Eight stories of decline, despair,
Iron beds and hand-washed underwear
Above us and our leatherette
Chattels, still grounded on the wet
Grey tessellated lobby floor.
Soon, through a dingy, numbered door,
We'll enter into our new home,
Provincials in Imperial Rome
To seek their fortune, or, at least,
To find a job. The wedding feast,
Digested and metabolized,
Diminishes in idealized
Group photographs, and hard today
Shunts us together and at bay.
Outside the soot-webbed window, sleet
Scourges the vista of Eighth Street;
Inside, the radiators clack

And talk and tell us to go back
Where we came from. A lone pecan
Falls from our lunch, a sticky bun,
And bounces on the trampoline
Of the torn bedspread. In the mean
Distance of winter, a man sighs,
A bedstead creaks, a woman cries.

IV. JULY 14, 1951

A summer lull arrives in the West Village,
Transmuting houses into silent salvage
Of the last century, streets into wreckage
Uncalled-for by do-gooders who police
The moderniqueness of our ways, patrol
The sanitation of our urban soul.
What I mean is, devoid of people, all
Our dwellings freeze and rust in desuetude,
Fur over with untenancy, glaze grey
With summer's dust and incivility,
With lack of language and engagement, while
Their occupants sport, mutate, and transform
Themselves, play at dissembling the god Norm
From forward bases at Fire Island. But—
Exceptions proving rules, dissolving doubt—
Young Gordon Walker, fledgling editor,
My daylong colleague in the corridors
Of Power & Leicht, the trade-book publishers,
Is at home to the residue in his
Acute apartment in an angle of
Abingdon Square. And they're all there, the rear-
Guard of the garrison of Fort New York:
The skeleton defense of skinny girls
Who tap the typewriters of summertime;
The pale male workers who know no time off
Because too recently employed; the old
Manhattan hands, in patched and gin-stained tweeds;
The writers (Walker's one), who see in their

City as desert an oasis of
Silence and time to execute their plots
Against the state of things, but fall a prey
To day succeeding day alone, and call
A party to restore themselves to all
The inside jokes of winter, in whose caul
People click, kiss like billiard balls, and fall,
Insensible, into odd pockets. Dense
As gander-feather winter snow, intense
As inextinguishable summer sun
At five o'clock (which it now is), the noise
Of Walker's congeries of girls and boys
Foregathered in their gabbling gratitude
Strikes down the stairwell from the altitude
Of his wide-open walk-up, beckoning
Me, solo, wife gone north, to sickening
Top-story heat and talk jackhammering
Upon the anvils of all ears. "Christ, Lou, you're here,"
Whoops Walker, topping up a jelly jar
("Crabapple," says the label, still stuck on)
With gin and tonic, a blue liquid smoke
That seeks its level in my unexplored
Interior, and sends back a sonar ping
To echo in my head. Two more blue gins.
The sweat that mists my glasses interdicts
My sizing up my interlocutor,
Who is, I think, the girl who lives next door,
A long-necked, fiddleheaded, celliform
Girl cellist propped on an improbably
Slim leg. Gin pings are now continuous.
The room swings in its gimbals. In the bath
Is silence, blessed, relative, untorn
By the cool drizzle of the bathtub tap,
A clear and present invitation. Like
A climber conquering K.28,
I clamber over the white porcelain
Rock face, through whitish veils of rubberized
Shower curtain, and at length, full-dressed, recline

In the encaustic crater, where a fine
Thread of cold water irrigates my feet,
To sleep, perchance to dream of winter in
The Village, fat with its full complement
Of refugees returned to their own turf—
Unspringy as it is—in a strong surf
Of retrogressing lemmings, faces fixed
On the unlovely birthplace of their mixed
Emotions, marriages, media, and met-
Aphors. Lord God of hosts, be with them yet.

JOHN HOLLANDER

Born in this city in 1929, John Hollander attended Columbia University, and his first collection of poems, *A Crackling of Thorns* (1958), won the Yale Series of Younger Poets. Since then he has published many volumes of poetry and criticism, translated Yiddish poets (several in this collection), and edited numerous books, including *The Oxford Anthology of English Literature* (1973) and the Library of America's two-volume *Nineteenth-Century American Poetry*. He is the former chancellor of the Academy of American Poets and currently the Sterling Professor of English at Yale University. The selection here is an excerpt narrating the poet's return home after a long absence.

from NEW YORK

In smaller cities, nothing much can be
Private, and all one finds is secrecy.
A crowd is not a mob, nor makes one die
A death of self inside it, with a sigh.
Only in anonymity and crowds
Can urban wanderers unwind their shrouds,
Unchained by nature in their final quest
Where largest, deepest cities are the best.
Green foliage and a backwoods road or two

Hide Appalachian poverty from view:
In the Metropolis, the hopeless poor
Decently plain, are by no means obscure.
High towers with dingy walkups at their backs
Are found disposed on both sides of the tracks;
And even urban rustics, those who live
Not in the city, but in primitive
Villages scattered in among its blight
Are led out, no great distance, into light.

Now as for homecomings—*mirabile factu!*— ☆
New York's the only city to come back to;
Reaching Manhattan, high over the tossed
Water at Spuyten Duyvil which I crossed
Once in a kayak when I was nineteen;
Turbulent thoughts impressed upon its screen
Of surface, glittering with overlaid
Transparencies of memory, filtering shade
And repetitions animate a view
That I am more than just returning to.

Thus I live here again. My brother Mike
Has moved next door; and in a way, I'm like
Some old agrarian conservative:
The half-mile distance between where I live
And where I did when I was ten, feels never
Once like a shackle I should want to sever
Now, but like an extension of my own,
A tap-root run through asphalt, pipe and stone—
Plenty of continuity for an
Otherwise rootless cosmopolitan.
But memory has its hearsay too: my great-
Grandfather came in 1848,
Fleeing from fuzz and new defenestrations
In Prague, to wander here among the nations,
Bring up his dozen children, make cigars,
And live for me in anecdote, like stars,
Those tiny innuendoes, piercing night,

From which a child infers a plain of light.
My grandfather and I walked in the park
Around the frozen lake, in growing dark;
In 1888, he said, the year
Of the great blizzard, we crossed without fear.
I listened as the bundled skaters skimmed
The gray ice on the safe part that was rimmed
With benches, cut across the reflex of
A starry park lamp on the bridge above.
Who was remembering, and who had merely
Heard of the past? For each it gleamed as clearly.

Now nested memories open up again:
My older daughter, at the age of ten.
Hears of the old Met Opera House from me,
Some half-formed fiction she will never see,
As at the same age, I was quite at home
With a remembrance called the Hippodrome—
Phased, similar emblems of the city's quest,
Moving beyond historic palimpsest,
For instant self-fulfillment. One night late,
Six years ago in August, through the great
Newly revealed vaults in a ruined, weird
Penn Station, winds sang and faint stars appeared
Above columnar bases; broken gloom
Swallowed the crystal-palace waiting room
In gaping Piranesian pits—all seemed
Somehow created for this, and redeemed
By that great wind-swept moment. Then I passed
Out onto the hot pavements, to be gassed
By buses, bumped by derelicts, away
From dreams of change to contact with decay.—
But so much more decay because we've got
Riches to moulder, and so much to rot.

Tim lives downtown, and makes a long commute
(To Queens, to work) as long as is the route
Deep into Westchester; he gets to go

Home to a lovely place on Bank Street, though;
Not the benighted suburb, Middle Ridge
Where affluence is underprivilege.
Jim lives in Athens; there's no need to roam;
Our ruins-and-fig republic here at home
Will mellow us, as things go to the bad,
And lend us patience that we've never had.
Then, as our science fails and our arts rot,
Instead of huddling in some minor spot
On the torn outskirts of a little town
(Where more than here, old buildings are torn down,
And metal siding fronts for honest wood)
We'll see the ending out from where we should:
With nothing working, services gone slack,
Mushrooms on the abandoned subway track,
Telephones silent between twelve and two,
Thousands of cats reclaim an empty zoo.

West in Manhattan where the sun has set
The elevator rises calmly yet
In my dark tower, against the tower-dimmed sky,
Whose wide, old windows yield my narrower eye
Images no revision can defeat:
Newspapers blown along the empty street
At three A.M. (somewhere in between 'odd,'
A guru told me long ago, and 'God');
Calm steam rising from manholes in the dark;
Clean asphalt of an avenue; the spark
Of gold in every mica window high
On westward faces of the peaks; the sky
Near dawn, framed in the zig-zag canyon rim
Of cross-streets; bits of distant bridge, the dim
Lustrous ropes of pale lights dipping low;
Rivers unseen beneath, sable and slow.

Gardens? Lead me not home to them: a plain
Of rooftops, gleaming after April rain
In later sunlight, shines with Ceres' gold

Sprung up, not ripped, from earth; gained as of old.
Our losses are of gardens. We create
A dense, sad city for our final state.

RICHARD HOWARD

Richard Howard was born in Cleveland, Ohio, in 1929 and received a B.A. from Columbia University. The 1970 winner of the Pulitzer Prize for *Untitled Subjects* and author of eleven books of poetry, he has translated the great French poets, winning an American Book Award for his translation of Baudelaire. Currently poetry editor for the *Paris Review* and teaching at Columbia University, he writes here of a passing tradition in New York, the Italian bowlinglike game of boccie on a street in Greenwich Village where he has lived for many years.

THE OLD MEN PLAYING BOCCIE ON LEROY STREET ☆

A sense of Fall without the trees
That make their rot so decorous,
A lot of ashes in the air
Tasting oddly of surrender—
This is the place, appropriate
For such unsightly men as these,
Dispossessed and almost holy,
Almost depraved, playing games
Against each other for the long
Chances of a little gain
This afternoon upon the clay.

The river hauls its burdens down,
Lapping greedily like doubt
Between the banks of ashes. Here
They are playing, the mad ruined tribe:
Ignorant, not innocent, and yet

So terribly sure of who they are.
For them it must be difficult
Believing in death, at least before
The sunset, when the opportune light
Hangs like a victim so long in the sky
That all reminders of the dark are dumb.

The old men play until I think
Their laughter is the bravest sport
I ever listened to in nature;
For if their triumph gathers out
Of what is merely argument
To us, the very ground on which
They play is merely graves to them.
Ask of their broken faces, How
Do you savor life? Do you enjoy?
And as one mouth each scar will answer,
Crying, 'I appreciate pain.'

Listen to their voices, words
Echoing over the gritty court:
Something has been given up
But they are playing. While I stand
And watch their game, the western clouds
Accumulate and the world turns back
Into its empty sky, judging
Not as the judge judges, but as
The failing light decides, falling
At last with the exhausted sun
In shadows round a helpless thing.

ADRIENNE RICH

Born in 1929 in Baltimore, Adrienne Rich graduated Radcliffe in 1951, winning the Yale Series of Younger Poets for *A Change of World* that same year. Active against racism and anti-Semitism among other social issues, she gave her strongest alliance to the women's movement, as demonstrated in her powerful collection *Daughter-in-Law* (1963). She moved to New York City soon after. Fiercely principled and independent, she won the 1974 National Book Award for *Diving Into the Wreck* but refused the 1997 National Medal for the Arts award "while the people at large are so dishonored."

from TWENTY-ONE LOVE POEMS

I

Wherever in this city, screens flicker

with pornography, with science-fiction vampires,
victimized hirelings bending to the lash,
we also have to walk . . . if simply as we walk
through the rainsoaked garbage, the tabloid cruelties
of our own neighborhoods.
We need to grasp our lives inseparable
from those rancid dreams, that blurt of metal, those disgraces,
and the red begonia perilously flashing
from a tenement sill six stories high,
or the long-legged young girls playing ball
in the junior highschool playground.
No one has imagined us. We want to live like trees,
sycamores blazing through the sulfuric air,
dappled with scars, still exuberantly budding,
our animal passion rooted in the city.

GREGORY CORSO

Part of the Beat Generation, Gregory Corso (1930–2001) was born in a tenement on Bleecker Street across from the famous San Remo restaurant in New York. He spent time in an orphanage,

Bellevue, and jail before meeting Allen Ginsberg in a lesbian bar on W. Fourth Street, and he, like Ginsberg, often wrote about the dark visions of the city, "right in the heart of the horror," he said after moving to E. Fifth Street and Avenue C.

ON THE DEATH OF THE LUCKY GENT

Of the homerless young after dark with no purpose of fantasy
waiting the stinkstreets pimpled gangtide
the insecure the boypack (this way they're more scarey than
the humanslayer hanging humans like deer in a shed)
O incredible untellable gathering!
The Harlem thunder! The Bronx wonder!
They come from tenements like tenements
and more and more to the street and they become the street!
O Boywar! O rumble passion pure!
I hear in the distance the song the crazydance of gangwar!
I see the might of their stomage on the earth!
Of deathmuch sequence the tuneless moon the apes of kill
and all is locked searchry—here is no rank dominion
no fun
Of deathmakery & socialscrew the police roundup
Switchblade reward! 20 to life! Death!
Here no kingdom cared no infinity but infinite pain
the shame
The Lucky Gent's seraphim stab
Mad shot at Godhead—nothing but heavenair
There never was a St. Nicholas Ave. beyond ☆
nor a round world
The earth should have been flat!
The dot on the horizon never an empire
Columbus a liar!
A coin dropped behind a boy's coffin
—the solution of sunset

GARY SNYDER

Born in San Francisco in 1930, Gary Snyder received bachelor degrees in literature as well as anthropology. He's been a logger, merchant marine, fire lookout, and the 1975 Pulitzer Prize winner for *Turtle Island*. Profoundly influenced by Zen, he believes the poet has two faces: one of people and language, the other of nature and non-verbal. As in this poem, he often writes of man's relationship to nature, even in New York City.

WALKING THE NEW YORK BEDROCK ALIVE IN THE SEA OF INFORMATION

Maple, oak, poplar, gingko
New leaves, "new green" on a rock ledge
Of steep little uplift, tucked among trees
Hot sun dapple—
          wake up.

Roll over and slide down the rockface
Walk away in the woods toward
A squirrel, toward
Rare people! Seen from a safe distance.
A murmur of traffic approaching,
Siren howls echoing
Through the gridlock of structures,
Vibrating with helicopters,
   the bass tone
                    of a high jet.

        Leap over the park stone wall
        Dressed fast and light,
        Slip into the migrating flow.

New York like a sea anemone
Wide and waving in the Sea of Economy,
Cadres of educated youth   in chic costume
Step out to the nightlife, good food, after work—

In the chambers of prana-subtle powder-pumping
Heartbeat buildings   fired
Deep at the bottom, under the basement,
Fired by old merchant marine
Ex-fire-tenders   gone now from sea

to the ships stood on end on the land:
ex-seamen stand watch at the stationary boilers,
give way to computers,
That monitor heat and the power
webs underground;   in the air;
In the Sea   of Information.

Brisk flesh, keen-eyed, streams of people
Curve round the sweep of street corners
cardboard chunks tossed up in truckbed.
Delicate jiggle, rouge on the nipple,
kohl under the eye.

Time and Life buildings—sixty thousand people—
Wind ripples the banners
stiff shudder shakes limbs on the
planted trees growing new green,

Glass, aluminum, aggregate gravel,
Iron. Stainless steel.
Hollow honeycomb brain-buildings owned by

Columbia University, the landlord of
Anemone
colony
Alive, in the Sea of Information

"Claus the Wild man"
Lived mostly with Indians,
Was there as a witness when the old lady
"Karacapacomont"
Sold the last bit of Washington Heights, 1701

Down deep grates hear the watercourse,
Rivers that never give up
Trill under the roadbed, over the bedrock.
A bird angles way off a brownstone
Couloir that looks like a route.

Echo the hollowing darkness.
Crisscrossing light threads
Gleam squeals up the side streets,
One growl shadow
in an egg of bright lights,
Lick of black on the tongue.
Echoes of sirens come down the walled canyons
Foot lifts to the curb and the lights change—

And look up at the gods.
Equitable god, Celanese god, noble line,
Old Union Carbide god,
Each catching shares of the squared blocked shadow
Each swinging in sundial arc of the day
more than the sum of its parts.
The Guggenheims, the Rockefellers, and the Fricks,
Assembling the art of the world, the plate glass
Window lets light in on "the water lilies"
Like fish or planets, people,
Move, pause, move through the rooms,
White birch leaves shiver in breezes
While guards watch the world,
Helicopters making their long humming trips
Trading pollen and nectar
In the air
of the
Sea of Economy,
Drop under the streetworld
Steel squeal of stopping and starting
Wind blows through black tunnels
spiderwebs, fungus, lichen.

Gingko trees of Gondwanaland. Pictographs,
Petroglyphs, cover the subways—
Empty eye sockets of buildings just built
Soulless, they still wait the ceremony
    that will make them too,
        new, Big
        city Gods,
Provided with conduit, cable and plumbing,
They will light up, breathe cool air,
Breathe the minds of the workers who work there—
The cloud of their knowing
As they soar in the sky, in the air,
Of the Sea
Of Information,

  Cut across alleys and duck beneath trucks.
  "Under Destruction"—trash chair at the curb—
  Stop to gaze on the large roman letters
  Of writing on papers that tell of Economy,

Skilsaw whine slips through the windows
Empty room—no walls—such clear air in the cellar
Dry brick, cooked clay, rusty house bodies
Carbide blade Skilsaw cuts bricks. Squalls
From the steps leading down to the subway.
Blue-chested runner, a female, on car streets,
Red lights block traffic but she likes the
Beam of a streetlight in the whine of the Skilsaw,
  She runs right through.
  A cross street leads toward a river
  North goes to the woods
  South takes you fishing
  Peregrines nest at the thirty-fifth floor

Street people rolling their carts
  of whole households
Or asleep wrapped in light blue blanket
    spring evening, at dusk, in a doorway,

Eyeballing arêtes and buttresses rising above them,
con domus, dominiom,
domus,
codominate, condominium
Towers, up there the
Clean crisp white dress white skin
women and men
Who occupy sunnier niches,
Higher up on the layered stratigraphy cliffs, get
More photosynthesis, flow by more ostracods,
get more sushi,
Gather more flesh, have delightful
Cascading laughs,

—Peregrine sails past the window
Off the edge of the word-chain
Harvesting concepts, theologies,
Snapping up bites of the bits bred by
Banking
ideas and wild speculations
On new information—
and stoops in a blur on a pigeon,

As the street bottom-feeders with shopping carts
Slowly check out the air for the fall of excess,
Of too much, flecks of extra,
From the higher-up folks in the sky

As the fine dusk gleam
Lights a whole glass side of
Forty some stories

Soft liquid silver,
Beautiful buildings we float in, we feed in,

Foam, steel, gray

Alive in the Sea of Information.

DEREK WALCOTT

Born 1930 on Saint Lucia, a volcanic island that was once a British colony, Derek Walcott grew up in a mixture of two worlds, African and European. Both of his grandmothers were descendants of slaves. As a young man he studied theater in New York then founded the Trinadad Theatre Workshop in 1959. Winner of the 1992 Noble Prize for Literature, he teaches at Boston University.

A VILLAGE LIFE

[FOR JOHN ROBERTSON]

I

Through the wide, grey loft window,
I watched that winter morning my first snow
crusting the sill, puzzle the black,
nuzzling tom. Behind my back
a rime of crud glazed my cracked coffee cup,
a snowfall of torn poems piling up,
heaped by a rhyming spade.
Starved, on the prowl,
I was a frightened cat in that grey city.
I floated, a cat's shadow, through the black wool
sweaters, leotards, and parkas of the fire-haired,
snow-shouldered Greenwich Village *mädchen*,
homesick, my desire
crawled across snow
like smoke, for its lost fire.

All that winter I haunted
your house on Hudson Street, a tiring friend,
demanding to be taken in, drunk, and fed.
I thought winter would never end.

I cannot imagine you dead.
But that stare, frozen,
a frosted pane in sunlight,

gives nothing back by letting nothing in,
your kindness or my pity.
No self-reflection lies
within those silent, ice-blue irises,
whose image is some snow-locked mountain lake
in numb Montana.

And since that winter I have learnt to gaze
on life indifferently as through a pane of glass.

II

Your image rattled on the subway glass
is my own death mask in an overcoat;
under New York, the subterranean freight
of human souls, locked in an iron cell,
station to station cowed with swaying calm,
thunders to its end, each in its private hell,
each plumped, prime bulk still swinging by its arm
upon a hook. You're two years dead. And yet
I watch that silence spreading through our souls:
that horn-rimmed midget who consoles
his own deformity with Sartre on Genet.
Terror still eats the nerves, the Word
is gibberish, the plot Absurd.
The turnstile slots, like addicts, still consume
obols and aspirin, Charon in his grilled cell
grows vague about our crimes, our destination.
Not all are silent, or endure
the enormity of silence; at one station,
somewhere off 33rd and Lexington,
a fur-wrapped matron screamed above the roar
of rattling iron. Nobody took her on,
we looked away. Such scenes
rattle our trust in nerves tuned like machines.
All drives as you remember it, the pace
of walking, running the rat race,
locked in a system, ridden by its rail,
within a life where no one dares to fail.

I watch your smile breaking across my skull,
the hollows of your face below my face
sliding across it like a pane of glass.
Nothing endures. Even in his cities
man's life is grass.
Times Square. We sigh and let off steam,
who should screech with the braking wheels, scream
like our subway-Cassandra, heaven-sent
to howl for Troy, emerge
blind from the blast of daylight, whirled
apart like papers from a vent.

III

Going away, through Queens we pass
a cemetery of miniature skyscrapers. The verge
blazes its rust, its taxi-yellow leaves. It's fall.
I stare through glass,
my own reflection there, at
empty avenues, lawns, spires, quiet
stones, where the curb's rim
wheels westward, westward, where thy bones . . .
Montana, Minnesota, your real
America, lost in tall grass, serene idyll.

PEGGY L. SHRIVER

Born in Muscatine, Iowa, in 1931, Peggy Leu Shriver, in her own words, is "concerned with preserving the human race in the nuclear age . . . [and] work[ing] for the church to serve God and neighbor." Although often portrayed as hard and heartless, New York also possess the spirit demonstrated in this tender, compassionate poem.

THE SPIRIT OF 34TH STREET

Doors opened with a silent scream,
    like photographs of anguish.

The subway paused, shed cargo
and raged on.

She lurched aboard,
sagged into a vacant seat,
frail weight of her gray years
hunched with cold.

Numb fingers plucked at rags,
drawn close against raw misery.
Knuckles, cracked and swollen white,
clutched into a plea for warmth.

He, dark and lithe,
swung down the aisle,
taut jeans dancing
rhythmically.

With Latin grace
he, sidling past
her patient form,
in one smooth gesture

disappeared through subway doors,
leaving in her lap,
like folded dove wings,
his black leather gloves.

JOHN UPDIKE

A contributor to *The New Yorker*'s "Talk of the Town" since the 1950s, John Updike—one of the poets in this anthology who has stayed in the Algonquin Hotel—was born in a small Pennsylvania town in 1932. He has written some of the most successful contemporary prose, known for its sense of place and life presented here.

SUMMER: WEST SIDE

When on the coral-red steps of old brownstones
Puerto Rican boys, their white shirts luminous,
gather, and their laughter
conveys menace as far as Central Park West,

When the cheesecake shops on Broadway
keep open long into the dark,
and the Chinaman down in his hole of seven steps
leaves the door of his laundry ajar,
releasing a blue smell of starch,

When the curbside lines of parked cars
appear embedded in the tar,
and the swish of the cars on the Drive
seems urgently loud—

Then even the lapping of wavelets
on the boards of a barge on the Hudson
is audible,
and Downtown's foggy glow
fills your window right up to the top.

And you walk in the mornings with your cool suit
sheathing the fresh tingle of your shower,
and the gratings idly steam,
and the damp path of the street-sweeper evaporates,

And—an oddly joyful sight—
the dentists' and chiropractors' white signs low
in the windows of the great ochre buildings on Eighty-sixth
    Street
seem slightly darkened
by one more night's deposit of vigil.

YEVGENY YEVTUSHENKO

Born in 1933 in a Siberia town along the Transiberian railway, Yevgeny Yevtushenko studied geology, then literature in Moscow. Greatly influenced by both Walt Whitman and Vladimir Mayakovsky, the poet came to New York in the mid-1960s and became fascinated particularly by the Empire State Building and the Beatniks of Greenwich Village.

NEW YORK ELEGY

TO S. MITMAN

At night, in New York's Central Park,
chilled to the bone and belonging to no one,
I talked quietly to America:
both of us were weary of speech,
I talked with my footsteps—
unlike words, they do not lie—
and I was answered with circles
dead leaves uttered, falling onto a pond.

Snow was falling, sliding embarrassed
past bars where noisiness never ceases,
settling tinted on the swollen neon veins
on the city's sleepless brow,
on the incessant smile of a candidate
who was trying, not without difficulty, to get in
somewhere, I don't remember just where,
and to the snow it didn't matter where.

But in the Park it felt undisturbed:
the snowflakes descended cautiously
onto the softly sinking leaves,
soggy multicolored floats;
onto a pink and tremulous balloon
childishly fastened with chewing gum

to the trunk of an evergreen
and sleepily rubbing its cheek against the sky;
onto someone's forgotten glove,
onto the zoo, which had shown its guests out,
onto the bench with its wistful legend:
PLACE FOR LOST CHILDREN.

Dogs licked the snow in a puzzled way,
and squirrels with eyes like lost beads
flickered between cast-iron baskets,
amidst trees lost in the woods of themselves.
Great juttings of granite stood about
morosely, preserving in mineral calm
a silent question, a reproach—
lost children of former mountains,

Behind a wire fence, zebras munching hay
peered, at a loss, into striped darkness.
Seals, poking their noses from the pool,
caught snow in midflight on their whiskers;
they gazed around them, quizzical, confused,
forsaken children of Mother Ocean
taking pity, in their slippery style,
on people—lost children of the Earth.

I walked alone. Now and then, in the thicket,
the crimson firefly of a cigarette
floated before an unseen face—
the staring pupil of Night's wide eye.

And I felt some stranger's feeling of being lost
was searching embarrassed
for a feeling of being lost like my own,
not knowing that this is what I longed for.

At night, beneath this snowfall,
its whispered secret having made us one,

America and I sat down together
in the place for lost children.

1967

TRANS. JOHN UPDIKE AND ALBERT C. TODD

TED BERRIGAN

Born in Providence, R.I., in 1934, Ted Berrigan moved to the Lower East Side in 1960. Part of the second generation of New York school poets, he uses specific time and place, recalling the work of Frank O'Hara, though he himself became a model for young poets who followed him. He taught poetry workshops at St. Mark's until his death in 1983. His *Sonnets* was published by Grove Press. Much-loved in the neighborhood, a city walker and generous spirit, he is remembered in *Nice to See You* by Anne Waldman.

XXXVI

AFTER FRANK O'HARA

It's 8:54 a.m. in Brooklyn it's the 28th of July and
it's probably 8:54 in Manhattan but I'm
in Brooklyn I'm eating English muffins and drinking
pepsi and I'm thinking of how Brooklyn is New
York city too how odd I usually think of it as
something all its own like Bellows Falls like Little
Chute like Uijongbu
I never thought on the Williams-
burg bridge I'd come so much to Brooklyn ☆
just to see lawyers and cops who don't even carry
guns taking my wife away and bringing her back
No
and I never thought Dick would be back at Gude's
beard shaved off long hair cut and Carol reading
his books when we were playing cribbage and
watching the sun come up over the Navy Yard

across the river
                I think I was thinking when I was
ahead I'd be somewhere like Perry street erudite
dazzling slim and badly loved
contemplating my new book of poems
to be printed in simple type on old brown paper
feminine marvelous and tough

AUDRE LORDE

Born in New York City from Grenadian immigrants in 1934 and raised in Manhattan, Audre Lorde published her first poem in *Seventeen* while still in high school. She attended Hunter College (where she later taught), then Columbia University. *First Cities* appeared in 1968. A cofounder of Kitchen Table: Women of Color Press and a founding member of Sisters in Support of Sisters in South Africa, she received the Walt Whitman Citation of Merit and was declared poet laureate of New York before she died in 1992.

NEW YORK CITY 1970

How do you spell change like frayed slogan underwear
with the emptied can of yesterdays' meanings
with yesterdays' names?
And what does the we-bird see with
who has lost its I's?

There is nothing beautiful left in the streets of this city.
I have come to believe in death and renewal by fire.
Past questioning the necessities of blood
or why it must be mine or my children's time
that will see the grim city quake to be reborn perhaps
blackened again but this time with a sense of purpose;
tired of the past tense forever, of assertion and repetition
of the ego-trips through an incomplete self
where two years ago proud rang for promise but now

it is time for fruit and all the agonies are barren—
only the children are growing:

For how else can the self become whole
save by making self into its own new religion?
I am bound like an old lover—a true believer—
to this city's death by accretion and slow ritual,
and I submit to its penance for a trial
as new steel is tried
I submit my children also to its death throes and agony
and they are not even the city's past lovers. But I submit them
to the harshness and growing cold to the brutalizations
which if survived
will teach them strength or an understanding of how strength is
  gotten
and will not be forgotten: It will be their city then:
I submit them
loving them above all others save myself
to the fire to the rage to the ritual scarifications
to be tried as new steel is tried;
and in its wasting the city shall try them
as the blood-splash of a royal victim
tries the hand of the destroyer.

II

I hide behind tenements and subways in fluorescent alleys
watching as flames walk the streets of an empire's altar
raging through the veins of the sacrificial stenchpot
smeared upon the east shore of a continent's insanity
conceived in the psychic twilight of murderers and pilgrims
rank with money and nightmare and too many useless people
who will not move over nor die, who cannot bend
even before the winds of their own preservation
even under the weight of their own hates
Who cannot amend nor conceive nor even learn to share
their own visions
who bomb my children into mortar in churches

and work plastic offal and metal and the flesh of their enemies
into subway rush-hour temples where obscene priests
finger and worship each other in secret
and think they are praying when they squat
to shit money-pebbles shaped like their parents' brains—
who exist to go into dust to exist again
grosser and more swollen and without ever relinquishing
space or breath or energy from their private hoard.

I do not need to make war nor peace
with these prancing and murderous deacons
who refuse to recognize their role in this covenant we live upon
and so have come to fear and despise even their own children;
but I condemn myself, and my loves
past and present
and the blessed enthusiasms of all my children
to this city
without reason or future
without hope
to be tried as the new steel is tried
before trusted to slaughter.

I walk down the withering limbs of my last discarded house
and there is nothing worth salvage left in this city
but the faint reedy voices like echoes
of once beautiful children.

GRACE SCHULMAN

Born in New York City in 1935, poetry editor for the *Nation*, distinguished professor at Baruch College of the City University of New York, and editor of *The Poems of Marianne Moore*, Grace Schulman reaches into the city's early origins to write of twenty-three Jews who were driven from Recife, Brazil, during the Spanish Inquisition and arrived in New Amsterdam in 1654 despite Governor Peter Stuyvesant's fervent attempts to prevent it.

NEW NETHERLAND, 1654 ☆

Pardon us for uttering a handful
of words in *any* language, so cut loose
are we from homes, and from His name that is still
nameless, blessed be He. We raised a prayer house—

that is, we broke new wood for one, but some
tough burned it, snarling: "Carve only stones for the dead."
Damp ground, no fire, no psalm we all remember.
But tall ships anchor here, and at low tide,

people with wheat-colored hair look out to sea,
just as we'd searched for land. "Pray if you must,"
my father said, "and when prayer fails, a story—
if it is all you have, will do." Months past,

we left Recife's force-worship laws in the Year
of *their* Lord, sixteen-hundred and fifty-four, for our new
world, old-country Amsterdam. Leagues seaward,
Spanish pirates slaughtered our scant crew,

and all that was left of us (friends wheezed
their last while they ragged us on) rose up on deck
and tossed our bags in the sea. We watched the wake
turn silver: kiddish wine cups, hanging bowls,

a candelabra for the promised altar,
carved pointers. Books' pages curled and sank,
prayer shawls ballooned, and, soaking, spiraled downward.
Just as we stared, again we heard sword clank—

a French ship, the Ste. Catherine (her prow had shone
gold on a gray horizon) came to our
port side and rescued us. In that commotion
on deck, we crouched below—not out of fear,
I swear, but stunned by luminous words

that echoed oddly—beautifully—like lightning
flickering through palls of thickset clouds.
A jaunty captain rasped to us in hiding:

"Where are you bound?"
"Amsterdam. Old country."
"Where?"
"Amsterdam."
"Antilles?"
"No, Amsterdam."

"Yes, yes. Nieuw *Am*sterdam. I'll see
you get there safely." He meant well, bless him.

St. Catherine sailed to land at its tip no larger
than a meadow, fanned out at its sides:
Manhattan Island. Our new master,
Stuyvesant, lashed us with phrases, *wheffs*, *guzzads*,

that stung but were not fathomed, mercifully,
when we came on a Sabbath, more than twenty
men, women, a baby born at sea.
Still cursing, he let us land, and heard our praise,

then disappeared among lank citizens
with faded skin who stride to the bay and brood
on water that we trust and dread, and listen
to tales unstamped by laws and never sacred.

JUNE JORDAN

June Jordan (1936–2002) was born in Harlem, where she remained an active worker for social reform and won the Architectural Design Award for her joint proposal of an African American burial ground in New York. Her first book of poetry, *Who Look at Me*, was originally an unfinished project of Langston Hughes. In *Soldier: A Poet's Childhood* (1981), she explores her troubled, formative years. This poem reaches back in the city's troubled past and the efforts, amid uncontrolled greed and the misery it caused, to achieve some basic human dignity.

47,000 WINDOWS

The Lower East Side of New York City offers, in itself, a history of American contradiction, devotion to profit, and the failure of environmental design for human life. People had to pass a law in order that ventilation and minimal, natural light be available to the immigrants who had no money for decent housing. Instead of tearing down the tenements that were unfit for human habitation when they were first erected, the reformers satisfied themselves by legislating phony windows blasted into the bricks. That was a hundred years ago. People still have to live in those Lower East Side hellholes. This is a poem about the law that passed some light and air into that deliberated slum.

1. There were probably more Indians alive
than Jews and Italians in that whole
early American place of New York
when the city began being big:
a perfect convergency confirmed
congested with trade
creating tolerance for trade requires
abject curiosity or general indifference
to anything that sells not well enough
to tell somebody else about it. And
at the beginning of New York
the world was selling well and so was
tolerance along with trade that
provocation to a polyethnic population
trading every bit of time for money
made the city made me take
your eye for mine according to extreme
prosperity and appetite.

2. In 1830 then the blurring crowd
that overwhelming beggarly blur of people came
they pushed into the seaport cornucopia of New York
small many people forced
from land from farms from food from family forced
like seasons dictatorial
the people fled
political hostilities and hunger
people fled
that soon consuming triumph
of elimination
that machinery for triumph
by a few.

3. Then in 1830 the Astors and the Vanderbilts left.
They rode by carriage from the uproar
trouble from arrival by the millions
shoved their ships that wandered
with the sea to make their glad delivery
of travelers penniless and hellbent toward
the welcoming coast of always America.

Those other ones
they came
not trading things
but lives.

4. Unskilled millions crammed old mansions
broke apart large rooms and took a corner
held a place a spot a bed a chair a box
a looking glass
and kept that space (expect for death)
a safety now for fugitives
from infamy and famine
working hard to live.

5. In place of land that street the outhouse
tenement testimonies
to a horrifying speculation that would quarter
and condemn
debase and shadow and efface
the privacies of human being.

6. Real estate arose as profit spread
to mutilate the multitudes and kill them
living just to live.
What can a man survive?
They say: The poor persist.

7. O the Chinese and the Irish and the names!
The names survived.
Likewise some families.

8. 1867 after the first and only Civil War
men look at others
men again
not targets.
Looked at latrines six stories high
people paralyzed by penury immobilized
and children docked
and hopes untied and
lying loose and less than skeleton
at the dirty waters
by the building of a dollarbill
venality
near to nothing
at the doorway nothing
only life and speculation:
What can a man survive?

9. Men looked at other men again
not targets
and in 1869 they passed a law ☆
about the nightmare rising as they saw

sick men and women nurse their babies
although love
is not enough to eat.

10. The Tenement Act of 1869
was merciful, well-meant, and fine
in its enforcement
tore 47,000 windows out of hellhole
shelter of no light.

It must be hard to make a window.

JAYNE CORTEZ

Though born in Arizona in 1936, Jayne Cortez grew up in the Watts ghetto of Los Angeles, where she eventually became the director of the Watts Repertory Theatre Company. She has spent most of her adult life in New York, and, like Whitman and many others who move here, she feels a strong identity with the city and embraces all aspects of it.

I AM NEW YORK CITY

i am new york city
here is my brain of hot sauce
my tobacco teeth my
  mattress of bedbug tongue
legs apart   hand on chin
  war on the roof   insults
pointed fingers   pushcarts
my contraceptives all

look at my pelvis blushing

i am new york city of blood
police and fried pies

i rub my docks red with grenadine
and jelly madness in a flow of tokay
my huge skull of pigeons
my seance of peeping toms
my plaited ovaries excuse me
this is my grime my thigh of
steelspoons and toothpicks
  i imitate no one

i am new york city
of the brown spit and soft tomatoes
give me my confetti of flesh
  my marquee of false nipples
my sideshow of open beaks
  in my nose of soot
in my ox bled eyes
in my ear of saturday night specials

i eat ha ha hee hee and ho ho

i am new york city
never change never sleep never melt
my shoes are incognito
cadavers grow from my goatee
look i sparkle with shit with wishbones
my nickname is glue-me

take my face of stink bombs
my star spangled banner of hot dogs
take my beer can junta
my reptilian ass of footprints
and approach me through life
approach me through death
approach me through my widow's peak
through my split ends my
asthmatic laugh   approach me
through my wash rag

half ankle   half elbow
massage me with your camphor tears
salute the patina and concrete
of my rat tail wig
face up   face down   piss
into the bite of our handshake

i am new york city
my skillet-head friend
my fat-bellied comrade
citizens
break wind with me

MARGE PIERCY

Born in 1936, novelist and poet Marge Piercy has fused her work with political statements and the ideals of feminism since becoming an organizer for Students for a Democratic Society in the 1960s. She wrote of those experiences as well as her troubled childhood in her memoir, *Sleeping with Cats* (2002).

I WOKE WITH THE ROOM COLD . . .

I woke with the room cold and my cat
Arofa kneading my belly.
I had been walking around the lower east side
while from every alley and fruit market and stoop,
out from under the ravaged cars,
the cats came running to me.
All the cats had heard I was moving to the country
because of my lungs
and they began to cough and sneeze and whine.
All the starving rat-gnawed rickety spavined cats
of the lower east side with their fleas and worms
and their siren of hunger

followed me through the teeming blocks.
They threw themselves under the wheels of trucks
in an effort to keep up.
They were rubbing my ankles and yowling
that I must take every one of them along.
They wanted to breathe air that was not stained.
They wanted to roll on wet grass.
They wanted to chase a bird that wasn't a dirty pigeon.
Then the demands of the cats were drowned out.
As I ran, all of the eleven and twelve and thirteen year olds
who had died of skag in the smoking summer
began to miaou and miaou and miaou
till all of New York was white with pain like snow.

MARVIN BELL

Born in New York City in 1937, Marvin Bell has been teaching in the Iowa Writers' Workshop since 1965. In this poem, he writes about the hearty gingko tree, imported from Asia and popular in the city because of its ability to survive pollutants.

THESE GREEN-GOING-TO-YELLOW ☆

This year,
I'm raising the emotional ante,
putting my face
in the leaves to be stepped on,
seeing myself among them, that is;
that is, likening
leaf-vein to artery, leaf to flesh,
the passage of a leaf in autumn
to the passage of autumn,
branch-tip and winter spaces
to possibilities, and possibility
to God. Even on East 61st Street

in the blowzy city of New York,
someone has planted a gingko
because it has leaves like fans like hands,
hand-leaves, and sex. Those lovely
Chinese hands on the sidewalks
so far from delicacy
or even, perhaps, another gender of gingko—
do we see them?
No one ever treated us so gently
as these green-going-to-yellow hands
fanned out where we walk.
No one ever fell down so quietly
and lay where we would look
when we were tired or embarrassed,
or so bowed down by humanity
that we had to watch out lest our shoes stumble,
and looked down not to look up
until something looked like parts of people
where we were walking. We have no
experience to make us see the gingko
or any other tree,
and, in our admiration for whatever grows tall
and outlives us,
we look away, or look at the middles of things,
which would not be our way
if we truly thought we were gods.

WILLIAM BORDEN

William Borden was born in Indianapolis, Indiana, in 1938, received a B.A. from Columbia University, and is now the Chester Fritz Distinguished Professor Emeritus at the University of North Dakota. The remarkable building of the poem's title is Frank Lloyd Wright's only important commission in the city, originally called the Museum of Non-Objective Painting.

GUGGENHEIM

At the Guggenheim Museum of Modern Art in New York City
a young woman in a wheelchair gyres down the ramp
past Chinese porcelain, swoops by terra cotta soldiers,
dodges walkers and gawkers, swirls gracefully around
standers and ponderers—descends backward in time
the Wright giant snail shell, right down
to the terra firma of the Café and Gift Shop.

And so we whirl downward, some say, from spirit to flesh
and back again, a vicious circle or a sublime progression,
depending on one's view, or faith, or experience.
We take the elevator up to the ethereal heights, then
wheel down to blood and bones again, hoping each trip
we're moving forward in time but who can tell, really?

Maybe our spirits welcome this airy time-out,
after the hurly burly of bardos and whatever
waiting rooms we loaf in between incarnations,
Grand Central Stations of the astral plane,
fraught with cancellations and reroutings,
so many embodiments and planets to choose from.

It must be a terrifying descent,
a train wreck of the soul,
a cataclysm of subtle matter.
No wonder we forget, put it out of mind,
recall only in dreams and fantasies.
"We're here to learn," people say,
but I think we're here to forget,
take a breather from the rush hours
of those dizzying, whirligig journeys.

ROBERT PHILLIPS

Born in Delaware in 1938, Robert Phillips moved to Manhattan in 1962 for an advertising career. He has published criticism on Lewis Carroll, Delmore Schwartz (Phillips is Schwartz's literary executor), and the "confessional poets," and is professor of English at the University of Houston. This poem is told by an aging survivor of one of New York's most haunting tragedies.

TRIANGLE SHIRTWAIST FACTORY FIRE ☆

(NEW YORK CITY, 1911)

I, Rose Rosenfeld, am one of the workers
who survived. Before the inferno broke out,
factory doors had been locked by the owners,

to keep us at our sewing machines,
to keep us from stealing scraps of cloth.
I said to myself, What are the bosses doing?
I knew they would save themselves.

I left my big-button-attacher machine,
climbed the iron stairs to the tenth floor
where their offices were. From the landing window

I saw girls in shirtwaists flying by,
Catherine wheels projected like Zeppelins
out open windows, then plunging downward,
sighing skirts open parasols on fire.

I found the big shots stuffing themselves
into the freight elevator going to the roof.
I squeezed in. While our girls were falling,

we ascended like ashes. Firemen
yanked us onto the next-door roof.

I sank to the tarpaper, sobbed for
one-hundred-forty-six comrades dying

or dead down below. One was Rebecca,
my only close friend, a forewoman kind to workers.
Like the others, she burned like a prism.

Relatives of twenty-three victims later brought suits.
Each family was awarded seventy-five dollars.
It was like the Titanic the very next year—
No one cared about the souls in steerage.

Those doors were locked, too, a sweatshop at sea.
They died due to ice, not fire. I live in
Southern California now. But I still see

skirts rippling like parachutes,
girls hit the cobblestones, smell smoke,
burnt flesh, girls cracking like cheap buttons,
disappearing like so many dropped stitches.

CHARLES SIMIC

Charles Simic was born in Belgrade, Yugoslavia, in 1938 but raised in Paris and Chicago before settling in New York City in 1954. With a B.A. from New York University, he was a housepainter, shirt salesman, and bootlegger, then a teacher at the University of New Hampshire since the early 1970s. He won the 1990 Pulitzer Prize for *The World Doesn't End*. Concerned with the small, rarely noticed aspects of life—his first collection is modestly titled *What the Grass Says* (1967)—he writes with a street-smart eye as he walks history through a morning stroll.

EARLY MORNING IN JULY

The streets were cool
After the heat of the night.
The dives, their doors open,
Smelled of stale beer.
Someone swept the floor
With even strokes.
He was pale as Confucius.
Martha Washington, her hair in a beehive,
Yawned in a glass booth
Of a movie theater.

Yesterday I saw Ulysses
Make Greek pastry.
Joan of Arc was at the dry cleaner's
Standing on a chair
With pins in her mouth.
St. Francis sold piranhas in a pet store.
At midnight Circe's daughters
Flew on a motorcycle.
Thomas Alva Edison
Roamed the streets in white socks
And blood on his shirt.

And now this sea breeze,
This unexpected coolness.
The small, sickly tree on your block
Hasn't grown much in years.
It shivers with happiness
With its few remaining leaves,
As if Emanuel Swedenborg
Was now whispering to the spirits
On Eighth Avenue.

FRANK LIMA

Born in 1939 in New York. attending Brooklyn College and later Columbia University where he received an M.F.A., Frank Lima for a while was a chef instructor at the New York Restaurant School and a cofounder of the Lower East Side Tenements' Project at St. Mark's Church. Although not quite celebrating New York's gritty underside, he embraces it with insightful passion.

INVENTORY—TO 100TH STREET

TO JOHN BERNARD MYERS ☆

In the corner lot
where they parked
green banana tricks
fruits
palmed in paper straw
I smell
bedbug & kitchen-cockroach
summer afternoons
Somewhere
tailless
one-eyed cats
doting in fat garbage cans
screaming with the stench
of rice & beans
strawberry tampax
piled
high as the smell
(I was small & slick)
the covers tilted
like the hat of a rock-look wino
in a deep
knee-bend nod
on a beer
can-street
Sunday morning

There were always
time-thick
empty nights
of nothing to do
but listen to the
ethereal
(she lived on the top floor)
I-go-for more screams
of Charlie's pimp's woman
when he beat her
for his good
business principles
joy-pop the block
with morning-talk

I hear the dim iron dawn yawning
(I lived on Third Ave.)
rattle
nights into
Saturday morning
flag-bloomer
eclipses
just before the hunt—
they were as big—
the cats
like jungle bunnies
fierce with fleas & sores

I see window-people
sweating
hanging out of gooey-stick slips
strange
below-the-button drawers
crouched junkies in hallways
with monkey backs
eating cellophane bananas
on a g-string
waiting

for that last bust
Spics with cock-comb
hair fronts
ear-gulping mambo music
eye-lapping peperican flower
crotches

I can hear the streets whispering
in the ears of yelping kids

in the fun-gushing that
rippled my blood
in the pump
but the kids
are dying in the lot
like the tarry-blown feet
of the rain
jingling
on the rusty-green
of yesterday's
fire-escapes.

BILLY COLLINS

One of America's most recognized and popular poets, having recently served as the nation's poet laureate, Billy Collins was born in New York City in 1941, prefers not to walk the streets with earphones, and found spelling "Thelonious" the most difficult part of writing this poem.

MAN LISTENING TO DISC

This is not bad—
ambling along 44th Street
with Sonny Rollins for company,

his music flowing through the soft calipers
of these earphones,

as if he were right beside me
on this clear day in March,
the pavement sparkling with sunlight,
pigeons fluttering off the curb,
nodding over a profusion of bread crumbs.

In fact, I would say
my delights at being suffused
with phrases from his saxophone—
some like honey, some like vinegar—
is surpassed only by my gratitude

to Tommy Porter for taking the time
to join us on this breezy afternoon
with his most unwieldy bass
and to the esteemed Arthur Taylor
who is somehow managing to navigate

this crowd with his cumbersome drums.
And I bow deeply to Thelonious Monk
for figuring out a way
to motorize—or whatever—his huge piano
so he could be with us today.

The music is loud yet so confidential
I cannot help feeling even more
like the center of the universe
than usual as I walk along to a rapid
little version of "The Way You Look Tonight,"

and all I can say to my fellow pedestrians,
to the woman in the white sweater,
the man in the tan raincoat and the heavy glasses,
who mistake themselves for the center of the universe—
all I can say is watch your step

because the five of us, instruments and all,
are about to angle over
to the south side of the street
and then, in our own tightly knit way,
turn the corner at Sixth Avenue.

And if any of you are curious
about where this aggregation,
this whole battery-powered crew,
is headed, let us just say
that the real center of the universe,

the only true point of view,
is full of the hope that he,
the hub of the cosmos
with his hair blown sideways,
will eventually make it all the way downtown.

STAN RICE

An established painter with eight collections of poetry, Stan Rice (1942–2002) taught many years at San Francisco University. He married the novelist Anne Rice, and his *False Prophets* was published posthumously in 2003.

LOOKING FOR AN APARTMENT IN NEW YORK

Who is the Korean grocer,
        by what light does he sleep, who are
The doves who serve coffee with Arabic accents,
        moving among each other and the steel stools
        like kleenex in airwells, who
Is the condo saleslady in the stiletto heels
        when she is not composed,

Who is the wealthy woman on 5th Ave
    with the ability to speak of the weather
    as though it were holy and the days were numbered,
Who are these people,
And how long will it take me
To sing songs with them in them?

SHARON OLDS

Born in San Francisco in 1942, Sharon Olds moved east in 1964, and received her Ph.D. from Columbia. Her book *The Dead and the Living* (1984) won both the Lamont Award and the National Book Critics Circle Award. A teacher at New York University, she writes here of what Scott Fitzgerald called "the most magnificent of towers."

THE EMPIRE STATE BUILDING AS THE MOON ☆

I walk the city, my eyes on her so she
comes out from behind buildings,
rising sideways, bright, fierce,
grayish, chambered. I hardly see the
unlit column like a grandfather clock that
holds the great orb up but
only the silvery even craters
bathed in cold light. Unpeopled,
brilliant, afloat—I look for her
wherever I am, and when she rises late I
walk to see her rise. Not good,
not bad, with no dark side, she
swims over the buildings as if out of pity
but mostly for the pleasure of swimming,
the single blazing breast stroke
above New York.

RON PADGETT

Ron Padgett from Oklahoma was born in 1942, received a B.A. from Columbia University, has translated the poems of Apollinaire as well as Pierre Reverdy (what Frank O'Hara carried in his pocket in "A Step Away from Them"), and, along with David Shapiro, edited *An Anthology of New York Poets* (1970). A great friend of Ted Berrigan and director of the St. Mark's Poetry Project for many years, he lives on the Lower East Side, some of which is captured in this personal, evocative poem.

STRAWBERRIES IN MEXICO

At 14th Street and First Avenue
Is a bank and in the bank the sexiest teller of all time
Next to her the greatest thing about today
Is today itself
Through which I go up
To buy books

They float by under a bluer sky
The girls uptown
Quiet, pampered
The sum of all that's terrible in women
And much of the best

And the old men go by holding small packages
In a trance
So rich even they can't believe it

I think it's a red, white and blue letter day from them too
You see, Con Ed's smokestacks are beautiful ☆
The way Queens is
And horses: from a pleasant distance

Or a fleet of turkeys
Stuffed in a spotless window
In two days they'll be sweating in ovens

Thinking, "How did I ever get in a fix like this?"

Light pouring over buildings far away
Up here when someone says "Hey!"
In the street you know they aren't going to kill you
They're yelling to a friend of theirs named Hey
John David Hey, perhaps
And even the garbage goes out
In big white billowy plastic bags tied at the top
Even the people go out in them
Some, now, are waiting
At bus stops (for a probably nonexistent bus . . .)
I thought it was the garbage!
It's so pretty!

If you're classless or modern
You can have fun by
Walking into a high-class antique store
So the stately old snob at the desk will ask
In eternity
"You're going where?"
You get to answer "Up."

I like these old pricks
If you have an extra hair in the breeze
Their eyes pop out
And then recede way back
As if to say, "That person is on . . . dope!"
They're very correct

But they're not in my shoes
In front of a Dubuffet a circus that shines through
A window in a bright all-yellow building
The window is my eye
And Frank O'Hara is the building
I'm thinking about him like mad today
(As anyone familiar with his poetry will tell)
And about the way Madison Avenue really

Does go to Heaven
And then turns around and comes back, disappointed

Because up here you can sneer at a Negro
Or pity the man
And rent a cloud-colored Bentley and
Architecture's so wonderful!
Why don't I notice it more often?
And the young girls and boys but especially the young girls
Are drifting away from school
In blue and white wool
Wrapped in fur
Are they French? They're speaking French!
And they aren't looking for things to throw
Skirts sliding up the legs of girl who can't keep from grinning
Under beautiful soft brown American eyes
At the whole world
Which includes their plain Jane girlfriends
She even smiled at me!
I have about as much chance of fucking her as the girl at the bank
But I stride along, a terrifying god
Raunchy
A little one day old beard
And good grief I really did forget to brush my teeth this morning
They're turning red with embarrassment
Or is that blood
I've been drinking—I ordered a black coffee
Miss

And then a black policeman comes in
Unbuttoning his uniform at the warmish soda fountain
While I pull the fleece over my teeth
And stare innocently at the books I've bought
One a book with a drawing
By Apollinaire called "Les fraises au Mexique"
"Strawberries in Mexico"
But when I open the book to that page
It's just a very blue sky I'm looking at

ALFRED CORN

Alfred Corn was born in Georgia in 1943. He received an M.A. from Columbia University and is presently with its Graduate Writing Program. He is a frequent contributor to the *New York Times Book Review* and *Art in America*. Much of his 1978 collection of poems, *A Call in the Midst of the Crowd*, is about New York, as is this haunting poem of the immigrant experience of Ellis Island a century ago.

PHOTOGRAPHS OF OLD NEW YORK

They stare back into an increate future,
Dead stars, burning still. Air how choked with soot
One breathed then, the smudged grays and blacks impressed
In circles around East European eyes,
Top hats, a brougham, the laundry that hung
Like crowds of ghosts over common courtyards.
Dignity still knew how to thrust its hand
Into a waistcoat, bread plaited into shapes
How to dress a window, light under the El
Fall as negative to cast-iron shadows.
Assemble Liberty plate by plate—so ☆
This giant dismembered arm still emerges
From folds of bronze and floats over the heads
Of bearded workmen riveted in place
By an explosion of magnetism they've learned
To endure. Then, Union. Rally. March. Strike.

And still the wretched refugees swarming
Out from Ellis Island, the glittering door,
To prosper or perish. Or both . . . The men
Don't see the women; or see how deftly hems
Can be lifted at curbs—well, any eye would
Be caught by that tilt of hat, profile, bearing.
Others strive to have mattered too, stolid
Forms that blush and crouch over sewing machines,
Haunt the libraries, speak on platforms.
Did they? And did this woman, who clearly still

Speaks no English, her head scarf, say, Russian?
A son stands at her side, crop-haired, in clumpy
Shoes. She stares straight forward, reserved, aware,
Embattled. The deep-set eyes say something
About the emptiness of most wishes; and
About her hopes. She knows the odds are poor.
Or, the odds are zero, counted from here.
That past survives its population
And is unkind. Triumph no more than failure
In the longest run ever fails to fail.
Is that the argument against shuffling,
Dealing, and reshuffling these photographs?
They are not mementos of death alone,
But of life lived variously, avatars
Energy, insight, cruelty took—and love.
Variousness: the great kaleidoscope
Of time, its snowflake pictures, form after
Form, collapsing into the future, hours,
Days, seasons, generations that rise up
And fall like leaves, each one a hand inscribed
With the fragile calligraphy of selfhood;
The human fate given a human face.

NIKKI GIOVANNI

Born in Knoxville, Tennessee, in 1943, Nikki Giovanni studied at Columbia University. She founded the press Niktom Limited in 1970, and is now a professor at Virginia Polytechnical Institute. This poem blends African American voices, both urban and Southern, heard on the streets of Harlem.

THE NEW YORKERS

In front of the bank building
after six o'clock the gathering
of the bag people begins

In cold weather they huddle
around newspapers
when it is freezing they get
cardboard boxes

Someone said they are all rich eccentrics
Someone is   of course   crazy

The man and his buddy moved
to the truck port
in the adjoining building
most early evenings he visits
his neighbors awaiting
the return of his friend
from points unknown to me
they seem to be a spontaneous
combustion these night people
they evaporate during the light of day
only to emerge at evening glow
as if they had never been away

I am told there are people
who live underground
in the layer between the subways
and the pipes that run them
they have harnessed the steam
to heat their corner
and cook their food
though there is no electricity
making them effectively   moles

The twentieth century has seen
  two big wars and two small ones
  the automobile and the SST
  telephones and satellites in the sky
  man on the moon and spacecraft on Jupiter
How odd to also see the people
of New York City living

in the doorways of public buildings
as if this is an emerging nation
though of course it is

Look at the old woman
who sits on 57th Street and 8th Avenue
selling pencils
I don't know where she spends the night
she sits summer and winter
snow or rain humming
some white religious song
she must weigh over 250 pounds
the flesh on her legs has stretched
like a petite pair of stockings
onto a medium frame
beyond its ability to fit
there are tears and holes
of various purples in her legs
things and stuff ooze from them
drying and running again
there is never though a smell
she does not ask you to buy
a pencil nor will her eyes
condemn your health
it's easy really to walk by her
unlike the man in front
of Tiffany's she holds her pencils
near her knee
you take or not
depending upon your writing needs

He on the other hand is blind and walking
his german shepherd dog
his sign says THERE
BUT FOR THE GRACE OF GOD
GOES YOU and there is a long
explanation of his condition

It's rather easy for the Tiffany shopper
to see his condition
    he is Black

Uptown on 125th Street is an old blind Black woman
she is out only in good
  weather and clothes
her house is probably spotless
as southern ladies are wont to keep house
and her wig is always on straight
  You got something for me, she called
  What do you want, I asked
  What's yo name? I know yo family
  No, you don't, I said laughing   You don't know anything
    about me
You that Eyetalian poet ain't you? I know yo voice. I seen you on
    television
I peered closely into her eyes
  You didn't see me or you'd know I'm black
  Let me feel yo hair   if you Black   Hold down yo head
I did and she did
  Got something for me, she laughed
  You felt my hair that's good luck
  Good luck is money, chile, she said
  Good luck is money.

DANIEL HALPERN

Daniel Halpern, born in Syracuse, New York, in 1945, is the author of seven collections of poems and editorial director of the Ecco Press, and he—along with Paul Bowles—started the journal *Antaeus*. The chair of the graduate writing division at Columbia University, he lives both in New York City and Princeton, New Jersey.

STREET FIRE

It is past midnight in a thick fog when sirens
call us to the terrace.
We look down onto the blossoms of bright fire
opening from manholes on Fifth Avenue.
There are men standing and smoking in rubber jackets
outside a garment-district café,
the lights fluttering, the fire
offering us its electric smoke.
In bare feet and robes—the cat
and dog at our feet—we hear
the heat pound tubes stuffed with wire.
And somewhere down there, under the softening blacktop,
the gas mains wait to take in the whole block.
We bring the two or three small relics of our lives,
the dog and cat, and the elevator to the street.
There is a cold wind and ice in the gutters.
There is the street's midnight population
leaning against the wall of Reverend Peale's Sunday church. ☆
We note the taxis that deliver strangers
to watch with us as the street shrivels and begins
to flow around the manhole covers.
They are all there: men of the brigade, the police,
women from nearby hotels, their furred men,
the strangers from the city.
What we see is the tip of the iceberg,
they tell us—and underneath
the tubes alive with flames.
For an hour we watch from the corner—
in this weather tragedies are distant.
The elevator back up contains the momentary explosion
in the eye where disasters flare—
our section of New York, between the flowers and furs,
is full of bright red petals.
We reach the ninth floor and step into air
powdered with radiator heat.

The tiny, muffled beats of fire below the street
pant through the window an even pulse.
The dog moves into the living room where the fire is dying
on bricks. The cat takes the warm tiles
of the bathroom. We stand silently, listen
a few minutes, then move to each other.
Our own fire is watered by the conviction
that things are right. Later, we listen to the small puffs
of heat spit from the manhole outside, smell
the smoke from the live wires
bound with rubber that smolders into morning.

MIGUEL PIÑERO

Born in Puerto Rico in 1946 and emigrating to New York at the age of four, Miguel Piñero was a poet, actor, author of the play *Short Eyes*, a prisoner on Rikers Island, a cofounder of the Nuyorican Poets' Theater on the Lower East Side, and a major force in creating a new street poetry until his death in 1988.

A LOWER EAST SIDE POEM ☆

Just before I die
I want to climb up on a
tenement sky
to dream my lungs out till
I cry
then scatter my ashes thru
the Lower East Side

So let me sing my song tonight
let me feel out of sight
and let all eyes be dry
when they scatter my ashes thru
the Lower East Side.

From Houston to 14th Street
from Second Avenue to the mighty D
here the hustlers & suckers meet
the faggots & freaks will all get
high
on the ashes that have been scattered
thru the Lower East Side

There's no other place for me to be
there's no other place that I can see
there's no other town around that
brings you up and keeps you down
no food little heat sweeps by
fancy cars & pimps' bars & juke saloons
& greasy spoons make my spirits fly
with my ashes scattered thru the
Lower East Side . . .

A thief, a junkie I've been
committed every known sin
Jews and Gentiles . . . Bums and Men
of style . . . run away child
police shooting wild . . .
mother's futile wails . . . pushers
making sales . . . dope wheelers
& cocaine dealers . . . smoking pot
streets are hot & feed off those who bleed to death . . .
all that's true
all that's true
all that is true
but this ain't no lie
when I ask that my ashes be scattered thru
the Lower East Side

So here I am, look at me
I stand as proud as you can see
pleased to be from the Lower East Side
a street fighting man

a problem of this land
I am the Philosopher of the Criminal Mind
a dweller of prison time
a cancer of the Rockefeller's ghettocide
this concrete tomb is my home
to belong to survive you got to be strong
you can't be shy less without request
someone will scatter your ashes thru
the Lower East Side

I don't wanna be buried in Puerto Rico
I don't wanna rest in long island cemetery
I wanna be near the stabbing shooting
gambling fighting & unnatural dying
& new birth crying
so please when I die . . .
don't take me far away
keep me near by
take my ashes and scatter them thru out
the Lower East Side . . .

CLAUDIA MENZA

Born in Canada in 1947, Claudia Menza—former assistant editor at the *Evergreen Review* and general editor of Grove Press—heads a literary agency in New York. Her collection *The Lunatics Ball* explores "the physical, psychological, and spiritual New York," wrote Ishmael Reed, and in the tradition of Whitman and Frank O'Hara, she is uneasy anywhere for long but the city.

YOU SAY YOU LIKE THE COUNTRY

You say you like the country,
how the pond snuggles up to your house
and birds hold forth at the picture window.
You say the sky is

full of stars, constellations
to light your way.

You say you like the quiet, the peace,
but your waterfall kept me
sleepless,
until at last a nod came on
only to be beaten back by
cicadas drumming like migraines
and thunderstorms which shook the bed
like a rattle.

I prefer a twilight street in rain,
the long, slow swish of cars,
a slick of rainbows in their wake,
voices refracted through silvery sheets
like parents in another room,
eerie yet comforting,
protection as night comes on.

I prefer my apartment at 6:00 a.m.,
a single Mourning Dove cooing in
the primitive arms of the Ailanthus.
Clock radios burst into song,
the giant rolls out of bed,
joggers pace the street,
leopards in spandex,
then the dogs come sniffing,
pulling sleepy companions to
secrets in concrete.

I like an outdoor café,
the symmetry of umbrellas
drawing sun to their crowns,
The intimacy of lunch
in their generous shade.

I live for a cab driver with
a snappy line,
a walk though Chinatown,
each telephone booth a pagoda for one,
restaurants defended by dragons
(you don't get dragons in the country anymore),
fish so fresh they're
jumping in their baskets.
And if I liked mimes (Annoying creatures.
Everybody hates them but nobody wants to say so.)
then a mime in Central Park.

It's no Currier and Ives but
how many ponds with skaters
can you look at? I'd rather
the Christmas windows at Lord & Taylor,
watching children with
mittens of chestnuts
press to a scene from
Currier and Ives,
faces bright with cold, with curiosity.

You want me to trade this in for
a babbling brook?
Brooks are nice, but brooks are easy to celebrate,
the proverbial good without evil,
no attempts at your core,
nothing that scrapes to the bone
like the collective frenzy of
a lunatics' ball,
a kaleidoscope gone mad.

Paddle this stream and
you can throw away your meditation pillow
'cause two weeks in New York is worth
sixty years of a hilltop in Tibet.

And if it's the miracle of nature you want,
which is more the miracle:
that field of daisies behind your house
or that one crocus pushing up though
the sidewalk on Bank Street?

Peace of mind is what I mean,
this quilt of roofs
our lively patchwork,
this urban potpourri,
this hybrid vigor,
no constraint of
white picket fence,
not how much space you have but
how much space you are.

DIANE ACKERMAN

Born in a northern suburb of Chicago in 1948, Diane Ackerman has been a social worker in New York and a teacher at both Columbia University and New York University. Apart from her poetry, she has written on nature and the natural world, as in her collection of essays *The Moon by Whale Light, and Other Adventures among Bats, Penguins, Crocodilians, and Whales*. This poem tells the experience of many millions of immigrants who entered New York with a dream still dreamt today.

HUNGARIAN WOMAN ON ELLIS ISLAND, 1907

PHOTOGRAPHED BY LOUIS HINE

Rumbled from steerage,
she wears an embroidered blouse
and seventeen petticoats
whose hems hide money,
documents, even love letters.

Renewal is the private fortune
she brings, learned partly
in steerage's carnival of filth
where five hundred sailed for weeks
in one shuddering, bolting room,
seasick all the way
on soup and stale biscuits;
gagging on bad air, tobacco,
fruit rinds, garlic, and sweat;
sleeping on cork life preservers,
but mainly awake for rats
and the rhythmic clatter
of metal railings and hawsers.

She half expected to find
a golden turnstile ahead,
or two gigantic gates spread open
in embrace, not an island fortress
floating in mist off Manhattan
whose skyline she first mistook
for a mountain range.

Clean-shaven American men
herded her through mazes and exams,
at one low lifting her eyelids
with buttonhooks, at another
feeding her ladlefuls of prunes.
When they chopped her name
it was a kind of circumcision.

What else had she left
but her only heirloom, *Grenstovak?*
Green fell from the clouds
and she slipped it on,
because America was her open sesame
to a world honeyed with drama,
full of dreamers and risk takers,
and Ellis Island the eye of a needle

through which she wished
to pass the camel of her hope.

In this photograph
posed with stoic candor
outside the Main Hall
where all wait for the ferry ride
through slick waters,
she holds her bundles and child
as if balancing separate thoughts.
Dark as horse chestnuts,
her eyes seem to shout.

She does not know that she will give birth
to poets and farmers,
astronauts, sales corps, tamers of cities.
All that is distant haze in 1907.
When the photographer finishes,
she looks at the mint-green saint in the harbor,
and vows that its long gesture
from earth to sky
will be the path she blazes,
her torch to time.

DAVID LEHMAN

Born in New York City in 1948, founder and series editor of the Best American Poetry series, author of *The Last Avant-Garde*—the story of the poets and painters of the 1950s in New York—and poetry coordinator of the New School Writing Program in New York, David Lehman, like many New Yorkers, had little affection for the Twin Towers until the first attack on February 28, 1993.

THE WORLD TRADE CENTER (1993)

I never liked the World Trade Center.
When it went up I talked it down
As did many other New Yorkers.
The twin towers were ugly monoliths
That lacked the details the ornament the character
Of the Empire State Building and especially
The Chrysler Building, everyone's favorite,
With its scalloped top, so noble.
The World Trade Center was an example of what was wrong
With American architecture,
And it stayed that way for twenty-five years
Until that Friday afternoon in February
When the bomb went off and the buildings became
A great symbol of America, like the Statue
Of Liberty at the end of Hitchcock's *Saboteur.*
My whole attitude toward the World Trade Center
Changed overnight. I began to like the way
It comes into view as you reach Sixth Avenue
From any side street, the way the tops
Of the towers dissolve into white skies
In the east when you cross the Hudson
Into the city across the George Washington Bridge.

MICHAEL BLUMENTHAL

Born in 1949 to German-refugee parents, Michael Blumenthal has a law degree from Cornell but abandoned his practice for poetry. He has published six books of poetry and translated the poems of Peter Kantor from Hungarian. Formerly the director of creative writing at Harvard, the poet lives now in Texas but writes with heartfelt recollection about his old neighborhood on Manhattan's Upper West Side.

WASHINGTON HEIGHTS, 1959 ☆

Even the bad news came slowly and was afraid.
Grandmothers tapped their way up the steep hill
to Bennett Park, gradual as mealybugs along
the stem of a coleus. A pink rubber ball, some
small boy's humble playground, would roll by,
and some gray girl would lift to where the mind
said step but the old legs wouldn't answer.

Trees danced their lonely dance in fields of concrete.
Each one we came to, we called: country. What grass
we knew lived by the river, a place our mothers called:
don't play there, it isn't safe anymore. Safety
was the day's dull wisdom, their past a net we swam
against, a high tide. Risk was small and fragile, tied
to a wave called future, sinking every laugh it came upon.

Fishing, our bait was bubble gum and daydreams,
our creels filled with old beer cans wished to bass,
prophylactics weaving like white eels in a Hudson
we dreamt clean as a mountain river. Five old bottles
meant a chance to find your hero and a piece of bubble
gum besides, snow a chance to claim your arms again.

Childhood reading was obituaries in *Aufbau*: name,
maiden name, place of birth, surviving relatives,
death the one occasion we were sure of. Black ties
meant another neighbor wouldn't be there anymore,
candles that memory would find us. Scarred bricks
held auditions for home plate, lines on pavement
drew a floor for dancing.

Saturday was Sabbath and the slow turned slower.
Those who couldn't carry with their arms grew heavy
with their faith. Each year, we set the table
for a man who never came, ate bitter herbs,
read aloud some dreams that never quite rang true.

Constancy was Mario, tapping his Cats Paw heels to walk
on old cloth shoes stretched wide with aching. His
deep black hair turned gray with years, but the sound
of hammer to rubber to steel stayed firm with a sense
of praying. Friends died and aging backs bent towards
the earth, slow and predictable as corn husks in November.
As long as the mail kept coming, we smiled, waited
for the ice truck, buried the dead, called it home.

ANDREA CARTER BROWN

Born in Paterson, New Jersey, in 1949, Andrea Carter Brown moved to New York and edited the periodical *Barrow Street*, living downtown until forced from her neighborhood after the terrorist attacks on the World Trade Center, which is the subject of this poem—told in couplets, like the Twin Towers, which are never mentioned. This poem originally appeared in *Poetry After 9/11*, and recently Ms. Carter won the 2004 River Styx Poetry Prize for her sonnet crown *September 12*.

THE OLD NEIGHBORHOOD ☆

Where is the man who sold the best jelly donuts and coffee
you sipped raising a pastel blue Acropolis to your lips? Two

brothers who arrived in time for lunch hour with hot and cold
heroes where Liberty dead ends at the Hudson? The courteous

small-boned Egyptian in white robe and crocheted skullcap
in the parking lot behind the Greek Orthodox shrine whose

bananas and dates you could always count on? How about
the tall, slim, dark brown man with dreadlocks cascading

to his waist who grilled Hebrew National franks to perfection
and knew just the right amount of mustard each knish wanted?

The cinnamon-skinned woman for whose roti people lined up
halfway down Church, the falafel cousins who remembered

how much hot pepper you preferred? Don't forget the farmers
who schlepped up from Cape May twice each week at dawn

to bring us whatever was in season at its peak: last August,
blueberries and white peaches. What about the lanky fellow

who sold green and red and yellow bears and fish and snakes
in plastic sandwich bags with twist ties; his friend, a block

away, who scooped still warm nuts from a silver cauldron
into pal-sized wax paper sacks he twisted at the corners

to close? The couple outside the post office with their neatly
laid out Golden Books, the shy Senegalese with briefcases

of watches except in December when they sold Christmas
trees? The Mr. Softee who parked every evening rush hour

by the cemetery to revive the homeward hurrying crowd?
I know none of their names, but I can see their faces clear

as I still see everything from that day as I ride away from
the place we once shared. Where are they now? And how?

C. D. WRIGHT

Born in a small Arkansas town in 1949, C. D. Wright received an M.A. from the University of Arkansas. She has published ten volumes of poetry as well as two state literary maps, one of Arkansas and the other Rhode Island, where she was named state poet from 1994 through 1999. She teaches at Brown University.

SPRING STREET GIRLFRIEND (#8) ☆

In the snug harbors, helicopters and electric eel
blink like stringlight in the pathetic, exhaust-resistant trees.
There has to be one more night like this, and then
peace and prosperity will reign for an even minute.
The vendor's hands don't look very clean, but we knew
it was a dirty city. The chestnuts smell deceptively good; we're
hungry even though they are mealy, and then
she comes down in her otis elevator holding a cricket cage.
She purposely wears the purple terrycloth robe of nobility.
The music scarcely changes up until now, and then
with the tiniest monogrammed scissors we snip
a ribbon of undergraduate hair.
She offers the food of her breasts.
She does not give a fig for our depression
glass; she's not into collectibles.
She does not rust or crack; up to this point
we know no more than two of the names under which she wrote
nor her intellectual milieu. The buddha
in the takeout emanates an unknown strain of mercy,
and then we get suddenly scared and tell the driver
we want transfers to the real world
where the fish smell like fish and the cheese like cheese.

TOM SLEIGH

Tom Sleigh was born in 1953 in Texas, and since producing his first collection, *After One*, in 1983, he has emerged as a strong, new voice in contemporary poetry, sharply mixing, as he does here, people and place. The title alludes to the visionary, merciless Commissioners' Plan of 1811 that flattened the middle of Manhattan and established an orderly, rectangular—some critics say inhuman—pattern of streets and avenues.

THE GRID

☆

Faces swell, then flatten into the million-celled grid
of windows that keeps replicating day and night
until no part of the sky remains unlit.

Words spoken between chasms of the avenues
are sucked up into stillness after rain:
Is my strength the strength of stones? Is my flesh of brass?

Lying on the sidewalk, tendons bulging in his wrists,
he stares straight into the armada of rush hour shoes,
his head lolling backward at a hard right angle to his neck

as the police hoist him by his armpits and sockless ankles.
Under the purple blackness of his face
a jaundiced pallor shadows the whites, unblinking, of his eyes.

The waters wear the stones. My face is foul with weeping
and on my eyelids is the shadow of death.
Sunlight steams up from humid pavement,

the subway air-shafts warmly breathe,
the parapets of the bridge towers gleam
through mist swirling off the water's satin-sheen.

Smoking, joking, he used to recline on one elbow
in front of the storefronts' steel-grated doors,
his boutique laid out on the sidewalk: A child's overalls,

soggy magazines, jewelry nicked and scratched . . .
Down river, huddled on the thin ledges of granite
the fledging kestrels reach toward their mothers' beaks,

the traffic blare funneling up past the office windows
to expand and mingle with the brine-tinged air,
the tugboats lifting and falling in the swell
that rolls beneath the heaving pier. Now another vendor

spreads out his wares in the same square of sidewalk, his hands
gently laying out each cast-off garment.

The other's goods still lie on the cement-damp
canvas laundry sack that each day he carefully unpacked.
By midnight his sack will be scavenged clean,

the aura of his hands on the canvas
already fading beneath the warmth of another's palms,
his square of the city washing back into the grid

that arranges and rearranges into the lights and darks
of numbered faces pressed into the coroner's files. . .
Hast thou entered into the springs of the sea?

Have the gates of death been opened unto thee?
When I looked for good, then evil came unto me.
The river's mouth widens, pouring out past

the harbor to open ocean, black swells
running off the freighters' hulls. Drifting in the mist
looms the island where they hung the mutineer,

up river lies the entrance to the tunnel
that runs beneath the waters,
those cuttings mark the tracks that radiate outward

toward the cities spread out across the plain,
and there under the mountain through lightless caverns,
the sun at night makes its smoldering way.

KIM ADDONIZIO

Now a teacher and writer in California, Kim Addonizio was born in Washington, D.C., in 1954. Her poem concerns matters dear to the children of immigrants' children, the second generation Americans who seek, a little wistfully, their origins more through their grandparents than their own parents. For most of us, the search is inevitably through New York.

GENERATIONS

Somewhere a shop of hanging meats,
shop of stink and blood, block and cleaver;

somewhere an immigrant, grandfather, stranger
with my last name. That man

untying his apron in 1910, scrubbing off
the pale fat, going home past brownstones

and churches, past vendors, streetcars, arias,
past the clatter of supper dishes, going home

to his new son, my father—
What is he to me, butcher with sausage fingers,

old Italian leaning over a child somewhere
in New York City, somewhere alive, what is he

that I go back to look for him, years after his death
and my father's death, knowing only

a name, a few scraps my father fed me?
My father who shortened that name, who hacked off

three lovely syllables, who raised American children.
What is the past to me

that I have to go back, pronouncing that word
in the silence of a cemetery, what is this stone

coming apart in my hands like bread, name
I eat and expel? Somewhere the smell of figs

and brine, strung garlic, rosemary and olives;
somewhere that place. Somewhere a boat

rocking, crossing over, entering the harbor. I wait
on the dock, one face in a crowd of faces. Souls

disembark and stream towards the city,
and though I walk among them for hours,

hungry, haunting their streets,
I can't tell which one of them is mine.

Somewhere a steak is wrapped in thick paper,
somewhere my grandmother is laid in the earth,

and my young father shines shoes on a corner,
turning his back to the old world, forgetting.

I walk the night city, looking up at lit windows,
and there is no table set for me, nowhere

I can go to be filled. This is the city
of grandparents, immigrants, arrivals,

where I've come too late with my name,
an empty plate. This is the place.

BARBARA ELOVIC

Barbara Elovic was born in 1954. Her poems have appeared in several anthologies, including *Walk on the Wild Side: Urban American Poetry Since 1975* (Scribner's) and *Lights in Many Windows* (Milkweed, 1997). She published a chapbook, *Time Out*, in 1996.

BROOKLYN BOUND

As if posed for a picture called "Restless Youth"

three kids stand on the footbridge
that spans the Stillwell Avenue station
and look out past the trains and the concession

stands of Coney Island—Nathan's Famous, a shrine built ☆
to the hot dog, and Disco Beat Bumper Cars—
toward the ocean and the subtler blue of the sky.

Did they catch the Mermaid Parade
that afternoon on the Boardwalk?
Women and girls in glitter and green blankets
enthroned in wagons and wheelchairs,
flapped their fin-bound legs
when reminded by their mothers

welcoming summer to Brooklyn shores.
As the mermaids rolled by, the Aqua String Band played along
pulling everyone's attention off the water, the horizon

and its promise of no limits.
It's Saturday, only four o'clock—what else have they to do?
Hours of daylight before them, the kids

hesitate before boarding the train
that bends achingly, as beautiful in the arc of its tracks
as the flight of any bird, away from the water.

EVE PACKER

Born in the Bronx in 1955 and educated at the University of Michigan, the London School of Economics, and NYU, Eve Packer has taught at Queens College and the New School. She occasionally performs her poems with jazz and dance accompaniment. Her collection *Playland: Poems, 1994–2004* (Fly By Night Press) records the dangerous, gritty, yet thrilling character of Times Square decades before it became a safe, corporate part of town.

PLAYLAND

Playland it was called playland hector valentine took me
well I guess I was 14 hector valentine used to sit in the back of
math class
throw spitballs you know he was tall & thin I just thought
he was cool anyway he took me to playland I dont remember a
thing
except we got pizza I vomited in the gutter—well I mean
you didnt go to 42nd there were whores

& pimps & thiefs & stuff, you didnt even look at
the neon cause it was just too dangerous to glance
at what it might be saying well a little later in spring
probably kurt who was black so I cldnt take him home
& he certainly wasnt gonna take me home we used to go
to the movie houses they were $2 they must have
been a dollar or less no they must have been a dollar

& sit up in the black row of the balcony & make-out cause
where else were we gonna make-out, I think we were totally
oblivious to the activities arnd us & they were probably
oblivious to us—before I see 42nd again
I was in college I was in europe then when I
came back

I got to be an actress & you just live
at 42nd I used to think it was so strange you know here you
are in this 'respectable profession' I guess you can see
its roots esp for women are definitely in whoredom cause thats
the district so there you are going to yr audition on those streets
in the w. 50's but you gotta walk by the 40's on the way to the

subway, & you sorta squinch yrself up make yr field of vision
tiny like
a mini-horse w/blinders so you dont see the secret shame
marquees but also so noone will see or hit on you before you
manage to get downstairs toss yr token in the slot
ride home & say oh no that place doesnt exist, oh no my life has
nothing
to do w/42nd—
playland—it was called playland—

MARTIN ESPADA

Martin Espada was born in Brooklyn in 1957. A former bouncer, tenant lawyer, and editor for *Ploughshares*, he is now a professor at the University of Massachusetts–Amherst. His 1993 *City of Coughing and Dead Radiators* is set in both New York and Puerto Rico. In these poems he writes first of magic found in the most familiar and neglected places, then of the dark cautions and inexhaustible hope of children in the city's neglected neighborhoods.

THE OWL AND THE LIGHTNING

—BROOKLYN, NEW YORK

No pets in the projects,
the lease said,
and the contraband salamanders
shriveled on my pillow overnight.
I remember a Siamese cat, surefooted
I was told, who slipped from a window ledge
and became a red bundle
bulging in the arms of the janitor.

This was the law on the night
the owl was arrested.

He landed on the top floor,
through the open window
of apartment 14-E across the hall,
a solemn white bird bending the curtain rod.
In the cackling glow of the television,
his head swiveled, his eyes black.
The cops were called, and threw a horse blanket
over the owl, a bundle kicking.

Soon after, lightning jabbed the building,
hit apartment 14-E, scattering bricks from the roof
like beads from a broken necklace.
The sky blasted white, detonation of thunder.
Ten years old at the window, I knew then that God
was not the man in my mother's holy magazines,
touching fingertips to dying foreheads
with the half-smile of an athlete signing autographs.

God must be an owl, electricity
coursing through the hollow bones,
a white wing brushing the building.

DAY OF THE DEAD ON WORTMAN AVENUE

Halloween in Brooklyn:
wearing the baggy costumes
of monsters, we were not allowed
to fill our bags
outside the sullen brick building
where we lived,
because, the voices said,
real monsters peered
between the slats of benches
in the projects.
One shot the grocer, and the witness,
a woman who worshipped a dry God,
needed rum for the first time.

At 245 Wortman Avenue
bedsheet ghosts pounded doors
that opened on a leash of chain,
then banged shut to shield hermits
with white hair and burglarized faces,
stunned at night by the slapped-mouth madrigal
of a woman somewhere in the building.

From doorways suspicious hands
lifted the masks of comic book heroes
to avoid feeding the same hero twice,
index fingers lecturing on gratitude
to children who pissed
in a malicious shower
from 10th-floor terraces
of concrete and chicken wire
on other nights.

Drunk on chocolate,
shoving and bickering,
we sorted the bags by night's end,
wary of pins and razors,
trashing unwrapped possible poison
in the hallway incinerator,
crematorium of dead cats.

So the Day of the Dead
was celebrated on Wortman Avenue
with the lust of a paranoid
for the enemy,
beating steam pipes with a broom
for silence overhead,
growling threats at the ceiling.

BROOKE WIESE

Born in Norwalk, Connecticut, in 1957, Brooke Wiese received an M.F.A. from Columbia University and works as an administrator for a nonprofit social service organization in East Harlem. Her writing has appeared in various journals and anthologies, and, as is true with other love poems set in New York, it's unclear who, or what, is the object of the love, a person or the city.

GOING HOME MADLY

I walked the two blocks from the subway down
the hill toward the mosque beside the new
Islamic school to my tumble-down
tenement just off Second Avenue.

The moon was new, a sliver rising over
Queens. The sky was plush as crushed velvet—
a midnight blue wedding lapel purpling over
the East River like the inside of a clamshell.

The scythelike moon atop the minaret
was silhouetted black against the sky
and I, going home madly
in love with you, in debt up to my eyes

and needing succor badly, and repair,
and almost lost, almost broken,
with nothing but my ragged heart to offer—
a warm and bloody token beating there

in my outstretched palm like some Edgar Allan Poe prize—
saw the crescent of the real moon rise
up over the solid dark dome of the mosque
with its mirror-image sickle moon on top.

Behind, the East River (oily, black as a bassoon)
boiled up in its banks like a *Cubop* tune,

and in the air, suspended, a double strand ☆
of lights going over, and Queens, darkly beyond.

Sometimes this city chokes me up with all
her jagged beauty, and sometimes I am made new,
like tonight, when I walked back up the hill
and 'round the block again because of you.

TONYA BOLDEN

Born in New York in 1959, Tonya Bolden graduated magna cum laude at Princeton before receiving a master's from Columbia. She is the author or editor of more than twenty books, most for children and teens, including *33 Things Every Girl Should Know* as well as *Wake Up Our Souls: A Celebration of Black American Artists*. She lives in the Bronx.

BELLA

I.

he has my nine-ninety-nine per pound parmesan in hand
grate it?
no, i smile
he smiles back, weighs the wedge

i've got seven-forty-nine worth and he,
still a smile as he slaps the price onto plastic wrap

grazie, bella
grazie, i nod, i smile

an elderly italian who
slices cold cuts
weighs cheese

scoops up salads: quarter-pound, half-pound, whatever-the-
customer-wants—
this man
without leer to the lip
without a tease of sleaze in his eyes
has made my day

bella

do i look the part?

nose still cold from the cold
eyes still in sorta-shock from so much white trudged
through, by
to reach this bronx met food
bundled in a five- six- nine-year-old
soldier-green
parka-type coat, head
swaddled in autumnal-patterned shawl-scarf
capped by cheap black knitty
spirit chapped
grungy red gloves inside the wnyc canvas tote i
tote to the market
so as not to take up so many plastic bags
so as not to contribute
(so much)
to the trashing of america
bella

when you are over forty and have lost your mother and
finally understand why
when you were young
women older than your mother *always* had hand lotion
in their handbags—

when you come to see gray hair has a will of her own—

when *that's youth for you!* is common in your parlance—

when you wonder how you might contend with days of
depends and
attend to ads for undereye creams—

you are not nonchalant about a *grazie, bella*
i'm flashbacked to wonder years in a part of harlem where
eye-talians
part of the norm alongside ricans and
my people morphing from negro to black
bella

and i loved that carnival in july
herald of the festival starring a gigantor lady saint i never
prayed to
(not being catholic)
being carried round-around the block
and people cheered
and i ate five-cent fruit ices
bella

so nice
needed on the day i learned from aol
al qaeda might have holiday gifts for us
again? i wonder
as i've wondered other autumn, winter, spring,
summer, wintry autumn days
my hometown?
my still-bruised new york?
again?

shopping for food, provisioning up
calms my nerves

II.

sad but soothing on the way home
lapsing into memories of my city before

long before
the ugly day

back when the empire
the tallest
some subway seats still like wicker
tokens tiny like dimes

back when there was no cable
back when there was woolworths
back when there were no play dates instead
doorbell belled or
intercom buzzed—
can tonya come out-n-play?

back when yorkville
closer to quaint, dotted with descendants of old world shops,
where
mommy picked out special spices
delicacies for holiday meals or
seven-layer cake or
maybe marzipan
for my birthday or
just because
I was her child

back when an egg cream
not so uncommon
breakfast at dubrows a saturday morning extra when I ☆
went to work with daddy,
to the rag trade:
him working
me working
(stamp-stamp-stamping o'grady & bialer on
bills of lading, envelopes, boxes)
me taking my work serious
(daddy said it was important!)

me trying to stamp *real-real* straight
me hanging around by his side
me over the years
naturally, organically
learning
chanukah gilt, gefilte fish, whitefish, lox, sittin shiva
and having fond memories of redhead belle sending the family
a few pounds of her ownmade chopped liver in decembers

back when living multicultural
was not a work, an agenda, just
the everyday way of a life

and baychester had more bluejays
and some summer evenings the sharpening man
(scissors, knives, lawn mower blades)
cruised the block hoping for business
and eggs and milk a milkman delivered, really dressed in white

and mommy
dinnered us with chicken, turkey, ground round, pig
knuckles, sausage, mutton, from
gruff-but-nice-smiling
twinkle-eyed
accent-light-italian phil
who never called my mother *bella* i don't think:
hello, mrs. bolden, what can i get ya today, mrs. bolden?
i can orderem for ya, mrs. bolden

cornish hens i so loved, a sometimes or once-a-year treat, like
dinner in chinatown
sightseeing christmas lights in westchester
sightseeing the groovy in the village—
daddy, can we go to the bowery?

daddy sometimes obliging
not asking why baby girl likes to sightsee people it used to be
okay to call

bums, but
daddy
    (and mommy)
pearling the grim adventure into a lesson:
on counting your blessings
on praying for the less fortunate
on what not to be when you grow up

back when white castle car hops quick-snapped yellow trays onto
windows of cars
    (most without ac)
wore minis
even when the hawk was out
and nyc had drive-ins and a child could delight in a drive out to the
nearest mcdonalds
    (in jersey)
    (not much more to the menu than hamburger, cheeseburger,
        shakes,
fries)
    (nothing super-sized)
or to the paramus dairy queen, where
one july day we crowded around our long silver-gray
        oldsmobile, her
radio loud
cheering one man's one small step

and i reach home with provisions
a bit stronger, braver
braced for this twenty-first-century life.

JULIA KASDORF

A professor at New York University, Julia Kasdorf was born in Pennsylvania in 1962 to Mennonite parents who left their rural life for the city. Her sensual poem blends women, the past, and the present together in a part of New York that still survives.

LADIES' NIGHT AT THE TURKISH AND RUSSIAN BATHS ☆

Outside, it's any tenement on East Tenth Street;
at the head of the stairs I drop my watch,
keys, wallet into a slender metal box
and take a robe of thin cotton sheeting.
Past the case of smoked fish, I pull off
my clothes among napping strangers and descend
marble steps stained with a century's grit.

In the steam room, an old woman looks up;
slender gourds hang off the cage of her ribs,
and when she wrings the pink cloth on her crotch,
I see a bun, bald as a girl's, and think *crone*,
ashamed. She runs weary eyes down my form,
then closes them.

Along the plunge pool, supple women stroke
green mud on their cheekbones and stretch
their legs between plastic palms. Above them,
a compote of brilliant tile fruit and the name
of an Italian mason. I love to think of him
telling his son about this place, or how it was
in the thirties, filled with immigrants
from cold-water flats, one of them
with eyes like Franz Kafka could not afford
to come here, but did, breathing steam for hours,
not needing to remember the names of things,
only sweating out the soot of New York, safe
as I feel in the hot cave where women drape
between streaming spigots. Some murmur,
most are silent, except when one
grabs a bucket and dumps it onto her chest
with a groan. Our eyes meet and we grin,
grateful to show and view the real shapes
of ourselves: so many different breasts

and hips that get smoothed over by clothes,
none of us looking like we're supposed to!

And after, our hair wrapped up in towels,
we climb to a roof that faces the back
of Ninth Street where strangers pass by lit
windows, cooking dinner, opening letters.
We stretch out there on cots, and beside me
tears slide like sweat into the turban
of a stunning young woman. Whatever
the reason, I feel bound to her weeping,
eyes locked on our city's sky
aglow with all that lies beneath it.

DAVID BERMAN

Born in Virginia in 1967, David Berman published the first release of Open City Books, his poetry collection *Actual Air*, and he also writes and performs with the rock band Silver Jews. In this poem, a vision of a new city is haunted by an annoying, persistent problem.

NEW YORK, NEW YORK

A second New York is being built
a little west of the old one.
Why another, no one asks,
just build it, and they do.

The city is still closed off
to all but the work crews
who claim it's a perfect mirror image.

Truthfully, each man works on the replica
of the apartment building he lived in,
adding new touches,

like cologne dispensers, rock gardens,
and doorknobs marked for the grand hotels.

Improvements here and there, done secretly
and off the books. None of the supervisors
notice or mind. Everyone's in a wonderful mood,
joking, taking walks through the still streets
that the single reporter allowed inside has described as

"unleavened with reminders of the old city's complicated past,
but giving off some blue perfume from the early years on earth."

The men grow to love the peaceful town.
It becomes more difficult to return home at night,

which sets the wives to worrying.
The yellow soups are cold, the sunsets quick.

The men take long breaks on the fire escapes,
waving across the quiet spaces to other workers
meditating on the perches.

Until one day . . .

The sky fills with charred clouds.
Toolbelts rattle in the rising wind.

Something is wrong.

A foreman stands in the avenue
pointing binoculars at a massive gray mark
moving towards us in the eastern sky.

Several voices, What, What is it?
Pigeons, he yells through the wind.

JOEL BROUWER

Joel Brouwer was born in Michigan in 1968, attended Sarah Lawrence College and Syracuse University, and is associate professor at the University of Alabama. His first book, *Exactly What Happened*, appeared in 1999. This timeless conflict between the city and nature occurs just north of Seventy-second Street off Fifth Avenue, home to the Central Park Model Yacht since 1916.

CONSERVATORY POND, CENTRAL PARK, NEW YORK, NEW YORK

The model yachts contend in seas sheltered
from any wave while their captains fidget
on the concrete shore, fingers sticky

with ice cream and Cracker Jack, less intrigued
by the tiny jibs and rudders of their ships
than their grandfathers would like.

Beyond the armada, on the far shore,
a flock of birders flutters into view.
They snap together telescopes and tripods,

screw four-foot lenses into cameras,
and vanish in a thicket of magnification
just as their quarry, a red-tailed hawk, dives

from his nest high above Fifth Ave., snatches
a squirrel off the grass not ten feet away,
and banks into an oak to eat. Equipment

superfluous, the birders stare up rapt.
The crowd grows fast: yuppies on mountain bikes,
Haitian nannies pushing strollers, some drunks,

the young skippers, their rankled guardians.
Fifty heads tilt and swivel like radar
as the hawk drags its prey from branch to branch.

A woman in a filthy Mets sweatshirt
stops tossing popcorn to the chipmunks, screams
Drop it, fucker! Go back to the goddamn forest!

She hurls rocks, misses. But the hawk, flustered,
bobbles, and the torn gray rag falls
at her bandaged feet. Guts shiny with blood. Eyes

augered out. The crowd looks around. We see
how close we're standing, begin to inch apart.
In the pond, the abandoned boats collide, go down.

YVONNE C. MURPHY

Yvonne C. Murphy was born in 1968 and received an M.A. in creative writing from New York University and a Ph.D. in creative writing from the University of Houston. A member of the faculty of the Long Island Center of Empire State College, she writes in this poem of two New York legends—Marianne Moore and Coney Island's iconic roller coaster.

THE CYCLONE ☆

Marianne was fond of roller coasters; a fearless rider, she preferred to sit in the front seat.

—ELIZABETH BISHOP,
FROM HER ESSAY "EFFORTS OF AFFECTION"

Nautilus of wood and steel—tracks twisted
into an exoskeleton of spirals. World famous,
"Faster than Ever," the Cyclone's drops
and turns, speeds reaching sixty miles per hour.

Charles Lindburgh said it was "scarier than flying
the Atlantic solo," but Miss Moore, our poet-hero,
prefers the front seat. Her hands rest gently around
the safety bar, waiting for the first drop *as if they knew love*
is the only fortress strong enough to trust to . . .

The sailors in the car behind her punch and jab
each other, twist brass buttons in anticipation.
"Surfs up," seagulls cry between dives for hot dog
scraps scattered under benches. All this treasure,
lively amongst them. Marianne isn't looking back,
the loop-di-loops fling her forward, catapulting gusto.
The Dreamland flea-market glitters with sun, circus
freaks dangle charms to gawkers, screams from the coaster
weave in and out through tight layers of day.

Such structure supporting chaos, thrills engineered
to appear spontaneous. Marianne is in her element—
the sailors gasp as her hair clips pop into their laps.
The celebrated braid swings wild in the air. On the ground,
Kewpie dolls pucker while boys throw balls at bottles
arranged in towers. Marianne's hair dances its own miracle.
This is mortality, she sighs, *this is eternity . . .*

MARK WUNDERLICH

Born in 1968, Mark Wunderlich taught at Columbia University and is now professor of literature at Bennington College in Vermont. His collection *Voluntary Servitude* appeared in 2004. This chilling poem tells of the city's indifference that awaits some New Yorkers.

EAST SEVENTH STREET

I love to ride the D train just to emerge from the tunnel
and see the sun dipping, toxic, into New Jersey's petroleum
    shimmer,

beyond the yellow mass of taxis that cruise the streets like sharks.
When I think of Manhattan, I think of the baby carriage

on Second Avenue cradling a man's small family—
two dogs, a cat, and a goose in a milk crate, craning
her neck like some dangerous flower. All January
they worked the line at the cash machine, ankle deep

in a litter of receipts, clicking the security lock to the Avenue's
petulant slur. I spent my first winter here, five stories up,
smoking, at a hobbled kitchen table, laying out postcards
of cities I'd never live in, an imagined map of disappointments,

paper ghosts. One floor below a thin young man was being
burnt down
to an essence. I was neither keeper nor witness to it. We
never spoke.
Once I dreamed I leapt from the window ledge, spread crude
wings
and flew like the newspaper angels that ride the City's

air current whips. Below me, the streets were made luminous
as I pitched across valleys the buildings carve
through soot-particulated air, before I set down
on a rain-darkened, black-cobbled street. In 7-D

the young man died. No relatives came. Only medics
sterile with masks, their gurney chroming in the dim hallway,
to usher his cooling body to the street. For three days
his apartment door swung open while neighbors sifted

through his things in a city where someone's always poor enough
to covet what's been cast off, and where the mirror
I took from the apartment reflects my face instead of his.
Outside, today, the season tightens into its more contemplative
notes,

breaking from summer's excess, while locusts
cut their last swaths through the park's unmowed field.
In the subway tunnels, the arriving train carries with it
a whisper of smoke. Somewhere underground a fire is burning.

KEVIN COVAL

Born in Chicago in 1975, Kevin Coval appeared four times in HBO's *Def Poetry Jam* and is founder of the Chicago Teen Poetry Festival. He is the author of *Slingshots (A Hip-Hop Poetica)*. This poems reaches for the eternal wonder, conflict, and endless variety found on the city's streets.

LURED BENEATH YOUR GOLDEN, CALLING LIGHTS

AFTER CARL SANDBURG FOR BI AND SHL

it is impossible to know you,
impossible to gather all i can
in my arms and claim to have an idea
of your immensity.

even when i see you
on Broadway, in white knit Kangols
and circus hoop silver bangles, your sweet roast
almond scent. even when you pull my body flat
against yours i still feel foreign, or that you
are a foreigner or that sometimes this experiment
will not last. at some point the Nigerian doctors
picking up used straws in the Angelica film center
or the Pakistani cabbie or Chilean hot pretzel vendor
or my midwestern uncle working three jobs
for child support, will collapse in your lap
with white flag or fire.
i've been tempted

to rent an apartment in morning-
side heights, but
                                        you are an impossible dream
                                        i scream myself awake in.
too immense,
        intense,
never mine to grasp,
a Coney Island carousel
        of images,
you whirl too fast.

you are an express train,
i never know which track you'll be on:

the Indian restaurant at 94th and Amsterdam
its slide metal gates on glass windows,
i can no longer look in and see
the table we first sat at.

the all night diner
where you ordered rice pudding
in Union Square, is a Sports Club
for people who can afford one.

you have changed,
have always been
changing.
                  but
damn! you look good,
                                        new york
you court me,
                  again.
                                      (again?, new york)

at 3rd and Mercer
we felt like tea, and i knew you
would suggest Cafe Reggio,
though i had not been there

since '94 and couldn't remember
its location or name but felt its windows
would open to the street and be perfect
after-dinner in spring, sitting
in metal-wire chairs, blackberry supreme
pot steeping on the two-top wooden table,
i knew i could love you again, (though I know you are not
    mine alone
& chicago will not want to hear this, but . . .)

your civilized all-hour tomatoes!
your fresh flower fields littering the fronts of bodegas!
your subway lines: vast and democratic!
your bootlegs sleeping on blankets like dominos!
your two model per train car city ordinance!
all those mixed babies blurring neighborhood lines!
your gold space pharaohs slanging veg patties on 125th St.!
your corner kids up late blaring Biggie out 6th floor apartment
    windows!
my grandfather's anglicized name tucked in a book on your
    Ellis Island!
your Grandmaster Flash mash-ups! your Grandwizrad Theodore
    scratch bombs!
your afro-diasporic puerto rican borough global exports!
your shtick, new york, each one of you sounds like a jew
and even italians know how to make good bagels!
you are the ultimate reality / check! the last of bastion
of schmer and empire. the american ideal gone
                                        mad

and perfect

NOTES TO THE POEMS

ACKERMAN, DIANE: "Hungarian Woman on Ellis Island." The most feared part of the inspection on Ellis Island was the examination, done with a buttonhook, for trachoma, an incurable eye disease.

BELL, MARVIN: "These Green-Going-to-Yellow." *Gingko trees* also appear in the poems (not included) "Oh the Gingkos" by Edward Field and Claudia Menza's "Gingkos." See Gary Snyder's "Walking the New York Bedrock Alive in the Sea of Information."

BERRIGAN, TED: "XXXVI." The *Williamsburg Bridge* crosses the East River, was designed by Leffert L. Buck, and opened in 1903. It connects Delancey Street on Manhattan's Lower East Side to Marcy Avenue in Williamsburg, Brooklyn. *Perry* is a Greenwich Village street named for Oliver N. Perry, commander of the American fleet in the War of 1812 at the Battle of Lake Erie.

BLACKBURN, PAUL: "Bryant Park." Once the city's reservoir, the park behind the New York Public Library suffered—like much of the city—from drug dealing and crime in the 1970s (when it was known as Needle Park), but the Bryant Park Restoration Corporation remade it as a beautiful Midtown oasis.

BLUMENTHAL, MICHAEL: "Washington Heights, 1959." Named for Fort Washington, which was built by the Continental Army during the American Revolution, *Washington Heights* (or Harlem Heights) is a northern Manhattan neighborhood, rural until the early twentieth century. The table setting *for a man who never came* is for the prophet Elijah, whose spirit visits the Seder table during Passover. *Aufbau*, founded in 1934, was a weekly paper published by the German-Jewish community of New York.

BOLDEN, TONYA: "bella." *Dubrow's*, at 515 Seventh Avenue, was a legendary cafeteria in the garment district.

BORGES, JORGE LUIS: "The Cloisters." Sculptor George Gray Barnard spent years in France finding medieval art in ruined churches, monasteries, barns, and even pigsties, then displayed the items in a building on Fort Washington Avenue in 1914. The Metropolitan Museum of Art, with funds from the Rockefellers, bought the collection in 1925. Shortly afterward, the Fort Tryon property was given to the city by the Rockefeller family. To display the art work, the *Cloisters* was built on a four-and-a-half-acre site made to resemble a medieval cloister, with chapels, halls, and gardens completed in 1938. To insure a good view for the museum's patrons, the Rockefellers acquired and left undeveloped the land directly across the Hudson River. "Der Asra" is the poem by Heinrich Heine (1797–1856) where the Sultan's daughters "wander[ed] in the evening to the fountain" (Louis Untermeyer, trans.). See John Logan's "Manhattan Movements."

BRANCH, ANNA HEMPSTEAD: "New York at Sunrise." The *Tombs* is the common name given to the first (there have been three) Manhattan House of Correction for Men at 100 Centre Street, which resembled an Egyptian tomb taken from an illustration in John L. Stephens's book *Travels* (1837). Junius Henri Browne wrote in *The Great Metropolis* (1869) that the Tombs' "gloomy semblance gave it the name it still bears, and will bear while one block of the dingy stone stands upon another."

BROWN, ANDREA CARTER: "The Old Neighborhood." *Cape May* is in southern New Jersey. *Liberty* and *Church* are streets near the World Trade Center. See David Lehman's "World Trade Center (1993)."

CIARDI, JOHN: "George Washington Bridge." "The most splendid of all Manhattan bridges" (*WPA Guide to New York*) was built in 1931 by Othmar Ammann and spans the Hudson River from 179th Street in Manhattan to Fort Lee, New Jersey. The little red lighthouse from Hildegarde Hoyt Swift's children's tale stands at the base of its eastern tower. Ammann also built the Triboro Bridge and the tremendous Verrazano Narrows Bridge. From his penthouse window he spent much of his old age looking at his glorious work through a telescope.

CLAMPITT, AMY: "Times Square Water Music." The *IRT* is a subway line, the Interborough Rapid Transit Company. *BMT* is the Brooklyn-Manhattan Transit Company. The *N*, *RR*, *Q*, and *B* are subway train lines.

CORN, ALFRED: "Photographs of Old New York." The *Statue of Liberty* was assembled plate by copper plate, all 300 of them. The "glittering door" alludes to Emma Lazarus's "New Colossus."

CORSO, GREGORY: "On the Death of the Lucky Gent." *St. Nicholas Avenue* winds through Harlem from Central Park North (110th Street) to 160th Street and for a while passes through the beautiful district nicknamed "Strivers' Row."

CRANE, HART: "The Tunnel." *Columbus Circle*, at Broadway, 59th Street, and Eighth Avenue (where Central Park West begins) was once a place for trolleys to "circle" and head back up- or downtown. *Floral Park* is in the Flatbush section of Brooklyn where the Culver train line once ran until taken over by the Long Island Rail Road. *Gravesend Manor* is a neighborhood in southwest Brooklyn; *Chambers Street* is in Lower Manhattan; and though "*Wop*" is now a derogatory name for an Italian, the tag originally referred to people, many from Italy, who passed through Ellis Island "with out papers" or W.O.P.

DRAKE, JOSEPH RODMAN: "The Bronx." The *Bronx*—the city's northernmost borough and the only part of New York City connected to mainland America—was named for Jonas Bronck, a Swedish sea captain who settled there in 1639 and is the subject of Elizabeth Akers Allen's poem "The Ballad of the Bronx" (not included).

ELOVIC, BARBARA: "Brooklyn Bound." *Nathan's* ("From a Hot Dog to an International Habit") is a hot dog stand that opened in 1916 on Surf Avenue and had sold more than one million dogs by 1991. The *Mermaid Parade* along the boardwalk began in 1982 as part of Dick Zigun's revival of Coney Island.

FELDMAN, IRVING: "The Handball Players at Brighton Beach." With primarily a Russian Jewish population since the late 1970s, *Brighton Beach* is a neighborhood in southwest Brooklyn between Coney Island and Manhattan Beach, named in 1878 for the resort in England.

FERLINGHETTI, LAWRENCE: "Meet Miss Subways." Elected every eight months by passenger vote—her picture was displayed in all the cars for the next three months—she was immortalized as "Miss Turnstiles" in the 1944 musical *On the Town*. Recently, the idea has been revived.

GINSBERG, ALLEN: "*Rhapsody in Blue*": interview, in *Literary New York*, by Susan Edminston and Linda D. Cirino.

"THE CHARNEL GROUND." *Christine's* is a popular neighborhood Polish restaurant at First Avenue and Twelfth Street. The poet's photograph hangs on the wall. *Stuyvesant Town* is a housing project (population 20,000) from Twentieth Street down to Fourteenth Street and from First Avenue to Avenue C. The *Catholic Church* at Fourteenth Street is the Immaculate Conception Church just east of First Avenue.

GREENBERG, ELIEZER: "Visiting Second Avenue." *Second Avenue* from Fourteenth Street downtown to Houston Street was once referred to as the Jewish Rialto because of its many Yiddish theaters. A most famous meeting place for Jewish intellectuals and unemployed actors was the Café Royal at Second Avenue and Twelfth Street. Leon Trotsky once visited the Monopole on Second Avenue and Ninth Street. Second Avenue is the subject of both paintings and poems, most notably in poetry by Frank O'Hara's epic and experimental *Second Avenue*, which he was writing in Kenneth Koch's "Time Zone."

GROSS, NAFTALI: "The Cemetery at Chatham Square." Founded in 1655, Congregation Shearith-Israel, the oldest Jewish congregation in America (Emma Lazarus was a member), owns three small cemeteries in Manhattan: the first is the subject of Gross's poem; the second, opened in 1805 and closed in 1829, is on W. Eleventh Street just east of Sixth Avenue (of note, though not included, is Grace Schulman's "Jewish Cemetery, Eleventh Street"); and the third is at W. Twenty-first Street off Sixth Avenue. *East Broadway*, once a distinguished avenue with wide sidewalks and beautiful houses, primarily Latin by the 1950s but now almost entirely absorbed by Chinatown, was home to the *Jewish Daily Forward* (at 175, ninth floor) as well as Goodman and Levine's Café, the center for the Yiddish poets who referred to themselves as Di Yunge (the Young Ones).

HALLECK, FITZ-GREENE: "Song." In response to the city's more exclusive clubs, *Tammany Hall* was formed in 1788 and evolved from an organization supporting craftsmen as well as immigrant Irish and Jewish minorities to the city's most powerful—and notoriously corrupt—political machine, including in its membership Mayor Fernando Wood, William "Boss" Tweed, James "Jimmy" Walker, and Alfred E. Smith. Its power was eventually defused with the election of Fiorello LaGuardia.

HALPERN, DANIEL: "Street Fire." Reverend Norman Vincent *Peale* (author of the popular *Power of Positive Thinking*) was pastor of the Marble Collegiate Reformed Church on Fifth Avenue at Twenty-ninth Street.

HOLLANDER, JOHN: *from* "New York." "*Mirabile factu*" (wonder to do or make) is a variation of Virgil's "*mirabile dictu*" (wonder to tell). *Spuyten Duyvil* is a neighborhood in the northwest Bronx. Its name, from the Dutch, means "spirit of the devil." The *Hippodrome* at Sixth Avenue and Forty-third Street was the world's largest theater until it closed in 1939. *Penn Station* (the original, opened in 1910 as "the largest and handsomest [station] in the world," said the *New York Times*), on Seventh Avenue between Thirty-first Street and Thirty-third Street, set "the standard of style, elegance and grandeur . . . of Western man," believed architect critic Ada Louise Huxtable. It was a station where "the voice of time remained aloof and unperturbed," wrote Thomas Wolfe, "a drowsy and eternal murmur below the immense and distant roof." Its waiting room, based on the ancient Roman baths of Caracalla, was as large as the nave of St. Peter's. Designed by McKim, Mead, and White (designers of the New York Post Office across the street on Eighth Avenue), the station was demolished in 1963, its loss eventually leading to the passage of the Landmark Preservation Law. *Ceres*, Roman goddess of agriculture, also appears in Jacob Steendam's "The Complaint of New Amsterdam to Its Mother."

HOWARD, RICHARD: "Old Men Playing Boccie on Leroy Street." *Boccie* is an Italian bowling game somewhat resembling lawn bowling and shuffleboard, at one time so popular that a world championship was first held in Genoa, Italy, in 1951. Boccie courts remained on the predominantly Puerto Rican East First Street until the mid 1990s. *Leroy Street* in Greenwich Village was once part of an Italian neighborhood and was named for Jacob Leroy, a worldwide trader who made huge profits running the British blockade in the War of 1812.

HUGHES, LANGSTON: "The Heart of Harlem." The *Schomberg* is the Schomberg Center for Research in Black Culture, now at 515 Lenox Avenue. The *Apollo*, at 253 W. 125th Street, is still vibrant since opening in 1934, though for a while in the 1970s it was a movie theater. The *Rennie* was the Renaissance Ballroom at Seventh Avenue and 133rd Street. The *Savoy Ballroom* at 596 Lenox, said to be the most beautiful ballroom in the world, closed in 1958. *Small's Paradise* at Seventh Avenue and 135th Street was a nightclub catering mostly to white patrons.

Edgecombe Avenue, from W. 135th Street to W. 155th, is part of "Sugar Hill," where affluent African Americans moved in the 1920s. Thurgood Marshall lived at 409 Edgecombe.

JORDAN, JUNE: "47,000 Windows." The first *Tenement House Act* (plagued with loopholes and inadequate methods of enforcement) passed the state legislature in 1867 and required tenements to have fire escapes and, for every twenty inhabitants, water closets connecting to cesspools—when possible.

JUSTICE, DONALD: "Manhattan Dawn (1945)." *Hudson* and *Horatio* are Greenwich Village streets.

KASDORF, JULIA: "Ladies' Night at the Turkish and Russian Baths." Still active since opening in 1892 and more popular now than in decades, the Tenth Street Baths between First Avenue and Avenue A once played an important part in a community of cold-water flats. Indoor plumbing greatly diminished the need for the more than forty such baths throughout the city, and now only a few remain, with one still at Coney Island.

KEROUAC, JACK: *from* "MacDougal Street Blues." Named for Alexander MacDougal, Revolutionary War general and later the first president of the Bank of New York, *MacDougal Street* in Greenwich Village is one block east of Sixth Avenue and runs from W. Eighth Street to a few blocks below Houston Street. *Joe Gould*, a Greenwich Village bohemian eccentric from the 1920s into the 1950s who imitated seagulls for drinks, is remembered in Joseph Mitchell's "Professor Sea Gull" (*The New Yorker*, December 12, 1942) and *Joe Gould's Secret*. He also appears in Tuli Kupferberg's "Greenwich Village of My Dreams" kissing Maxwell Bodenheim. Of note though not included is Edna St. Vincent's Millay's "Macdougal Street."

KINNELL, GALWAY: "The Avenue Bearing the Initial of Christ into the New World." The avenue referred to, Avenue C, is one of four—Avenues A through D—east of First Avenue running north and south from E. Fourteenth Street downtown to Houston Street and known as Alphabet City, once a rough part of town at the city's edge (see Miguel Piñero's "A Lower East Side Poem"). *Pitt Street* is what Avenue C becomes below Houston Street. The *Mirror* was the *New York Daily Mirror*, a morning newspaper first published in 1924 to compete with the *New York Daily News* but closed in 1963 despite having the second highest circulation of any newspaper in America. The French lines ("Jöis la cloche . . .") are from François Villon's "Legacy," translated by Kinnell himself: "I heard the bell of the Sorbonne / which always tolls at nine o'clock / The salutation the Angel foretold." *Hell Gate* is a narrow strait between Astoria, Queens, and Ward's Island, connecting the East River to Long Island Sound. The German epigraph translates to "the little alleyway was a world unto itself."

KOCH, KENNETH: *from* "A Time Zone." *Frank* is Frank O'Hara, and the *Cedar*—still on University Place, just west of Broadway—was the painters' bar that had, for poet Robert Creeley, "almost . . . a mythical dimension." *The Five Spot* was a club on Cooper Square. Though the poem is filled with Koch's painter and poet friends, at *home* is *Janice*, his first wife. *Boris Pasternak* won the Noble Prize in 1958. *George Washington Crossing the Delaware* is Koch's one-act play inspired by a Larry Rivers painting of the same name and owned by the Metropolitan Museum of Art. *"Stones"* was the only true collaboration between a poet and painter done at a time when many were attempted. *Tenth Street* and *Second Avenue* form the central crossroads of the East Village, and in the early 1950s a renaissance occurred in this neighborhood when the charm and popularity of Greenwich Village drove rents beyond the means of struggling poets and painters who found cheaper dwellings across town. In a 1959 article "East Tenth Street: A Geography of Modern Art," art critic Harold Rosenberg wrote that at least fifty prominent American artists had moved to East Tenth Street and were making "the first art to appear in this country without a foreign address" (*Art News Chronicle* 136). See Tuli Kupferberg's "Greenwich Village of My Dreams."

KUPFERBERG, TULI: "Greenwich Village of My Dreams." *Lewisohn Stadium* is the stadium for the City College of New York, though it was demolished in 1973. *Kleins* and *Ohrbachs* were department stores around Union Square. *Sheridan Square* is a small park in Greenwich Village between Sixth Avenue and Seventh Avenue South. *The Cedar* on University Place—setting for Jack Kerouac's *Subterraneans* (though transplanted to San Francisco)—and the *San Remo* a few blocks to the west were popular hangouts in the 1950s and 1960s. According to Frank O'Hara, the Cedar was primarily a painters' bar, while the San Remo was a writers' bar. "In the San Remo we argued and gossiped: in the Cedar we often wrote poems while listening to the painters argue and gossip. As far as I know nobody painted in the San Remo while they listened to the writers argue." *The Gaslight* was a Bleecker Street coffee house/bar. *The Limelight* was a café on Seventh Avenue South. *MacDougal Street* is just east of Sixth Avenue beginning at W. Eighth Street and running downtown. *Minetta's* is an upscale tavern on MacDougal and Minetta Lane and, legend has it, a favorite of Hemingway. See Kenneth Koch's "Time Zone," Jack Kerouac's "MacDougal Street Blues," and for a later perspective Edward Field's "The Last Bohemians."

LAZARUS, EMMA: "The New Colossus." With broken shackles at her feet, a tablet in her left hand inscribed with "July 4th MDCCLXXVI," and her torch three hundred feet above the sea, a national monument since 1924, the most famous statue in America was a gift from the people of France to celebrate "the alliance of the two nations in achieving independence of the United States of America, and attests their abiding friendship." To six-year-old David Schreiber, sailing past in 1902, "Until I met your grandmother, she was the most beautiful woman I had ever seen." The allusion in the poem to the Greek *giant* is to the ancient Colossus of Rhodes, an inspiration for Bartholdi himself. The *twin cities* are New York (Manhattan) and Brooklyn (the third largest city in the nation before consolidation in 1898).

LEHMAN, DAVID: "The World Trade Center (1993)". The *Twin Towers*, completed in 1974, were designed by Minoru Yamasaki with narrow windows because of his own fear of height. The *Chrysler Building*, "everyone's favorite" (affectionately referred to in James Sanders's *Celluloid Skyline* as the winner of the Best Supporting Skyscraper Award) was briefly the world's tallest building at seventy-seven stories until overtaken, and metaphorically overshadowed, by the Empire State Building. See Andrea Carter Brown's "Old Neighborhood" about the area around the World Trade Center, and "Shadow of a Vision of an Ode to New York" by Melech Ravitch for the Chrysler Building. David Lehman also wrote the poem "September 14, 2001" (not included; nor is Edward Field's "After the Fall" or "Names" by Billy Collins).

LIMA, FRANK: "Inventory—to 100th Street." The poem is dedicated to *John Bernard Myers*, the flamboyant art dealer of the innovative Tiber de Nagy Gallery on W. Fifty-seventh Street in the late 1950s that showed the works of young painters—Fairfield Porter, Jane Freilicher, Larry Rivers—who would soon become a major influence on the New York poets of that day: "Artists in any genre are . . . drawn to the dominant art movement in the place where they live," wrote James Schuyler. "In New York the art world is a painters' world; writers and musicians are in the boat, but they don't steer." Myers also edited the gallery's small press that published those painters' poet friends, among them James

Schuyler, Kenneth Koch, John Ashbery, and Frank O'Hara. In 1969 Myers edited the anthology *The Poets of the New York School*, published by Gotham Book Mart's press.

LOGAN, JOHN: "Manhattan Movements." *Fort Tryon Park* in northern Manhattan, designed by Fredrick Law Olmstead's son and named after Sir William Tryon (last English governor of New York before the Revolution), has the city's finest views of the Hudson River. It contains the Cloisters—the branch of the Metropolitan Museum of Art housing its medieval collection (see Jorge Luis Borges's "The Cloisters"). *Mother Cabrini* is Francis Xavier Cabrini, the first American to be canonized, though her remains lie in a shrine beneath an alter at Cabrini High School on Fort Washington Avenue. Photographer Harry Callahan (1912–1999) was known for his innovative photographs of commonplace scenes and objects. The *Lady*, of course, is the Statue of Liberty.

LOWELL, ROBERT: "Central Park." Having nothing to do with the queen of Egypt, *Cleopatra's Needle* is a seventy-one-foot obelisk taken over much objection from Egypt in 1881 and placed behind the Metropolitan Museum of Art, giving proof that New York was now truly an international city. Although the poem was written during a particularly tough time for the park and most of New York, Central Park's reputation as dangerous after dark extends back to the park's first murder in 1870, when William Kane, mistaken for an Irish Catholic gang member, was shot and stabbed on his way home through the park by a gang of Irish Protestants. Soon after that, the *Police Gazette* published its first article on the "Perils of the Park" and how "our beautiful city resort is polluted by foul tidings in human form."

MCGINLEY, PHYLLIS: "Valentine for New York." *Mr. Morgan* is most probably financier and New York benefactor John Piermont Morgan. *St. Thomas* is at Fifth Avenue and Fifty-third Street, where flowers once taken from the Easter service to St. Luke's Hospital (then a block uptown) began the traditional Easter Parade. *Barrow Street* is a pleasant, crowded street in Greenwich Village. *Powers* models, trained in methods developed by John Robert Powers, included Jackie Kennedy and Princess Grace. *Automats* were self-service restaurants operated by Horn and Hardart. They began in 1912, spread throughout the city, and, by the 1950s, had more than a quarter million customers every day. The rise of fast food joints ended automats forever. The last one at Second Avenue and Forty-second Street closed in 1991, though a new version of the old auotmat recently opened in the East Village.

Nedrick's, famous for its orange juice, was a chain of restaurants where "Good Food is never expensive." The *Planetarium* is at Central Park West and Eighty-first Street. *Schling's* was the renowned florist at the Savoy Plaza, at Fifth Avenue near Sixtieth Street. *Moses* is Robert Moses, master builder and controversial city planner. *Gimbels* was once Macy's competitor across the street. *Mott Street*, once the center of Little Italy, remains that neighborhood's last stand, as it is now almost entirely absorbed by Chinatown. *Ballroom Renaissance* is the Renaissance Ballroom, once in Harlem at Seventh Avenue and 133rd Street (also in Hughes's "Heart of Harlem"). *El Morocco* was a nightclub/ speakeasy that opened in 1931 at 154 E. Fifty-fourth Street. *Radio City* is the famous music hall at Forty-ninth Street and Sixth Avenue, while *Tammany Hall* was the political machine of the Democratic Party (see Fitz-Greene Halleck's "Song").

MELVILLE, HERMAN: "The House-top": Melville's own note to the poem reads: " 'I dare not write the horrible and inconceivable atrocities committed,' says Froissart, in alluding to the remarkable sedition in France during his time." Regarding the atrocities occurring in New York from July 13 through 16, several policemen were beaten; draft offices were destroyed and set afire, as were offices of the Republican Party, abolition editor Horace Greeley, and the Colored Orphan Asylum; and at least eleven black men were murdered and horribly brutalized. The *Wise Draco* of the poem is the establishment of severe penalties for civil offenses as advocated by the sixth-century B.C. Athenian legislator Draco. The *black artillery* refers to the five regiments of the Union Army force-marched from Gettysburg to restore order.

MENASHE, SAMUEL: "Old As the Hills." This poems refers to the city's aboriginal name "Manahatta" (Island of the Hills) before the Commissioners' Plan of 1811 flattened the island's middle.

"SHEEP MEADOW." Originally called the Green and intended for military parades, the Sheep Meadow is soft, rolling lawn on the park's west side at Sixty-seventh Street where—to give a more pastoral look to the park—sheep once actually grazed. Overnight they were housed in the Sheepfold, later converted to what is now Tavern on the Green, after Robert Moses, then parks commissioner, had the sheep exiled to Prospect Park. The "very rich hour / of the Duke of Berry" alludes to the illuminated manuscript *Les Tres riches heures du duc de Berri*.

MERRILL, JAMES: "As American as chiffon pie": from William Corbett, *New York Literary Lights*.

MILLAY, EDNA ST. VINCENT: "English Sparrows (Washington Square)." *Washington Square*, where Fifth Avenue begins, changed from a potter's field and public execution ground to the stylish park of Edith Wharton and Henry James novels in the late nineteenth century. Its *arch*, recalling the Arc de Triomphe, was designed by Stanford White. *Buses* once did pass "under the arch" because the park was bisected by Fifth Avenue until the 1960s.

MOORE, MARIANNE: "Granite and Steel." The Brooklyn Bridge, begun in 1869, was designed by German-born John Roebling, who was killed in an accident at the site that same year. His son, Washington, took his place but only a year later suffered so badly from caissons disease that even when the bridge opened on May 23, 1883, he was still too crippled to attend: "But I had a strong tower to lean on," he said of his wife, Emily. "O catenary curve" refers to the curve formed by a cable or rope hanging freely between two fixed points of support. See Vladimir Mayakovsky's "Brooklyn Bridge." Not included but of note are William Meredith's "View of the Brooklyn Bridge," Grace Schulman's "Brooklyn Bridge," and the entirety of Hart Crane's *The Bridge*.

MORLEY, CHRISTOPHER: "The Ballad of New York, New York." *Blatherskites* (bletherskates) are noisy, talkative fellows. At *Sardi's*, opening in 1921 at 246 W. Forty-fourth Street, then later at 234 W. Forty-fourth, Broadway cast members dined while waiting for the reviews in the morning papers. The *Stork* was the Stork Club at 3 E. Fifty-third and, according to Walter Winchell, "the New Yorkiest place in New York." *Nolle Pros* means a legal case won't be prosecuted. *Mappamond* is a map of the world or the world itself.

MURPHY, YVONNE C.: "The Cyclone." Coney Island's National Historic Landmark roller coaster took its first drop off the eighty-six-foot lift hill in the summer of 1927. "A ride on the Cyclone," said Charles Lindbergh, "is greater than flying an airplane at top speed."

NASH, OGDEN: "I Want New York." In the middle of the East River is Roosevelt Island, once known as Blackwell's Island (when it was the home of a notorious prison where Emma Goldman, Mae West, and Boss Tweed himself were incarcerated), and called *Welfare* Island from 1921 until the 1970s.

O'HARA, FRANK: "Steps." *St. Bridget's* rectory at 119 Avenue B (also appearing in Kinnell's "Avenue Bearing the Initial of Christ to the New World") had, for a while in the late 1950s, a seemingly unending steeple repair. The *Pittsburgh Pirates* won the World Series in 1960.

"A STEP AWAY FROM THEM." As in many poems from the New York school, several of the poet's friends make appearances. *Edwin Denby* was a poet and the dance critic for the *New York Herald*; *Bunny* was the poet Violet Lang, who had died of Hodgkin's disease; film producer *John Latouche* died of a heart attack; and the poet's friend *Jackson Pollack* was buried a day before O'Hara wrote the poem.

OLDS, SHARON: "The Empire State Building as the Moon." At Fifth Avenue and Thirty-fourth Street on the site of the old Waldorf-Astoria, designed by Shreve, Lamb, and Harmon, built under budget and under schedule at the beginning of the Depression, the *Empire State Building* is, for now, again New York's tallest building.

OSBORN, LAUGHTON: "Five Points 1838." *Five Points* was an intersection of five streets: Mulberry Street, Anthony Street (now Worth Street), Cross Street (now Park Row), Orange Street (now Baxter Street), and Little Water Street (also known as Dandy Lane but since built over). *Laurens Street* is now West Broadway. *Broome* Street runs just above Canal Street from Lafayette to Sixth Avenue. In 1842 Charles Dickens wrote of Five Points, "Debauchery has made the very houses prematurely old. See how the rotten beams are tumbling down, and how the patched and broken windows seem to scowl dimly, like eyes that have been hurt in drunken frays."

PADGETT, RON: "Strawberries in Mexico." Con Edison's *smokestacks* are at E. Fourteenth Street just east of Avenue D (also in Galway Kinnell's "Avenue Bearing the Initial of Christ Into the New World"). The reference to *Madison Avenue* is an allusion to Frank O'Hara's poem "Rhapsody" ("515 Madison Avenue / door to heaven?").

PAZ, OCTAVIO: "Central Park." *Alice* is José de Creeft's enchanting statue *Alice in Wonderland* at the northern edge of the Conservatory Pond. See Joel Brouwer's "Conservatory Pond."

PHILLIPS, ROBERT: "Triangle Shirtwaist Fire." The Triangle Shirtwaist Fire, March 25, 1911, was the worst factory fire in New York City history. One hundred and forty-six people, nearly all young women, mostly Jewish immigrants thirteen to twenty-three years old, died either crushed near the doors (which were chained from the outside), burned in the flames, or from leaping from the Asch building (still standing at the northwest corner of Washington and Greene streets just east of Washington Square in Greenwich Village). At the funeral on April 5, "the skies wept," said the *World*. The last survivor, Rose Freedman, died in February 2001 at the age of 107 and, like the *Rose* in this poem, lived in Southern California. The only person named *Rebecca* who perished in the fire was a seventeen-year-old Russian immigrant, Rebecca Feicishi (Feibish). There is still a service held at the site each March 25 where a small bell is struck 146 times. Though not included, other poems about this tragedy are "Ballad of Dead Girls" by Dana Burnet, "A Fifth Avenue Parade" by Percy Stickney Grant, and "The Triangle Shirtwaist Fire" by Edward Sanders.

PIÑERO, MIGUEL: "A Lower East Side Poem." Avenue *D*, the last eastern street in Manhattan before the FDR Drive, in a rough, neglected part of town, begins at E. Fourteenth and ends at Houston Street (see Galway Kinnell's "Avenue Bearing the Initial of Christ Into the New World"). Other poems in the collection about the Lower East Side include H. Leyvik's "Here Lives the Jewish People," Eliezer Greenberg's "Visiting Second Avenue," Allen Ginsberg's "Mugging," and Kenneth Koch's "Time Zone." Of note though not included is "Living on the Lower East Side During the Sixties: Or The Triumph of Surrealism Over the Forces of Repression" by Allen Planz.

RAVITCH, MELECH: "Shadow of a Vision of an Ode to New York." Designed by William Van Allen, completed in 1930, the Chrysler Building, "sparkling in its dazzling sheath of polished chrome steel" (*Architectural Forum*), is at Lexington Avenue and Forty-second Street. Once the home of the exclusive Cloud Club for the rich and powerful, the Chrysler Building, which topped out the Bank of the Manhattan Company building, is one of New York's great stories of competition, deception, and triumph. See David Lehman's "World Trade Center (1993)".

SASSOON, SIEGFRIED: "Storm on Fifth Avenue." Augustus Saint-Gauden's equestrian statue of William Tecumseh Sherman—unveiled at the Paris exposition in 1900—was placed in Grand Army Plaza, at the southeast entrance of Central Park at Fifth Avenue and Fifty-ninth Street, in 1903.

SCHULMAN, GRACE: "New Netherland, 1654." *Whiffs* is a flat fish or a bad smell, while *guzzads* refers to the gutter or perhaps a gluttonous person. See Aaron Zeitlin's "Peter Stuyvesant." Seventeenth-century Dutch poet Evert Nieuwehof's "To The Patrons of New Netherlands, 1654" (not included) also tells of this event: "Why mourn Brazil," he asks, when here are "such pleasant lands" and "loss brings gain, doubly rejoice."

SCHUYLER, JAMES: "Back." The *Frick* is the Frick Collection, adorning the former mansion of steel industrialist Henry C. Frick, at 1 East

Seventieth Street, designed by Carrère and Hastings, who designed the Public Library at Forty-second and Fifth Avenue. Joseph *Duveen* was an art dealer who guided Frick in his art purchases.

SHAPIRO, KARL: "Brooklyn Heights." Brooklyn Heights is a most picturesque area in northwest Brooklyn on high ground overlooking the Upper Bay. After construction of the Brooklyn-Queens Expressway in 1953 cut off much of the neighborhood, community groups had the neighborhood listed with the National Registry of Historic Places, the first historic district in New York City. *Murder Incorporated* was a criminal organization in the 1930s. A lieutenant in the organization turned stool pigeon, leading to Louis "Lepke" Buchalter's arrest, prosecution, and execution—the only member of Murder Inc. to be convicted. The informant, Abe "Kid Twist" Reles, mysteriously fell to his death shortly afterward from the Half Moon Hotel in Coney Island, 1941 (*Half Moon* was the name of Henry Hudson's ship). Lepke is the subject of Robert Lowell's poem (not included) "Memories of West Street and Lepke." *Columbia Heights* is a lovely street in Brooklyn Heights just east of the esplanade where, after stricken with caissons disease, Washington Roebling lived and worked during construction of the Brooklyn Bridge. See Hayden Carruth's "Hyacinth Garden in Brooklyn."

SISSMAN, L. E.: "The Village: The Seasons." The *Hotel Earle* was renovated and renamed the Washington Square Apartments.

SLEIGH, TOM: "The Grid." The Commissioners' Plan of 1811, also known as the Grid Plan, established an orderly, rectangular pattern of streets and avenues from First Street all the way to Washington Heights (where homes would not be built for nearly a century). The original plan, an eight foot-long map, can be seen in the I. N. Phelps Stokes Collection in the New York Public Library at Fifth Avenue and Forty-second Street.

STEENDAM, JACOB: "The Complaint of New Amsterdam to Its Mother." Though born of Amsterdam, the *child* too quickly abandoned had to fend for itself, all too soon suffering hardships. Though there were conflicts with *Indian neighbors* (which the Dutch were far more responsible for than the native Lenape Indians), the island's *wife* and *nurse* was *Ceres*, the Roman goddess of agriculture, who, along with the gifts of the "great Giver," blessed this rich, bountiful land and the two rivers surrounding it. The first report to the West India Company stated that "nothing is wanted but the labor and industry of man," but a colonist wrote soon afterward, "Our fields lie fallow. The crops which the Lord permitted to come forth . . . remain in the field standing and rotting."

STERN, GERALD: "Poem of Liberation." *Batsto* is a New Jersey river. *Amagansett* is a town near East Hampton on eastern Long Island. The Cathedral of *St. John* the Divine on Amsterdam Avenue at W. 112th Street in Manhattan is the largest church in the United States, the largest cathedral in the world, the principal church of the Episcopal Diocese of New York, and a center for community, environmental, and international matters. Peacocks roam free in the back gardens. The *pastry shop* across the street is called the Hungarian Pastry Shop.

STODDARD, CHARLES COLEMAN: "When Broadway Was a Country Road." Once an Indian trail running from the southern tip of the island to the most northern edge, winding around ponds and hills, through valleys and forests, later widened by the Dutch and called *Breede Wegh* and merely translated into English, *Broadway* is still the only street running the entire length of Manhattan, shifting from East Side to West Side where it once rounded a pond or hill. The city's first graded street, the first with brick sidewalks, addresses, a bridge (over the Collect Pool at Canal Street), and the first with electric streetlamps, Broadway established itself as the street for entertainment when a circus opened at Broadway and Worth after the Revolutionary War. Even before the Civil War the broad avenue was both the shopping and theater district from City Hall north to Houston Street. In *The Great Metropolis* (1869), Junius Henri Browne wrote that "Broadway is New York intensified . . . hustling, feverish, crowded, ever changing. . . . A walk through Broadway is like a voyage around the Globe . . . interesting every day and every hour of the seasons." See Carl Sandburg's "Broadway" and "The Old Apple Woman" by Christopher Pearse Cranch. Not included is Walt Whitman's "Broadway."

SWENSON, MAY: "Riding the A." Written by Harlem resident Billy "Swee' Pea" Strayhorn, the song "Take the 'A' Train" was made popular by Duke Ellington when the line opened in 1940.

TEASDALE, SARA: "From the Woolworth Tower." Completed in 1913, the Woolworth Building and its "terrible height" of sixty stories at 223 Broadway was New York's tallest building until the Chrysler Building was completed in 1930. Though referred to by Frank Winfield Woolworth as "the cathedral of commerce," the nametag did not please architect Cass Gilbert. The building also appears in E. E. Cummings's "at the ferocious phenomenon." Also see James Oppenheim's "New York, from a Skyscraper." Of note, though not included, is "Woolworth Building," by Yiddish poet Yehoash (Solomon Bloomgarden; 1870–1927).

WHITMAN, WALT: "Mannahatta." "Manahatta" is the name given to this island by its first inhabitants, the Lenape Indians, and meaning "island of the hills" although the poet believed the name meant "place encircled by many swift tides and sparkling waters."

From "Give Me the Splendid Silent Sun." In part 1 of this poem (not included), Whitman extols everything about Nature, especially its solitude, only to refute those sentiments in part 2.

From "Crossing Brooklyn Ferry." Written in 1856, this poem tells of the ferry, those "inimitable, streaming, never-failing, living poems" (from *Specimen Days*) that carried people between Brooklyn and Lower Manhattan. In fact, the ferry often failed to cross the half-mile strait during the frozen winter of 1867, when the notion of a great bridge took hold. That same year, running at five minute intervals, the ferry carried 48,000,000 passengers.

WHITTEMORE, REED: "Ode to New York." Among his many notorious exploits, *Steve Brodie* faked—and became famous for—jumping off the Brooklyn Bridge on July 23, 1886. A saloon he later opened on the Bowery featured a large painting of the stunt as "proof." In the 1933 film *The Bowery*, Brodie was played by George Raft. *Rahway* is a New Jersey town about five miles from Staten Island.

WIESE, BROOKE: "Going Home Madly." The "double strand of lights" is the Queensborough Bridge, also known as the Fifty-ninth Street Bridge, connecting Queens to Manhattan.

WILLIS, NATHANIEL PARKER: "City Lyrics." Beginning at Bowling Green—the oldest existing public park in New York City—the poet and his lady stroll up *Broadway*, passing first the *City Hotel*—New York's first quality hotel (five stories, 137 rooms, with dining, dancing, and an excellent wine cellar), opened in 1794 on Broadway just north of Trinity Church—then *St. Paul's* Chapel at Broadway and Fulton (completed in 1766, Manhattan's oldest public building still in use and a refuge for workers during the long cleanup after the destruction of the World Trade Center), and finally the *Astor* House at Broadway near City Hall, built in 1836, with six stories and 300 rooms—the grandest hotel of its day.

WRIGHT, C. D.: "Spring Street Girl Friend (#8)." *Spring Street* is two blocks below Houston Street, between the Bowery and Vandam in Soho, where a spring still flows beneath the street. *Otis*, the name seen in many elevators throughout the city, is the company started by Elisha Otis, who invented the "safety hoist" in 1854.

ZEITLIN, AARON: "Peter Stuyvesant." Appointed the first director general of New Netherland in 1647, *Peter Stuyvesant* had a farm at what is now Stuyvesant Park, at Second Avenue and Fifteenth Street, where stands an oddly undersized statue of the "peg leg" captain (his leg lost in a naval battle in the West Indies). He was buried beneath the chapel of his house, now St. Mark's Church in the Bowery at Tenth Street and Second Avenue. The "roar of wrath / at my brothers from Brazil" refers to Stuyvesant's demand to exclude Jews—driven from Recife, Brazil, in 1654—from New Amsterdam. The passage from Scripture appears in Ecclesiastes 8:10. See Grace Schulman's "New Netherlands, 1654."

ACKNOWLEDGMENTS

ACKERMAN, DIANE. "Hungarian Woman on Ellis Island," from *I Praise My Destroyer* by Diane Ackerman, copyright© 1998 by Diane Ackerman. Used by permission of Random House, Inc.

ADDONIZIO, KIM. "Generations" from *Tell Me* by Kim Addonizio. Copyright © 2000 by Kim Addonizio. Reprinted with the permission of BOA Editions, Ltd.

ANGELOU, MAYA. "Awaking in New York," copyright © 1983 by Maya Angelou, from *Shaker, Why Don't You Sing?* by Maya Angelou. Used by permission of Random House, Inc.

BELL, MARVIN. "These Green-Going-to-Yellow" from *Nightworks: Poems, 1962–2000* by Marvin Bell Copyright © 1981, 2000 by Marvin Bell. Reprinted with the permission of Copper Canyon Press, P.O. Box 271, Port Townsend, WA 98368-0271

BERMAN, DAVID. "New York, New York" was originally published in *Actual Air* by David Berman (Open City Books, 1999).

BLACKBURN, PAUL. "Bryant Park" from *The Collected Poems of Paul Blackburn*, ed. Edith Jarolin. Persea Books, 1985.

BLUMENTHAL, MICHAEL. "Washington Heights, 1959." Copyright Michael Blumenthal from *Sympathetic Magic*. Water Mark Poets of North America First Book Prize for 1980, Water Mark Press, N.Y.

BODENHEIM, MAXWELL. "New York City" from *Against This Age* by Maxwell Bodenheim. Copyright 1923 by Boni & Liveright, renewed

© 1950 by Maxwell Bodenheim. Used by permission of Liveright Publishing Corporation.

BOLDEN, TONYA. "'bella' (6 December 2002)" copyright © 2003 by Tonya Bolden. Used by permission of the author. An earlier version of this poem appeared in *Metropolis Found: New York Is Book Country Twenty-fifth Anniversary Collection* (2003).

BORDEN, WILLIAM. "Guggenheim." Reprinted with permission of the *South Dakota Review.*

BORGES, JORGE LUIS. "The Cloisters," translated by W. S. Merwin, copyright © 1999 by Maria Kodama. Translation © by W. S. Merwin, from *Selected Poems* by Jorge Luis Borges, edited by Alexander Coleman. Used by permission of Viking Penguin, a division of Penguin Group (USA) Inc.

BROUWER, JOEL. "Conservatory Pond, Central Park" from *Exactly What Happened* by Joel Brouwer. © Purdue University Press. Reprinted by Permission. Unauthorized duplication not permitted.

BROWN, ANDREA CARTER. "The Old Neighborhood" excerpted from *Poetry After 9/11: An Anthology of New York Poets*, edited by Dennis Loy Johnson and Valerie Merians. Copyright © 2002 by Dennis Loy Johnson and Valerie Merians. Reprinted by permission of the publisher, Melville House.

CARRUTH, HAYDEN. "The Hyacinth Garden in Brooklyn" from *Scrambled Eggs and Whiskey: Poems, 1991–1995*, by Hayden Carruth. Copyright © 1996 by Hayden Carruth. Reprinted with the permission of Copper Canyon Press, P.O. Box 271, Port Townsend, WA 98368-0271.

CIARDI, JOHN. "George Washington Bridge" from *The Collected Poems of John Ciardi*, edited by Edward M. Cifelli. Copyright 1941 by John Ciardi. Reprinted with the permission of the University of Arkansas Press, www.uapress.com.

CLAMPITT, AMY. "Times Square Water Music" from *The Collected Poems of Amy Clampitt* by Amy Clampitt, copyright © 1997 by the Literary Estate of Amy Clampitt. Introduction copyright © 1997 by Mary Jo Salter. Used by permission of Alfred A. Knopf, a division of Random House, Inc.

COLLINS, BILLY. "Man Listening to Disc," copyright © 2001 by Billy Collins, from *Sailing Alone Around the Room* by Billy Collins. Used by permission of Random House, Inc.

CONNELLAN, LEO. "Helpless, We Go Into This Ground, Helpless." Poem used by permission of Nancy A. Connellan, Shoreham, Vt.

CORN, ALFRED. "Photographs of Old New York," reprinted by permission of the author.

CORSO, GREGORY. "On the Death of the Lucky Gent" from *Elegiac Feelings American* by Gregory Corso, copyright © 1970 by Gregory Corso. Reprinted by permission of New Directions Publishing Corp.

CORTEZ, JANE. "I Am New York City," copyright © 2006 by Jayne Cortez.

COVAL, KEVIN. "lured beneath your golden, calling lights" from *Slingshot: A Hip-Hop Poetica*. Used by permission of the author.

CRANE, HART. "The Tunnel," from *Complete Poems of Hart Crane*, edited by Marc Simon. Copyright 1933, 1958, 1966 by Liveright Publishing Corporation. Copyright © 1986 by Marc Simon. Used by permission of Liveright Publishing Corporation.

CUMMINGS, E. E. "at the ferocious phenomenon." Copyright 1925, 1953, © 1991 by the Trustees for the E. E. Cummings Trust. Copyright © 1976 by George James Firmage, from *Complete Poems: 1904–1962* by E. E. Cummings, edited by George J. Firmage. Used by permission of Liveright Publishing Corporation.

ELOVIC, BARBARA. "Brooklyn Bound" originally published appeared in *Home Planet News*, Vol. 6, No. 2. Copyright © 1987 by Barbara Elovic. Reprinted by permission of the author.

ESPADA, MARTIN. "The Owl and the Lightning" from *Imagine the Angels of Bread* by Martin Espada. Copyright © 1996 by Martin Espada. Used by permission of W. W. Norton & Company, Inc. "The Day of the Dead on Wortman Avenue" from *City of Coughing and Dead Radiators* by Martin Espada. Copyright © 1993 by Martin Espada. Used by permission of W. W. Norton & Company, Inc.

FEARING, KENNETH. "Manhattan." Reprinted by the permission of Russell & Volkening as agents for the author. Copyright © 1948 by Kenneth Fearing, renewed in 1976 by the Estate of Kenneth Fearing.

FELDMAN, IRVING. "The Handball Players at Brighton Beach" from *Collected Poems: 1954–2004* by Irving Feldman, copyright © 2004 by Irving Feldman. Used by permission of Schocken Books, a division of Random House, Inc.

FERLINGHETTI, LAWRENCE. "Meet Miss Subways" from *A Coney Island of the Mind* by Lawrence Ferlinghetti, copyright ©1958 by Lawrence Ferlinghetti. Reprinted by permission of New Directions Publishing Corp.

FIELD, EDWARD. "New York" and "The Last Bohemians" reprinted with permission of the author.

GINSBERG, ALLEN: All lines from "Mugging" from *Collected Poems, 1947–1980* by Allen Ginsberg. Copyright © 1974 by Allen Ginsberg. Reprinted by permission of HarperCollins Publishers. "The Charnel Ground" from *Selected Poems, 1947–1995* by Allen Ginsberg. Copyright © 1996 by Allen Ginsberg. Reprinted by permission of HarperCollins Publishers.

GIOVANNI, NIKKI. "The New Yorkers" from *Cotton Candy on a Rainy Day* by Nikki Giovanni, copyright © 1978 by Nikki Giovanni. Reprinted by permission of HarperCollins Publishers William Morrow.

GREENBERG, ELIEZER. "Visiting Second Avenue," translated by John Hollander from *A Treasury of Yiddish Poetry*, edited by Irving Howe and Eliezer Greenberg, © 1969, 1997 by Irving Howe and Eliezer Greenberg. Reprinted by permission of Henry Holt and Company, LLC

GROSS, NAFTALI. "The Cemetery at Chatham Square" from *America in Yiddish Poetry*. Ed. Jehiel B. Cooperman and Sarah A. Cooperman. Exposition Press, 1967.

GUEST, BARBARA. "The Location of Things" by Barbara Guest from *Collected Poems*, Wesleyan University Press, 2008. Originally published in *Poems: The Location of Things*, *Archaics*, *The Open Sky*, Double Day & Co. Inc., 1962. © 1962 by Barbara Guest and reprinted by permission of Wesleyan University Press.

HALPERN, DANIEL. "Street Fire" from *Street Fire* by Daniel Halpern, copyright © 1972, 1973, 1974, 1975 by Daniel Halpern. Used by permission of Viking Penguin, a division of Penguin Group (USA) Inc.

HALPERN, MOISHE LEIB. "Song: Weekend's Over" by Moishe Leib Halpren, translated by John Hollander from *A Treasury of Yiddish Poetry*, edited by Irving Howe and Eliezer Greenberg, © 1969, 1997 by Irving Howe and Eliezer Greenberg. Reprinted by permission of Henry Holt and Company, LLC.

HOLLANDER, JOHN. "New York" from *Spectral Emanation: New and Selected Poems*. New York: Atheneum, 1978. Reprinted by permission of the author.

HOLMES, JOHN. "From Brooklyn" from *The Selected Poems of John Holmes* by John Holmes copyright © 1964. Reprinted by permission of Beacon Press, Boston.

HOWARD, RICHARD. "The Old Men Playing Boccie on Leroy Street" by Richard Howard from *Quantities*, Wesleyan University Press, 1962. © 1962 by Richard Howard. Reprinted by permission of Wesleyan University Press. www.wesleyan.edu/wespress

HUGHES, LANGSTON. "Good Morning" and "The Heart of Harlem" by Langston Hughes, from *The Collected Poems of Langston Hughes* by Langston Hughes, copyright © 1994 by The Estate of Langston Hughes. Used by permission of Alfred A. Knopf, a division of Random House, Inc.

JOHNSON, JAMES WELDON. "My City" by James Weldon Johnson, copyright 1935 by James Weldon Johnson, © renewed 1963 by Grace Nail Johnson, from *Saint Peter Relates an Incident* by James Weldon Johnson. Used by permission of Viking Penguin, a division of Penguin Group (USA) Inc.

JORDAN, JUNE. "47,000 Windows" by June Jordan. Copyright 2005 June M. Jordan, reprinted by permission of the June M. Jordan Literary Estate Trust, www.junejordan.com

JUSTICE, DONALD. "Manhattan Dawn (1945)" by Donald Justice, from *Collected Poems* by Donald Justice, copyright © 2004 by Donald Justice. Used by permission of Alfred A. Knopf, a division of Random House, Inc.

KASDORF, JULIA. "Ladies' Night at the Turkish and Russian Baths" from *Eve's Striptease*, by Julia Kasdorf, © 1998. Reprinted by permission of the University of Pittsburgh Press.

KEROUAC, JACK. "Macdougal Street Blues" by Jack Kerouac, reprinted by permission of Sll/sterling Lord Literistic, Inc. Copyright 1995 by John Sampas, Literary Rep.

KINNELL, GALWAY: "The Avenue Bearing the Initial of Christ Into the New World" from *What a Kingdom It Was: Poems by Galway Kinnell* © 1960, renewed 1988 by Galway Kinnell. Reprinted by permission of Houghton Mifflin Company. All rights reserved.

KOCH, KENNETH. "A Time Zone" from *Collected Poems of Kenneth Koch* by Kenneth Koch, copyright © 2005 by Kenneth Koch Literary Estate. Used by permission of Alfred A. Knopf, a division of Random House, Inc.

KUPFERBERG, TULI. "Greenwich Village of My Dreams" reprinted by permission of the author.

LEHMAN, DAVID. "World Trade Center (1993)" © David Lehman c/o Writers Representative, L.L.C. New York, N.Y. All rights reserved. This poem first appeared in *Valentine Place*.

LEVERTOV, DENISE. "The Cabdriver's Smile" by Denise Levertov, from *Poems, 1972–1982*, copyright © 1978 by Denise Levertov. Reprinted by permission of New Directions Publishing Corp.

LEYVIK, H. "Here Lives the Jewish People" from *America in Yiddish Poetry*. Ed. Jehiel B. Cooperman and Sarah A. Cooperman. Exposition Press, 1967.

LIMA, FRANK. "Inventory—to 100th Street" reprinted by permission of the author.

LOGAN, JOHN. "Manhattan Movement" from *John Logan: The Collected Poems*. Copyright © 1989 by the John Logan Literary Estate, Inc. Reprinted with the permission of BOA Editions, Ltd.

LORCA, FEDERICO GARCIA. "New York" from *Collected Poems* by Federico Garcia Lorca, *Collected Poems Revised Bilingual Edition* by Federico Garcia Lorca, translated by Christopher Maurer. Translation copyright © 1991, 2002 by Christopher Maurer. Reprinted by permission of Farrar, Straus and Giroux, LLC.

LORDE, AUDRE. "New York 1970" from *The Collected Poems of Audre Lorde* by Audre Lorde. Copyright © 1997 by The Audre Lorde Estate. Used by permission of W. W. Norton & Company, Inc.

LOWELL, AMY. "New York at Night" from *The Complete Poetical Works of Amy Lowell*, Boston: Houghton Mifflin, 1955.

LOWELL, ROBERT. "Central Park" from *Collected Poems* by Robert Lowell. Copyright © 2003 by Harriet Lowell and Sheridan Lowell. Reprinted by permission of Farrar, Straus and Giroux, LLC.

MAYAKOVSKY, VLADIMIR. "Brooklyn Bridge" from *The Bedbud and Selected Poetry* by Vladimir Mayakovsky, edited by Patricia Blake. Translated by Max Hayward and George Reavey. Copyright © 1980 by Harper and Row, Publishers, Inc. Reprinted by permission of HarperCollins Publishers.

MAYHALL, JANE. "Token" by Jane Mayhall from *Sleeping Late on Judgment Day* by Jane Mayhall, copyright © 2004 by Jane Mayhall. Used by permission of Alfred A. Knopf, a division of Random House, Inc.

MCGINLEY, PHYLLIS. "Valentine for New York" by Phyllis McGinley, copyright 1941 by Phyllis McGinley, from *Times Three* by Phyllis McGinley. Used by permission of Viking Penguin, a division of Penguin Group (USA) Inc.

MENASHE, SAMUEL. "Old As the Hills" and "Sheep Meadow" by Samuel Menashe from *New and Selected Poems* by Samuel Menashe, edited by Christopher Ricks, published by The Library of America 2005.

MENZA, CLAUDIA. "You Say You Like the Country" by Claudia Menza, from *The Lunatics Ball*, Mosaic Press, copyright © 1994 by Claudia Menza. Reprinted by permission of Claudia Menza.

MERRILL, JAMES. "164 East 72nd Street" by James Merrill, from *Collected Poems* by James Merrill, J. D. McClatchy and Stephen Yenser, editors, copyright © 2001 by the Literary Estate of James Merrill at Washington University. Used by permission of Alfred A. Knopf, a division of Random House, Inc.

MERTON, THOMAS. "Hymn of Not Much Praise for New York City" from *The Collected Poems of Thomas Merton*, copyright © 1977 by The Trustees of the Merton Legacy Trust. Reprinted by permission of New Directions Publishing Corp.

MERWIN, W. S. "227 Waverly Place" by W. S. Merwin, © 1999 by W. S. Mervin, permission of The Wylie Agency.

MILLAY, EDNA ST. VINCENT: "English Sparrows (Washington Square)" by Edna St. Vincent Millay. All rights reserved. Copyright 1939, 1967 by Edna St. Vincent and Norma Millay Ellis. Reprinted by permission of Elizabeth Barnett, Literary Executor, The Millay Society.

MOORE, MARIANNE. "Granite and Steel" and "Dock Rats" from *The Poems of Marianne Moore* by Marianne Moore, edited by Grace Schulman, copyright © 2003 by Marianne Craig Moore, Executor of the Estate of Marianne Moore. Used by permission of Viking Penguin, a division of Penguin Group (USA) Inc.

MORLEY, CHRISTOPHER. "Ballad of New York, New York" from *The Ballad of New York, New York and Other Poems, 1930–1950* by Christopher Morley. New York: Doubleday, 1950.

MORLEY, HILDA. "New York Subway" from *To Hold in My Hand: Selected Poems, 1955–1983*. New York: The Sheep Meadow Press, 1983. Used by permission of The Stefan Wolpe Society,

MOSS, HOWARD. "The Roof Garden" by Howard Moss. Reprinted with permission from the Howard Moss Estate.

MOSS, STANLEY. "SM" first published in *New and Selected Poems, 2006*, from Seven Stories Press.

MURPHY, YVONNE C. "The Cyclone." Reprinted with permission of the *South Dakota Review.*

NASH, OGDEN. "I Want New York" by Ogden Nash. Copyright © by Ogden Nash, renewed. Reprinted by permission of Curtis Brown, Ltd.

O'HARA, FRANK: "Steps" and "A Step Away From Them" by Frank O'Hara, from *Lunch Poems* © 1964 by Frank O'Hara. Reprinted by permission of City Lights Books.

OLDS, SHARON. "The Empire State Building as the Moon" first appeared in *The New Yorker*, February 16, 1987. Reprinted with permission of the author.

PACKER, EVE. "playland" by Eve Packer. From *Playland: Poems 1994–2004*. Published by Fly Night Press, 2005. Copyright © 2005 by Eve Packer. Reprinted by permission of the author.

PADGETT, RON. "Strawberries in Mexico" from *Great Balls of Fire*. Copyright © 1969, 1990 by Ron Padgett. Reprinted with the permission of Coffee House Press, Minneapolis, Minnesota.

PAZ, OCTAVIO. "Central Park" by Octavio Paz, Translated by Eliot Weinberger, from *Collected Poems, 1957–1987*, copyright © 1986 by Octavio Paz and Eliot Weinberger. Reprinted by permission of New Directions Publishing Corp.

PHILLIPS, ROBERT. "Triangle Shirtwaist Factory Fire" reprinted by permission of the author, Robert Phillips, © 2006.

PIERCY, MARGE. "I woke with the room cold . . . " by Marge Piercy, from *Circles on the Water* by Marge Piercy, copyright© 1982 by permission of Alfred A. Knopf, a division of Random House, Inc.

PIÑERO, MIGUEL. "A Lower East Side Poem" is reprinted with permission from the publisher of *La Bodega Sold Dreams* by Miguel Piñero, Houston: Arte Publico Press–University of Houston, © 1985.

RAVITCH, MELECH. "Shadow of a Vision of an Ode to New York" from *America in Yiddish Poetry*. Ed. Jehiel B. Cooperman and Sarah A. Cooperman. Exposition Press, 1967.

REZNIKOFF, CHARLES. "By the Well of Living and Seeing" by Charles Reznikoff. from *The Poems of Charles Reznikoff, 1918–1975*. Reprinted by permission of Black Sparrow Books, an imprint of David R. Godine, Publisher, Inc. Copyright © by the Estate of Charles Reznikoff.

RICE, STAN. "Looking for an Apartment in New York" by Stan Rice from *Fear Itself* by Stan Rice, copyright © 1995 by Stan Rice. Used by permission of Alfred A. Knopf, a division of Random House, Inc.

RICH, ADRIENNE: Poem 1 from "Twenty-One Love Poems." Copyright © 2002 by Adrienne Rich. Copyright © 1978 by W. W. Norton & Company, Inc. from *The Fact of a Doorframe: Selected Poems, 1950–2001* by Adrienne Rich. Used by permission of the author and W. W. Norton & Company, Inc.

RODITI, EDOURADO. "Manhattan Novelettes" from *Emperor of Midnight* by Edourado Roditi, Black Sparrow Press, 1974.

ROSENTHAL, M. L. "Geometries of Manhattan: Morning" from *Poems: 1964–1980* by M. L. Rosenthal, copyright © M. L. Rosenthal, 17 Bayard Lane, Suffern, New York 10901. Used by permission of Oxford University Press, Inc.

RUKEYSER, MURIEL. "The Ballad of Orange and Grape" from *The Collected Poems of Muriel Rukeyser*. Ed. Janet E. Kaufman and Anne. F. Herzog. University of Pittsburgh Press, 2005.

SANDBURG, CARL. "Broadway" from *The Complete Poems of Carl Sandburg*, copyright © 1970, 1969 by Lilian Steichen Sandburg, Trustee, reprinted by permission of Harcourt, Inc.

SASSOON, SIEGFRIED. "Storm on Fifth Avenue" from *Collected Poems of Siegfried Sassoon* by Siegfried Sassoon, copyright 1918, 1920 by E. P. Dutton. Copyright 1936, 1947, 1948 by Siegfried Sassoon. Used by permission of Viking Penguin, a division of Penguin Group (USA) Inc.

SCHULMAN, GRACE: "New Netherland, 1654" from *Days of Wonder: New and Selected Poems by Grace Schulman*. Copyright © 2002 by Grace Schulman. reproduced by permission of Houghton Mifflin Company. All rights reserved.

SCHUYLER, JAMES. "Morning" and "Back" from *Collected Poems* by James Schuyler. Copyright © 1993 by the Estate of James Schuyler. Reprinted by permission of Farrar, Straus and Giroux, LLC.

SCHWARTZ, DELMORE. "America, America!" by Delmore Schwartz, from *Last and Lost Poems*, copyright © 1979, 1989 by Kenneth Schwartz. Reprinted by permission of New Directions Publishing Corp.

SENGHOR, LÈOPOLD SÈDAR. "New York" from *Selected Poems*. Translated by John Reed and Clive Wake. Atheneum, 1964.

SHAPIRO, HARVEY. "Through the Boroughs" and "Brooklyn Heights" by Harvey Shapiro from *Selected Poems*, Wesleyan University Press, 1997. © 1997 by Harvey Shapiro. Reprinted by permission of Wesleyan University Press. www.wesleyan.edu/wespress

SHRIVER, PEGGY L. "The Spirit of 34th Street" from *The Dancers of Riverside Park and Other Poems*. © 2001 Peggy Shriver. Used by permission of Westminster John Knox Press.

SIMIC, CHARLES. "Early Morning in July" by Charles Simic from *Hotel Insomnia*, copyright © 1992 by Charles Simic, reprinted by permission of Harcourt, Inc.

SISSMAN, L. E. "The Village: The Seasons" from *Night Music: Poems by L. E. Sissman*, edited by Peter Davison. Copyright © 1999 by The President and Fellows of Harvard College. Reprinted by permission of Houghton Mifflin Company. All rights reserved.

SLEIGH, TOM. "The Grid" reprinted from *The Dreamhouse* by Tom Sleigh, courtesy of University of Chicago Press.

SNYDER, GARY. "Walking the New York Bedrock Alive in the Sea of Information." From *Mountains and Rivers Without End* by Gary Snyder, copyright © 1996 by Gary Snyder. Reprinted by permission of Counterpoint, a member of Perseus Books, L.L.C.

STERN, GERALD. "The Poem of Liberation" was originally published in *The Red Coal*, Houghton Mifflin, 1981, and appears with permission of the author.

SWENSON, MAY. "Riding the A" by May Swenson. Used with permission of the Literary Estate of May Swenson.

UPDIKE, JOHN. "Summer: West Side" by John Updike from *Collected Poems, 1953–1993* by John Updike, copyright © 1993 by John Updike. Used by permission of Alfred A. Knopf, a division of Random House, Inc.

WALCOTT, DEREK. "A Village Life" from *The Castaway* by Derek Walcott. Copyright © 1965 by Derek Walcott. Reprinted by permission of Farrar, Straus and Giroux, LLC.

WHITTEMORE, REED. "Ode to New York" from *The Past, the Future, the Present: Poems Selected and New.* Copyright © 1990 by Reed Whittemore. Reprinted with the permission of the University of Arkansas Press, www.uapress.com.

WIESE, BROOKE. "Going Home Madly" by Brooke Wiese first appeared in *The Laurel Review.*

WILLIAMS, WILLIAM CARLOS. "The Great Figure" by William Carlos Williams, from *Collected Poems: 1909–1939*, volume 1, copyright © 1938 by New Directions Publishing Corp. Reprinted by permission of New Directions Publishing Corp.

WRIGHT, C. D. "Spring Street Girl Friend (#8)" from *Steal Away: Selected and New Poems.* Copyright © 2002 by C. D. Wright. Reprinted with the permission of Copper Canyon Press, P.O. Box 271, Port Townsend, WA 98368-0271.

WUNDERLICH, MARK. "East Seventh Street" published by permission of the author.

YEVTUSHENKO, YEVGENY. "New York Elegy" from *The Collected Poems: 1952–1990*. Ed. Albert C. Todd. New York: A John Macrae Book, Holt Rinhart, 1991.

ZEITLIN, AARON. "Peter Stuyvesant" from *America in Yiddish Poetry*. Ed. Jehiel B. Cooperman and Sarah A. Cooperman. Exposition Press, 1967.

Although efforts have been made to find and contact all copyright holders, a few instances proved impossible. If notified, Columbia University Press will rectify any omissions in future editions.

I am most appreciative for the guidance and patience of Jennifer Crewe at Columbia University Press, and to John Hollander for his early directions and later contribution. Thanks to the skillful editing craft of Columbia's Michael Haskell; to Berkeley College for support and encouragement; to the tireless research of Corazon C. Estavillo, who was often as excited by her research discoveries as I was; and to Rupinder Kaur for her efforts and enthusiasm and for the free contributions from the mysterious Permdude. I am most grateful to Diane Ackerman, Kim Addonizio, Maya Angelou, David Berman, Michael Blumenthal, Tonya Bolden, Billy Collins, Nancy Connellan, Alfred Corn, Kevin Coval, Barbara Elovic, Martin Espada, Irving Feldman, Edward Field, Hadley Haden-Guest, John Hollander, Julia Kasdorf, Karen Koch, Tuli Kupferberg, David Lehman, Frank Lima, Jane Mayhall, Samuel Menashe, Claudia Menza, Stanley Moss, Sharon Olds, Eve Packer, Ron Padgett, Robert Phillips, Peggy Shriver, Tom Sleigh, Gerald Stern, Mark Wunderlich, Yevgeny Yevtushenko, the Wylie Agency, and New Directions Press, without whose generosity this collection would lack its breadth and scope.

Special thanks for the joyful assistance of Lily Wolf; for the company and comfort provided by Skylar Wolf while I typed late into the night; for the essential sustenance given by Don Fisher; for the guidance from my teacher, dissertation director, and friend Professor James Hurt at the University of Illinois; to the severe encouragement of Maynard Solomon; to Mom, from who I inherited a portion of her hopeful spirit; and, most especially, for limitless effort and unending faith of Nina Solomon, the angel at my shoulder, who swore eternal love even if this anthology was never published.

Finally, this collection is dedicated to Dave and Gussie Schreiber, whose spirits brought me home.